HELPING
PEOPLE

---

*A Handbook on Reconciliation-Focused
Counseling and Preaching*

Asa R. Sphar III

Argile Smith

University Press of America,® Inc.
Lanham · New York · Oxford

University Press of America,® Inc.
4501 Forbes Boulevard
Suite 200
Lanham, Maryland 20706
UPA Acquisitions Department (301) 459-3366

PO Box 317
Oxford
OX2 9RU, UK

ISBN 0-7618-2477-4 (paperback : alk. ppr.)
ISNN: 978-0-7618-2477-0

This book is dedicated to

our wives,

Donna Sphar

and

Connie Smith,

who believe in us.

Table of Contents

PART I. INTRODUCING THE RFC MODEL

Chapter

   An Overview of the Challenge
   A Theology of Emotional and Relational Problems
        as Revealed in the Creation Story

   Principle #1: Promote the Ministry of Reconciliation
   Principle #2: Prepare the Way for a Divine-Human
        Encounter
   Principle #3: Acknowledge the Need for Therapeutic
        Trialogue
   Principle #4: Maintain a Redemptive/Hopeful
        Attitude
   Principle #5: Make the Most Efficient Use of Time
   Principle #6: Emphasize Change in the Thoughts and
        Behaviors of the Counselee
   Principle #7: Be Both Collaborative and Directive

List of Figures and Tables

Preface

Thanks for picking up this book. It's about how counseling and preaching can work to help hurting people tear down the walls between them and God, other people, and even themselves. When walls come tumbling down, enemies become friends and hurting gives way to healing.

That's what reconciliation is all about. And that's what counseling and preaching should be about if we counsel and preach effectively.

The authors serve this book up to you with a twofold purpose in mind. First they want to show you a model for counseling that focuses on reconciliation. Then they want to show you how the model can be applied by ministers in the counseling and preaching settings.

In Part I you will be introduced to the Reconciliation-Focused Counseling (RFC) model. Dr. Asa Sphar developed the model, and he has taught it to students majoring in counseling and psychology at New Orleans Baptist Theological Seminary since 1994. When you read it, you will get the impression that you too are in his classroom. You will appreciate the depth of his research and the passion of his heart that produced the model.

In Part II you will see how the RFC model can be applied in a pastor's counseling ministry. You will read accounts of actual counseling situations that involve real people with real problems. The accounts will show you how a pastor can put the RFC model to work when people come to him for help.

The model will also be applied to a pastor's preaching ministry. Dr. Argile Smith, a preaching professor and one of Dr. Sphar's colleagues at the Seminary, has given consideration to applying RFC to a pastor's work in the pulpit. Based on his pastoral experience and homiletical research, Dr. Smith will suggest some issues for you to think about in terms of the common ground that preaching and counseling share in a pastor's ministry. He also will show you some reconciliation-focused sermon briefs.

Peruse the appendixes and you will notice more than enough material to help you put RFC into practice. The bibliography is extensive too, perhaps a little more thorough than what you might expect. It's provided to get you off to a good start as you dig deeper into the rich and rewarding study of reconciliation-focused counseling and preaching.

Acknowledgments

We have a number of people to thank for helping us write this book. New Orleans Baptist Theological Seminary granted us sabbatical leaves so we could work through the project and shepherd it to completion. Our faculty colleagues listened to us share our ideas, debated with us, read our manuscript, and offered suggestions on writing and publishing. Furthermore, they patted us on the back and told us that our project was important.

Our students made their mark on the manuscript as well. The material on the pages that follow started out as notes scribbled on paper. The passion to help counseling students help hurting people tear down walls moved the pencil to scribble the possibilities. In the fire of classroom interchange between professor and student, the material was purified into its present form.

We are also debtors to the hurting people we have tried to help. In counseling we struggled to find a way to help them. In preaching we ached to see the hurt give way to wholeness. No, we are not grateful for the pain these people have endured; we are most grateful, however, for the privilege they gave us to try to help them.

We share tremendous gratitude for our wives, Donna and Connie, and our respective children Chrissy and Bethany, . . . Josh, David, and Dustin, for the support, sacrifice, and inspiration they have provided in both our writing and our lives. They have all, in one way or another, shaped the ways that we think about relationships in profound and meaningful ways.

Most of all, we owe Jesus Christ. He lived, died, and rose from the grave so the walls could come down. We know first hand what He can do in people's lives so they can be reconciled with Him, other people, and even themselves. Not only have we witnessed His reconciling work in other people, we also experienced it personally when we made Him our Savior and Lord.

Introduction

The Potential of Reconciliation

Meet Martha. The ideas and images of reconciliation forged into the words of this book have been provided for the sake of people like her.

She's hurting. And she needs help.

Martha represents lots of people who come to churches and carry on conversations with ministers because they need someone to help them find a way out of their pain. She might be a single parent who struggles with raising her children on her own. She could be an up-and-coming corporate executive who endures the silent sting of depression. Or perhaps she has recently come to terms with the harsh reality that she has been nurturing an addiction.

The name of the person in pain may not be Martha. It could be Matt. Emotional or relational troubles have no particular respect for either gender. Matt could be trying to forgive some people who hurt him deeply, but so far he's losing the battle to anger and resentment. His marriage may be in trouble. Or he's confused and frustrated over the way that God doesn't seem to be listening to him when he prays.

Where do people like Martha and Matt go for help? Lord willing, they will turn to a minister. Suppose they do. What can a minister do to help them?

The answer to that question will be offered in the following pages, and it centers around one solitary term that comes right out of God's Word. You've probably heard it used in one sermon after another.

However, you might not have considered how deeply it runs through the emotional and relational pain people endure in order to bring healing and wholeness to them. Some people portray the term as a metaphor for salvation, a picture word used to describe what God has done for us through the death, burial, and resurrection of Jesus Christ. If you remember the title of this book, you recall the word: *reconciliation.*

They say that every word in the Bible can paint a picture or tell a story. That's certainly true when we study reconciliation. Unpack the word for reconciliation in the original language of the New Testament and you will uncover the precious treasure of God's work to tear down walls between people and Him, each other, and even themselves.

Put in its simplest terms, to reconcile means to change or exchange. Although such a simple definition of the term doesn't in itself make for a beautiful portrait or a compelling story, it's a good starting point. When you add human relationships as a backdrop, the image becomes clearer and more compelling.

Imagine two people at war with one another. Each person considers the other an enemy, and their relationship with one another can only be described as hostile. Over time, they build a wall between each other. On either side of the wall, each person lives in alienation from the other. A miserable way for people to live with each other, don't you think?

What if the wall has been built between a person and God! The isolation has got to be horrible and the outcome dreadful. Over time, the wall that goes up between a person and God can only get taller, thicker, deeper, and more insurmountable.

God did something about the wall because He knew we couldn't. According to Paul's remark in Romans 5:10, God made it possible for the wall to come tumbling down through His Son who died and rose again to be our Savior. When you receive Him, the wall comes down and a change takes place, a change that we refer to as reconciliation. In other words, He no longer sees you as His enemy. Instead, He makes you His friend.

Imagine the difference it could make in Martha's life to be able to put into practice the reality that God has made us His friends if we have received Christ. If she is a Christian, just think about the way that seeing herself as God's friend could help her to rewrite her personal story. It could make the same kind of difference in Matt's life as he portrays himself painted by God in warm colors of intimacy rather than cold dye of alienation.

But how can ministers help people like Martha and Matt appropriate all that it means to be reconciled with God?

Before we deal with that question, we should consider another realm in which reconciliation can make a difference: in our relationships with one another. If God can tear down the walls between us and Him, then it makes sense to think that the walls that separate people from one another can topple too. You might even say that our reconciliation with the Lord actually paves the way for reconciliation in our interpersonal relationships.

Jesus made reconciliation with one another an imperative for Kingdom citizens. In His Sermon on the Mount, for instance, He focused attention on reconciliation with one another as a way of curbing the sour side effects of unbridled anger.

When you read Matthew 5:21-26 you get the impression that Jesus considered anger a poison. The deeper it went and the longer it stayed, the more damage anger would do in the people who kept it inside them. That's why He instructed His disciples who harbored hard feelings toward one another to reconcile quickly. Before fermenting anger could build impregnable walls, a faithful follower of the Master would work toward reconciliation in his or her strained relationships.

The Master's mandate has not changed. Interpersonal relationships still remain a high priority for Him. Anger, betrayal, and misunderstanding can build walls in relationships with one another that look impossible to tear down. With Christ, though, anything is possible, even reconciling people to one another.

It can happen in Martha's relationships. If she and her father reconciled, for example, she might not be so driven to succeed in order to get his attention and approval. And it could be just the thing that Matt needs to do in order to get his relationship with his wife going in a more positive direction.

But how will a minister guide Martha and Matt so they can know what it's like to enjoy the sunshine of reconciliation in their relationships with important people in their lives?

Again, we will put off answering that question for now. Instead, think about the potential of reconciliation in the most intimate arena of all relationships: your relationship with yourself. Speech communication theorists, psychologists, and other social scientists give serious attention to what they refer to as intrapersonal relationships. So should we who are engaged in the ministry of reconciliation.

Jesus gave considerable attention to intrapersonal relationships. Do you remember the Great Commandment? Can you quote it? If you can, you might also be able to see just how vital Jesus considered this ingredient to be for healthy Christian living.

According to Luke 10:25-29, a lawyer who questioned Jesus about eternal life could quote it well, even though he still missed its meaning in his life. He cited the admonition to love the Lord with everything within him and to love his neighbor in the same way he loved himself, but he missed what it meant to be a neighbor.

Do you suppose that some people miss the part in the commandment about loving yourself? Of course, the commandment doesn't give us permission to be self-absorbed. Rather, it compels us to see ourselves in a healthy way, the same way God sees us. Remember that He sees us through eyes of divine love, a love for us that prompted Him to reconcile us to Himself through Christ.

Do you think that Martha could benefit from learning how to see herself in a healthy way? Could it be possible that the heart of Matt's pain could be the pitiful self-concept he carries around? Could a number of the serious problems we live with be associated with the need for reconciliation with ourselves? Do some hurting people who suffer from not being able to forgive, affirm, and be honest with themselves?

Now we return to the question that has already been raised two different times. How would a minister help Martha or Matt reconcile with themselves?

An answer awaits us in the Reconciliation-Focused Counseling (RFC) model. First described and then applied to pastoral counseling and preaching, RFC will show a minister how to help hurting people like Martha and Matt to move toward reconciliation.

Just imagine what could happen to them when the walls come down.

Part I

Introducing the RFC Model

Chapter 1

Reconciliation-Focused Counseling: In Search of a Lasting Foundation

An Overview of the Challenge

"The grass withers and the flowers fall, but the word of our God stands forever." (Isaiah 40:8 NIV)[1]

"Jesus Christ is the same yesterday and today and for ever." (Hebrews 13:8)

Someone once well said, "He who marries the spirit of the age will soon become a widower." Nowhere is the truth of this statement more evident than in a student's academic preparation for the counseling ministry.

Any adequate counselor preparation program requires that aspiring counselors be exposed to a wide variety of helping models in their training for ministry. Such exposure will expand not only their understanding but also their ability to utilize a variety of ministry interventions when approaching the helping task. However, this learning experience inevitably challenges students to begin asking the question, "Which of these helping models is the best and for what problems?" The answer to this question, it is believed, will then allow the student to use the optimal approach when dealing with some corresponding problem.

However, throughout this process a recurring development can be observed in the lives of student trainees. Faced with such a wide array of choices, they first become attracted to one theory of helping and then the next. Each approach, whether investigating various theories of personality or differing approaches to marriage and family therapy, seems to offer some unique insights not provided by the other. Each seems to be the "best" or at least offer a unique angle to address the particular problem(s) being considered. One student, distressed by the divergent ideas presented in competing approaches, lamented, "Just when I think I have discovered the theory or approach that has the most merit for a certain problem, I am presented with another and become disenchanted with the last. I just wish there was one approach where I could just hang my hat and focus."

Most students of counseling are well aware of the theoretical vacil-lation that occurs during the course of their academic preparation for ministry. Further complicating this process are the cross-disciplinary challenges involved in the study of theology, psychology, and spirituality. While most students find this preparation to be immensely rewarding, it is also stress producing as new and often-competing insights beckon for priority in the student's developing approach to helping people. The difficulties encountered in attempting to synthesize such diverse material can be very confusing and tension producing for the pastoral counselor candidate. Students often are left with an anxious sense that they are floating free in a sea of information and, understandably, desire some quick relief from this anxiety. Therefore, upon sensing a satisfactory path, they will attempt to anchor in these theoretical waters, only to find the anchor inevitably begins to slip as the currents of new competing theories begin to press upon them.

Interestingly, this same type of phenomenon can be witnessed sociologically, albeit in a more protracted fashion, when throughout this century we have witnessed at first the rise and then fall of professional favor concerning a variety of psychotherapeutic approaches. Initially psychoanalytic, then behavioral, and then humanistic/existential models of understanding and helping people were in vogue. In each case, one "spirit of the age" has yielded to the next in an endless succession of attempts to arrive at the "best." This is not to say that significant merit cannot be found in any of these helping models. Certainly this is not the case. However, the question is ultimately not one of merit but of lasting sufficiency.

Theoretical and technical pondering has its place in academic preparation for ministry. But in spite of the benefits that have come from the study of secular approaches to counseling, a new question inevitably confronts the developing counselor. The question is no longer just which approach or even combination of approaches is the best but what approach will provide what Wayne Oates refers to as a "lasting center"[2] in our efforts to help people. Larry Crabb, in his *Basic Principles of Biblical Counseling*, reflects a similar concern when he says, "Psychology's efforts, while enlightening in many ways, are about as useful to the counselor in search of an absolute foundation as floating anchors are to a ship in stormy waters."[3]

A wide range of Christian writers and practitioners in the field of pastoral counseling readily concede there is profit in the study of the secular. However, the question remains, "Which approach will provide that foundation for speaking to the deepest needs of humanity, not sacrifice any clinical efficacy, and at the same time withstand the transient nature of attempts to build a therapeutic 'tower of Babel'?"

This book represents our personal response to this question. Every minister who counsels and every vocationally called pastoral counselor desires to counsel from a framework that is both theologically grounded and clinically effective. Reconciliation-Focused Counseling (RFC) provides a working solution to this desire. RFC utilizes a theological/biblical foundation as the center upon which we then build our helping model. It is by no means exclusively "biblical" in that the influence of various theoretical models has flavored and illuminated our understanding of faith. What it does offer is a theological framework for understanding the development of emotional and relational problems in the church. This foundation will then serve to guide our pastoral assessments and interventions. You might say that this model reflects our conclusion that theology is decisive in trying to answer the questions that emerge in the counseling arena. However, our academic pursuits and work with people over the years have helped to stimulate and illuminate our understanding of the helping process. As Edward Thornton has so aptly stated in his *Theology and Pastoral Counseling*, "Counseling serves me at the point of both application and apprehension of theology. In fact, my theology is my theory of pastoral care and counseling, and reflection on pastoral functioning constitutes an important methodological aspect of my theological thinking."[4]

We are by no means the first to work toward this end. Veterans in pastoral theology laid a strong foundation early on for contemporary work in pastoral care and counseling. Our purpose is not to be dismissive of this rich heritage but to provide pastors and other ministers of counseling not extensively schooled in this tradition with accessibility to a theologically grounded and clinically effective model from which to counsel. Effective pastoral counseling requires careful attention to both. An excessive concentration on theology makes the counselor vulnerable to a type of "ivory tower" thinking, remote from the challenges of life and faith. Technical preoccupation devoid of a theological foundation will be inclined simply toward symptom reduction, failing to connect these life adjustment problems with the client's broader need to find meaning and purpose in life. In the end, helpers must prayerfully seek a balance between these competing tensions.

A Theology of Emotional and Relational Problems as Revealed in the Creation Story

Since the Fall we as human beings have struggled with estrangement from our Maker. The following pages offer a unique look at the nature of this separation and the resulting alienation that exists between and within people. This examination will show how the introduction of mistrust, shame, and a host of other negative emotional experiences have resulted in the loss of these need-satisfying relationships and had a profoundly detrimental impact on the human experience. People today carry personal hurts and an unfulfilled longing for connection stemming from the same destructive dynamics first experienced by this couple. Furthermore, we will see how the unique struggles people face reveal a common need for reconciliation in one or more of three relational domains.

Finally, persons seeking a scriptural basis from which to approach the helping process will find the reconciliation-focused model developed in succeeding chapters to be a sound and practical way to assist others in their journey toward wholeness. By embracing the universal call to promote reconciliation, both counselors and pastors can join hands in their efforts to assist hurting people. Together we can help restore the relational balance and harmony intended from the beginning.

The Fall—Balance Lost

The stage was set; the snare was laid. The unsuspecting couple was about to experience a mortal wounding of their souls. Never again throughout the course of human history would a man and a woman live in such harmony with one another or with God. Any utopian dream within the realm of humankind's imagination would have been epitomized by their existence. They lived in perfect balance within the whole of God's created order. The fact that they were not gods was not a concern to them. All their needs were perfectly supplied.

But all this was about to change. Within the garden one had come to destroy this condition of spiritual bliss. His intention was malignant from the beginning, born out of his own desperate condition, his rejected state. All he had to do in order to accomplish his seduction was to raise several key questions in the minds of this unsuspecting pair. In the coming pages, we will carefully examine the negative emotional and relational ramifications for the human race resulting from this fateful exchange. Notice how, through a carefully crafted question and subtle innuendo, the serpent managed to instill in this couple the seeds of mistrust and shame. In response to God's instruction not to eat from the tree, he inquired:

> "Did God really say, 'You must not eat from any tree in the garden'? . . .
> You will not surely die, . . . for God knows that when you eat of it your
> eyes will be opened, and you will be like God, knowing good and evil."
> (Genesis 3:1, 4-5)

The Invitation to Mistrust—
The Compromise of Faith

Immediately in the beginning of verse 1 we witness an invitation for this couple to question the trustworthiness of God.[5] The question "Did God really say, 'You must not eat from any tree in the garden?'" demonstrates the subtle yet amazingly effective way an individual can corrupt the faith potential of a listener by attempting to compromise the character and integrity of the messenger, in this case, God. Such attacks needn't be direct, such as "You can't trust God." Indeed, such an approach would likely invite more reluctance and circumspection from the listener due to the stark contrast it poses to immediate experience. The initial approach used by Satan presented a much more insidious challenge to God's integrity. It was like saying, "Have you considered that things may not be as they seem?" This lead-in was meant to snare the curiosity and naïveté of a couple who had only known or considered a God of good intentions. A thin shroud of innocence often veils such invitations to evil and mistrust. When the veil is removed, however, the person already has been lured in the wrong direction, carried by the momentum of considering the alternative.

But the couple was challenged to doubt not only the trustworthiness of God but the reliability of their own senses and judgment as well. Up to this point in their lives, their God-given ability to judge, discern, and listen had served them well. But the question "Did God really say . . ." suggested that their ability to trust their judgment, indeed their very hearing, was now being called into question.

To appreciate the significance of what is being suggested here is difficult for those who have never experienced the loss of these "faculties." But the aged know it well. By necessity, those compromised must choose to give up some if not all their decision-making authority since resources for reaching appropriate decisions are no longer reliable. The tragedy for this couple was that they were lured to doubt the reliability of their God-given senses, *prematurely*.

Taken a step further, the belief that one can hear a message clearly and accurately and can appropriately judge its meaning rests at the heart of issues such as personal security, accountability, and responsibility. Referred to by philosophers as "a priori beliefs" (Ray and Rivizza, 1985, 3-7), such presuppositions affirm the trustworthiness and reliability of our five senses. Only when these presuppositions are in place can we then go on to trust and bring order to the sensory impulses constantly surrounding us.

Conversely, to prematurely accept another's suggestion that our physical or spiritual hearing, or our judgment is compromised, is to make ourselves susceptible to the same malicious influence we witness in the garden. In summary, what we now see is that by questioning the trustworthiness of God, as well as the trustworthiness of Adam and Eve's God-given ability to hear and discern, Satan began to compromise the very resources necessary to establish and maintain need-satisfying relationships with God and others. Let's consider a more contemporary illustration.

Early in my clinical training I vividly recall an incident that served to highlight the role that trust plays in helping to facilitate our vital relationships. The event in question occurred one evening while working in a local psychiatric hospital on the adolescent chemical dependency unit. At the time, the unit was on "lock-down," meaning that no residents were allowed off the unit. As my group was preparing to begin a twelve-step meeting, we realized that there were not enough handouts for the group participants. As I was volunteering to run down the hall to the copy machine, one of the patients, a sixteen-year-old, rather petite and attractive female, offered to come along and help sort and staple the copies. Such "volunteerism" was not uncommon for the unit during "lock down" times since it gave patients an opportunity to get off the unit. And so off we went, down the hall and around the corner to the copy machine. Five minutes later, we were back and proceeded to go on with the meeting.

Following the group session, one of my co-workers approached me and, having observed this process, asked, "Have you noticed how seductive she tends to be?" Caught off guard by his comment, I awkwardly responded with, "I hadn't really noticed." He subsequently told me that during her admission, her social history had revealed a long pattern of promiscuity with men. As he continued to tell me about information from her past, a serious sense of concern began to overtake me. Had I been seduced as well, enticed by the willingness of her offer to help? In this case, was my notion of a "trip off the unit" really a convenient rationalization to legitimize proximity to her?

And then an even greater fear presented itself. The copier was around the corner and out of sight of any needed "corroborative witnesses." What if she, or someone else, were to make an accusation? Panic began to set in. I was early in my academic and clinical training. While this kind of problem can seriously threaten even a seasoned therapist, it can totally derail a trainee. And then there was my wife, Donna. What would her reaction be to this scenario and the possibility of such problems?

Clearly my naïveté and inexperience were being felt in a very acute way. While my best attempts at self-examination revealed no reason for appropriate guilt or personal failure, how would my wife respond if my worst fears materialized? How could I prove the innocence of my actions? The fact was, I couldn't. Complicating my worries at the time were the recent revelations regarding the sexual failures of Jimmy Swaggart and Marvin Gorman. I knew that in the minds of the general public, the only persons more suspect of sexual indiscretion than men were men who were also ministers.

Some readers may have the sense that this whole matter has been entirely overblown or exaggerated. Some may see a grand attempt to rationalize away latent illicit impulses. Others may find identity in this story. Still others may view my choices as not just careless but reckless, deserving of whatever consequences might be forthcoming. All I can say is that on my way home from work that evening, I desperately needed something from my wife. Just what that something involved was still not clear to me at that point, but the urgency of the need was clearly present.

Shortly after arriving home at around 10:30 P.M., I joined my wife, who had already gone to bed. Within moments, the silence of the dark room was broken when I heard her familiar greeting, "How was your evening?" Seizing the opportunity, I proceeded to share the concerns I was harboring, knowing that there was no proof of my innocence and wondering whether my explanation sounded as suspect to her as it did to the one offering it. After what I am sure must have been a five-minute monologue befitting a lawyer's closing argument, I paused and awaited some response. Without missing a beat and with a calm assurance which affirmed her sincerity, she said, "Don't worry sweetheart, . . I trust you." Comforted but not yet convinced I continued, "But what if . . . ?" She interrupted, "It doesn't matter what happens; I trust you."

Within a matter of seconds, my troubled spirit found the very thing that up to this point I had been unable to articulate—*trust*.[6] I cannot begin to tell you how critically important her words were to me that evening. But such mutual affirmations of trust have served to foster our relationship for almost twenty-five years now. Trust, I have learned, is something that can be cultivated over time but never fully earned. That's the nature of trust. There is always an element of choice in the matter. Not just because humans are created with freedom to choose, but also because none of us is truly trustworthy. As the old saying goes, "Lest for the grace of God, there go I." I am no more immune to sexual temptation than the next person and therefore guard this area, like any other, with appropriate diligence. Since we can never fully know a person's motivations or intentions, ultimately trust can find expression only when we *choose* to invest our support in the object of our trust.

In this sense trust is a gift, cultivated by the relationship but still bestowed from one person to the other based on a conscious choice on the part of the giver. Trust is an ingredient so essential to relationships that without it they will surely fail. My wife's choice to trust me that evening not only affirmed me personally for whatever qualities of fidelity I had attempted to exhibit; it affirmed our relationship as being of vital worth and importance to her. In her humanity, she could have chosen to doubt the sincerity of my actions. But instead she chose to trust me and by so doing demonstrated respect for my history of commitment and highlighted the value of our relationship. Because my good intentions, naïve though they may have been, were not overshadowed by a veil of suspicion, I found myself encouraged to be even more trustworthy. It was as if she had found something in me worthy of blessing and I was therefore even more committed to merit the gift of her trust. Such is the power of affirmation in and between the lives of God's people. Relationships grow and prosper when we seek to find qualities to bless rather than criticize in one another.

Conversely, the dynamic of mistrust not only injures our relationship with God and ourselves, but impairs our relationships with others as well.

Mistrust is like a cancer, permeating families, groups, organizations, cultures, and the international community at large. Within all of these realms, frequent, prominent, and pervasive violations of trust occur on a daily basis, damaging the way individuals interact with one another and severely limiting the potential for cooperative living. Within our Western society, it seems that there is more suspicion between the sexes, the races, and the socioeconomic classes than ever before. Clearly, the ramifications of the Fall regarding the perpetuation of mistrust throughout the whole of God's creation have been devastating for humanity. For Adam and Eve, the beginnings of this interpersonal fallout can begin to be seen in chapter 3, verses 11-12 of Genesis. "And he said, '. . . Have you eaten from the tree that I commanded you not to eat from?' The man said, 'The woman you put here with me—she gave me some fruit from the tree, and I ate it.'"

The picture painted here is played out over and over in relationships today. Imagine the dialog that must have taken place just prior to God confronting this couple. Now hiding behind the trees and bushes in the garden but still close enough to speak, Adam says to Eve, "What in the world have you gotten me into!" "Gotten you into!?" she replies. "I didn't make you eat that fruit! Don't you try to pin that on me!" At which point, God probably hears their bickering and approaches them only to have first one and then the other try to divert the blame onto another. The mistrust between this couple must have been so thick that you could have, as they say, "cut it with a knife." While denying his own complicity, Adam felt betrayed for having been misled by Eve. Eve, on the other hand, felt betrayed for being blamed. Both were still reeling from the messages of suspicion encouraged by Satan. Clearly, a foundational component of successful relationships had been sorely damaged.

One additional observation needs to be made regarding the problematic nature of mistrust. Mistrust is by implication the opposite of faith. Extreme examples of both mistrust and faith can be understood as resting on opposite ends of a continuum. In severe cases of mistrust, a person begins to doubt the very existence of God. For those of us who espouse a Christian worldview, this type of outcome is certainly a point of great concern. But another matter of concern, not initially apparent, is also revealed. The problem can best be highlighted by first raising a question. "How can two equally bright, insightful, analytic minds, when given the same set of facts about the Christian faith, come to diametrically opposite conclusions regarding its worth and meaning?" The answer lies in the awareness that the "facts," as we have come to know them, are not self-interpreting. In other words, each of us to some degree distorts the facts in our attempts to know something or to apprehend the truth of the matter.

Such distortions occur by virtue of the presuppositions that we bring to the matter at hand. For example, parents who believe their child is rebellious will interpret their adolescent's subsequent misbehavior more negatively than parents who interpret the same behavior as their adolescent's need for independence. Therefore, a person who brings the presupposition that "there is no God" to the facts about Christ will interpret them entirely differently than their God believing counterpart. Understanding this gives us a better appreciation for Christ's warning that "whatever is not from faith is sin." Faith in God is a necessary prerequisite to properly understanding the "facts" of life and our response to them. Jesus statement in Mark 8:18 (NAS), "Having eyes, do you not see? And having ears, do you not hear? . . . ," is a vivid reminder that our looking and listening in life must occur in the context of a faith in God. Any attempt to approach the interpretation of life without this belief or presupposition will lead one to errant conclusions and actions, in other words sin. Thus, the seed of mistrust further damages our lives both directly and indirectly through the insidious ways in which it compromises our judgment and therefore ultimately our relationships with God and others.

The Introduction of Shame:
An Image Marred

Having compromised the perceived trustworthiness of both the Creator and his creation, Satan in verses 4-5 continued to distort the integrity and goodness of both through his unfolding progression of deception. Having managed to introduce doubt into the minds of this unsuspecting pair, he then sought to strike a fatal blow to the God-affirmed goodness of their humanity. Backtracking for a moment in this story, verses 4-5 read, "You will not surely die!" the serpent said to the woman. "For *God knows* that when you eat of it your eyes will be opened, and you will be *like God,* knowing good and evil " [Genesis 3:4-5] (emphases added).

Like one who has just been made the brunt of a cruel joke, the question immediately haunts each of them: "Is there something that I am missing?" Or stated in the affirmative, "There must be something that I am missing." An awareness of the state of being incomplete or exposed, of feeling inadequate or lacking some unattainable quality, is the center of what is called shame. Fossum and Mason state:

Shame is an inner sense of being completely diminished or insufficient as a person. It is the self-judging the self. A moment of shame may be humiliation so painful or an indignity so profound that one feels one has been robbed of her or his dignity or exposed as basically inadequate, bad, or worthy of rejection.[7]

Echoing this view, widely recognized shame theorist Gershen Kaufman writes:

Contained in the experience of shame is the piercing awareness of ourselves as fundamentally deficient in some vital way as a human being. To live with shame is to experience the very essence or heart of the self as wanting. Shame is an impotence-making experience because it feels as though there is no way to relieve the matter, no way to restore the balance of things. One has simply failed as a human being. No single action is seen as wrong and, hence, reparable.[8]

Now notice the conclusions that are encouraged in this couple from the shameful implications concealed in Satan's ploy. These thoughts offer a sobering parallel to these definitions:

We must not only be blind but gullible. The serpent is right. How could we not see. We do lack knowledge, in particular the knowledge of good and evil, and this condition of not knowing is shameful. And come to think about it, we do lack power, in particular a power comparable to God, and this condition of lacking power is also shameful. We do lack transcendent presence, in particular the ability to transcend our human state and experience God in His spiritual realm, and this condition of being confined to the material is shameful.[9]

While hypothetical, this internal dialogue, or some variation thereof, set the wheels of shame in motion for all of humankind. And so the great lie, perpetrated to distort the perfect condition of the untainted image of God in humanity, has continued to plague his creation.[10] The lie is that the condition of being human, and therefore not being God, is shameful, as if such a comparison should be made in the first place.

If pride goeth before a fall,[11] then a comparison goeth before pride.[12] Like the familiar admonition to refrain from comparing "apples to oranges," some comparisons are not rightfully made. Man was never created to be "like" God. He never needed to be. He was loved by God. All of his needs were perfectly supplied.[13] Now obviously the making of comparisons between this couple and God had long been made. Certainly, they knew that they were not gods by virtue of the fact that they could not do the things God could do. But for the first time, their worth was being diminished in comparison to God's worth. While they couldn't do everything God could do, they never thought this meant they were worth less than God, at least not until now.

Some comparisons help to add perspective while others only tend to distort the truth. The guise proposed by Satan comparing a person's worth to that of God's was an illustration of the latter. The purpose of this strategic, ill-intentioned comparison is clear when seen in the context of shame—it was meant to cast a disparaging light on the human condition of this unsuspecting couple. It had its intended effect. Adam and Eve succumbed to the temptation. They were not guilty of choosing to compare their condition or worth to that of God. This was Satan's choice, his ploy. Their sin followed this comparison. By choosing to agree with Satan they, in essence, questioned God's trustworthiness and the goodness of their condition.

Collateral Damage: Guilt, Fear, Anger, and Distress

A host of other negative emotional experiences resulting from the Fall accompanied those previously mentioned.[14] New troubling feelings of guilt and fear are demonstrated by this couple's hiding in the garden. Distress and despair over the loss of their untainted relationship with God as well as privileged access to the garden were no doubt soon present. And while we certainly witness the damaging emergence of anger in chapter 4 in the account of Cain and Abel, no doubt anger was already resident in Adam's blaming of Eve and Eve's blaming of the serpent. Clearly, we begin to see a picture of colossal collateral damage stemming from the Fall.

We should note that while the emergence of negative emotions represented a decline in the quality of life for this couple, in a fallen world the ability to experience negative emotions is nevertheless crucial to survival. Negative feelings of fear, guilt, anger, mistrust, and so forth can serve a very useful role in life by providing guidance for persons making choices in a world compromised by sin.

For example, imagine the risks that would be encountered by a person who knew no fear and therefore took no precautions to avoid potentially dangerous situations. Or what if a man could not access his anger when witnessing his family being attacked by intruders. Doesn't this emotion propel and drive a protective response in those seeking to care for the ones they love? And consider physical pain or other types of emotional distress. Are they not useful in helping to inform the sufferer about issues that need attention? Don't they serve as barometers of self-care, providing critical information that can be used to guide a proper and remedial response? The point being encouraged here is that while God would have preferred for his creation to have avoided the pain and anguish of the Fall, in his perfect love and infinite wisdom he has provided the necessary resources for people not only to survive but to thrive in a fallen world.

An Image Marred—The Relational Fallout

We often fail to consider that what made the garden experience so completely satisfying to this couple was not just the overflowing provision of material goods but the undefiled nature of relationships. There was a harmony that existed between God and man, man and man, and man and himself. A thorough understanding of these three relational domains is central to an understanding of the Fall's impact on our world.

Alienation from God

Humankind was created with a need for spiritual relatedness. Psalm 42:1 states, "As the deer pants for streams of water, so my soul pants for you, O God." The early Christian theologian Augustine summarized it well in his prayer: "Thou has made us for Thyself, and the heart of man is restless until it finds its rest in Thee."[15]

Both the Scriptures and the widespread nature of humanity's religious strivings observed over the generations confirm that people have been created with a deep desire and personal need to live in a loving and affirming relationship with God. However, the presence of mistrust, shame, guilt, fear, distress, despair, anger, and a host of other negative emotions have placed a barrier between humankind and this life-giving relationship. We are introduced to these new relational realities when, immediately after the Fall, we see that ". . . they hid from the LORD God among the trees of the garden" (Genesis 3:8). When asked why he was hiding, Adam's response was ". . . I was afraid because I was naked; so I hid" (Genesis 3:10).

The behavior now witnessed in this unfolding drama represents the culmination of a cascade of negative emotional experiences pressing down upon this couple. Guilt, distress, despair, and so on, while not explicitly outlined here in these verses, are no doubt all beginning to weigh into their emotional and relational agony. However, the Scriptures highlight for us two emotional states that are central to an understanding of the behaviors being witnessed.

First, in the beginning of verse 10 we read that Adam "was afraid." Adam was literally in "no man's land." Like a ship in uncharted waters, fear of what now lay before them gripped both their minds. Fear, of course, can find expression only in an atmosphere where trust has been compromised. Clearly, their choice to compromise what was once a perfect trust between them and God is once again being felt. However, a second emotional experience that is directly related to their fear is highlighted later in verse 10 where we read that Adam was afraid because he "was naked." Since Genesis chapter two verse 25 clearly describes a nakedness absent of shame, the presence of fear now reveals that it is accompanied by shame.[16]

To further appreciate the significance of this response, a distinction should now be made between shame and guilt. Appropriate guilt is a feeling that results from acting in a way that violates God's standards for our behavior. Guilt relates to some action on our part, whether the action is reflected in either actual behavior or thinking. In essence, guilt is a value judgment on a person's behavior. Shame, on the other hand, is a value judgment on the person. No longer is just the behavior bad, the person is bad. The distinction is critical. Behavior that falls short of appropriate standards is something that a person can change. Being inadequate or deficient as a result of being human is another matter entirely.

Therefore, Adam's confession that he "was afraid" should not be explained only in terms of his guilt and fear of God's reprisal but also in terms of being "naked." His state or condition of nakedness must in turn be understood in light of the couple's previous exposure to shame. Adam's response reflects not just a loss of innocence, as is traditionally suggested, but to a loss of value. It speaks to the heart of what it means to be human. Adam was afraid to be seen in all of his humanness and the inadequacy and failing that it now represented. He was now alienated from God not only by his rebellious choices but also by a sense of personal unacceptability further amplified by these choices.

Alienation from Others

Not only were Adam and Eve ashamed of being seen by God but they were also ashamed of being seen by one another. Herein lies another dilemma. The Scriptures affirm humankind's need for interpersonal relatedness. God declared in Genesis 2:18 that "it is not good for the man to be alone." In spite of Adam's utopian environment, he needed the emotional, physical, and spiritual intimacy found in relating to another human being.

Set in this context, God's revelation makes it clear that humans were created with a need for not only intimacy with God but other people as well. Shame, however, limits the formation of these need-satisfying relationships. It increases one's commitment to isolation by giving persons the message that if they were truly known by others then they would be unacceptable and therefore must remain hidden.

Complicating the estrangement brought on by the shame that they now experienced was the expression of mistrust now witnessed in their inter-actions. We have already explored how mistrust was weaving its way into this couple's relationship, compromising their ability to remain close due to growing cycles of blame. But we, like this couple, are often deceived into believing that our feelings of mistrust are warranted due to the untrustworthiness of others.

Unfortunately, the untrustworthiness we witness in others is often only a reflection of what already exists in us. Satan's inference that God cannot be trusted we now see was in fact just projecting onto God what really existed in him. Or the Pharisees' claim that Jesus had a demon,[17] is really only a reflection of the evil that was resident within them. These are only a few of the numerous Old and New Testament examples where we witness this tendency. Jesus warned against such lacking circumspection by cautioning those who would seek to remove the "speck"[18] in their brother's eye to first check for a log in their own. Clearly these lessons should promote humility and self-examination in anyone seeking to find fault in another.

When the effects of shame and mistrust are taken together, a picture of the formidable obstacles to intimacy between people begins to emerge. We now see how shame and untrustworthiness permeate our very nature and, when placed together with the host of other negative emotional experiences stemming from the Fall, rob humankind of the ability to experience meaningful connection and the reciprocal need satisfaction intended to characterize human interactions.

Alienation from Self/Nature

A few of the dangerous implications of being alienated from oneself have already been seen in Adam blaming Eve and Eve blaming the serpent for their choice to eat from the tree. When a person feels they are unacceptable, they must avoid acknowledging responsibility for behaviors that might reveal their unacceptability. Many people conclude that the influence of guilt offers the best explanation for such behavior, that guilt often leads to the avoidance of self-awareness and therefore personal responsibility. But contrary to such popular notions, guilt does not motivate one to hide from "self" as much as shame. It is clear that guilt may join shame in promoting concealment from others in an effort to escape scrutiny or punishment, but the penalty of being exposed to oneself comes mainly from shame.

Guilt may bring contrition but not self-rejection. Guilt may even draw an individual closer to the One who can forgive. However shame alienates a person from himself or herself. By virtue of the message that one is too bad, too far gone for help, honest self-appraisal must be compromised. Therefore, an individual can no longer acknowledge guilt without the risk of triggering shame. Consequently, guilty behavior goes unchecked. Defensive strategies are then called on to assist in avoiding the level of honest self-appraisal that would be necessary to acknowledge personal shortcomings. In the final analysis, a faulty self-concept hinders both the personal accountability and self-acceptance necessary for an honest and growing relationship with God and others.

Complicating the intra-personal alienation promoted by shame is the position taken by some that all negative emotions, regardless of their form, are reflections of sin and are therefore to be censored and by implication avoided. Arguing that since negative emotions have resulted from the Fall and are based ultimately in distorted thoughts and beliefs about God, self, and others, they are intrinsically bad.

While such moral reductionisms are inviting due to their mere simplicity, such a global stigmatization of negative emotions is a highly risky proposition. First, as we have seen, negative emotions can help to serve as "barometers of self-care," giving individuals vital feedback necessary to direct and motivate corrective, protective, and redemptive responses to life's many difficult situations. Therefore, giving attention to rather than avoiding these provisional states is essential. Second, to frame all negative emotions as bad is like saying to an ill person that his elevated temperature is "bad" as opposed to the illness that it identifies. Negative emotions, like a person's physical temperature, are neither good nor bad.

It is what we do with these emotions and their underlying messages that will determine their merit.

In James 1:15, we see this principle highlighted where we read, "Then when lust has conceived, it gives birth to sin"(NAS). Clearly just the initial *emotion* of lust, while by implication a risky state, is not highlighted as the central focus of concern. It is when lust or temptation is allowed to develop or take hold that it becomes sin. Or in Genesis 4:6-7 we read, "Then the Lord said to Cain, 'Why are you angry? . . . Sin is crouching at the door; and its desire is for you, but you must master it'"(NAS). God did not say, "Because you are angry, you have sinned." What he was saying is that here is an alarm or warning to which you must respond appropriately. It is the *response* of Adam to this vulnerable state that invites our attention. Such is the nature of emotions. They are like alarms, unpleasant and even distressing at times, but nonetheless vital in providing the feedback which is necessary to properly manage our lives.

Furthermore, like the avoidance of guilt that we described earlier, recognizing all negative emotions as "bad" tends to discourage the level of self-awareness necessary to promote adequately our physical health. Attending to our negative emotional states helps us to maintain not only our emotional health but physical fitness as well. Many physical aliments are foreshadowed and subsequently identified by the presence of certain negative emotional states. For example, one of the early signs of hypothyroidism, or under-functioning thyroid, is the presence of a depressed or sad mood. To categorize all negative emotional states as spiritual failure or "bad" may well misdirect subsequent efforts to bring about a remedial response. So, rather than finding relief through the administration of appropriate medication, the individual is often further burden by the exaggeration of unwarranted guilt.

As we can see, the emotional alienation described above further highlights and complicates the physical and ecological alienation also resulting from the Fall. Genesis 3:8-24 reveals that humankind is now separated not only emotionally and spiritually from God, self, and others, but physically from self and nature. We are in a sense at odds with our now temporal bodies, struggling to resist the deterioration presented by illness and aging. We wrestle with nature, condemned to toil all the days of our lives with a ground that on the one hand resists us with "thorns and thistles"[19] and which we in turn neglect resulting in our further detriment. Truly, the balance originally evidenced in creation has been desperately compromised.

Their Remedy

So here they were, each created with a deep desire and personal need to live in a loving and affirming relationship with God, one another, and self, left without the relational qualities needed to satisfy this need. The image that made harmonious relationships possible had now been compromised and with it the delicate balance witnessed in the original created order. It was just such a dilemma that set the stage for the desperation that was to follow.

Following their interaction with the serpent, a shift in the focus of humanity's desire for God can clearly be seen. Our original desire to draw close to, to love, and to be loved by God was replaced by a desire to be like God.[20] Additionally, we now desire what has been created over the creator, the material over the spiritual, what can be seen over what cannot be seen. Genesis 3:6 highlights this shift in focus: "When the woman saw that the fruit of the tree was good for food and pleasing to the eye, and also desirable for gaining wisdom, she took some and ate it."

What is interesting to note is that by eating the fruit, Adam and Eve were attempting to remedy, on their own, the perceived untrustworthiness of God and the shameful state of their condition. They assumed that some action on their behalf, apart from God, would liberate them from this problem. This was, of course, the cardinal sin of pride . . . representing or acting like someone (in this case, God) who you are not.

To appreciate the full tragedy of pride, we need to recognize that it represents not only the height of arrogance but also the depth of self-reproach. It is striving to be something that you were never intended to be and despising what you were created to be. It calls into question our rightful place in relationship with God, a relationship that was intended to affirm both the value of God as well as the value of his creation. It is, as we now see, humanity's attempt to assume control of life and elevate unrealistically our sense of worth in response to feelings of shame.[21] Isn't it paradoxical that the original attempt by human beings to raise themselves up by eating of the tree resulted instead in their fall? How much do our own efforts apart from God do this today?

Jesus' Remedy: Balance Restored

Jesus was no stranger to the dilemma being described here. In fact, humanity's longstanding struggle with mistrust, shame, guilt, and so forth is central to Jesus' emphasis on forgiveness and an understanding of his discussion with the Pharisean lawyer in Matthew 22:36-40. When asked, "Which is the greatest commandment in the Law?"[22] Jesus summarizes the attitudes and actions required by the Law in what could be called the formula for how to live the balanced Christian life. His response reveals a concise outline intended to guide our journey back to wholeness and lead us to the restoration of divine balance lost at the Fall.[23]

> Jesus replied, 'Love the Lord your God with all your heart and with all your soul and with all your mind.' [38]This is the first and greatest commandment. [39]And the second is like it: 'Love your neighbor as yourself.' [40]All the Law and the Prophets hang on these two commandments.' (Matthew 22:37-40)

To further enhance our understanding of this passage, we might imagine the nature of the relationships described here as being represented by a pendulum of a clock (figure 1). According to this text, God is to serve as the preeminent or focal point of our love[24] and is therefore best seen as the pivot point on which all our relationships hinge. The love of self and others can be represented by opposite swings of the pendulum. Consequently, balance in the Christian life can be realized only when we not only recognize the pivotal role that God must play in all our decisions and relationships but when the pendulum of love is allowed to swing freely between self and others.

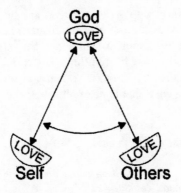

Fig. 1. Relationship Pendulum

The polarity of tensions that is created in trying to love both self and others at first seems irreconcilable. But it is these same tensions that remind us of our inherent need for God and our need to seek him for direction in all our choices. Only when we place God first as the object of our love and concern can these tensions find satisfaction and balance be achieved.

Given Christ's admonition toward what is defined here as divine balance, we are challenged to seek the restoration of relationships in all three areas. In my mind, this is the central task of the Christian counselor. We seek to set the stage for a divine-human encounter, in the midst of human tragedy and brokenness, in which grace is communicated and reconciliation is experienced in each relational domain. Not unlike the Christian community at large, we occupy the role of John the Baptist in preparing the way for a salvation experience in the lives of our clients. Thornton describes this process well when he states:

> God intends to meet us with salvation in every experience of life! This intention is present in the threat of destruction as well as in the promise of deliverance. Isaiah articulated this faith when he warned Ahaz of impending doom as a result of the king's alliance with Assyria. The prophetic sign of destruction was not the desertion of Israel by her Lord; the promised sign was the birth of a son named Immanuel: God is with us (Isaiah 7:14, 8:8). God is immanent in an event of judgment. The New Testament ascription of the name Immanuel to Jesus (Matthew 1:23) affirms that God is immanent in a decisive event of deliverance.[25]

For us, our ministry to people revolves around the recognition that ultimately we are to be ministers of God's grace in the midst of human suffering, seeking to promote a salvation experience that will facilitate reconciliation in all of our relationships. Notice the progressive call to reconciliation outlined by Christ in response to the Pharisean lawyer's question regarding what should be of ultimate concern?

Restoring a Relationship with God

> *"Love the Lord your God with all your heart and with all your soul and with all your mind." (Matthew 22:37)*

Christ's response demonstrates that our deepest need as human beings is to return to God as the center of our ultimate concern. Yet, learning to love God, to trust him, and to look to him for direction is hindered by the distorted messages and emotions resulting from the Fall. The sense of being unacceptable and unlovable permeates the shame-based individual's experience. These self-diminishing thoughts, in turn, tend to propel a person to seek self-deliverance through the pursuit of knowledge, money, sex, power, science, youth, anything but God. Messages of mistrust pervade relationships, tragically discouraging and ultimately preventing persons from experiencing the need-satisfying and life-giving relationships evidenced prior to the Fall. Instead, in the futility of isolation and separation, people seek to remedy that which can only come from a divine connection.

Emancipation from this vortex of human striving is possible only when one chooses to embrace, through faith, the grace of unconditional acceptance found in the cross. God's willingness to allow Christ to die and bear our shame demonstrated once and for all the trustworthiness of God and the value of his creation. To appropriate the love of God through Christ Jesus is to liberate an individual from the bondage of damaging messages and emotions and free him to embrace a new relationship with God. Thus, what was desperately grasped at in the fall has been given through the cross.[26]

Restoring a Relationship with Others

"Love your neighbor . . ." (Matthew 22:39)

The story of the Good Samaritan illustrates the truth that it is easier to say we love God than to demonstrate this love with our neighbor. It also reveals the roles that shame and mistrust play in perpetuating the alienation that exists in relationships between people. For one reason or another, issues of unacceptability, mistrust, and fear, dictate the relationships between all the characters in the story. Each reveals how the danger of involvement might not only risk injury or harm but also result in defilement and shame. For all but one, it was simply safer to remain distant.

So given the risks and obstacles we must face in reaching out to others, where do we find the ability to love demonstrated by the Good Samaritan? Paul challenged the Galatians to take seriously the resources found in their faith tradition, reminding them that their position in Christ offers the opportunity to partake of the fruit of the Spirit (Galatians 5:16-26). His rejoinder reminds us that when we live by the Spirit, we will be enabled to love our neighbor, to bless others rather than curse them, and to empower others rather than dominate them. Only then can the reciprocal love of God flow in relationships and allow freedom for people to experience mutual need satisfaction that was intended to characterize the nature of relationships from the beginning.[27]

Just as shame is born in the context of failed relationships, its remedy is likewise found in the context of restored relationships—relationships that communicate the love of unconditional acceptance and grace that we all so desperately need. While a perfect acceptance awaits those who discover their right relationship with God, it is through His creation that it finds its most similar and fundamental expression. We serve vicariously as His hands and feet, one body in Christ seeking to minister grace to the walking wounded in our midst. Likewise, injuries to our trust potential occur through violations and betrayals experienced in our relationships with others. And like before, our ability to move beyond these injuries to form satisfying, mutually trustworthy relationships depends on the corrective trust-engendering experiences discovered in healthy relationships with others. In both cases, God's people are called on to be conduits of the acceptance and trustworthiness we ourselves have experienced.

Restoring a Relationship with Oneself

". . . as yourself." (Matthew 22:39)

One might appropriately ask the question, "Is Christian self-love[28] legitimate or is it in fact an oxymoron?" Well, if self-love in this passage is not prescriptive, as some have argued, it most certainly is assumptive and permissive. However, while the notions of loving God and others are readily accepted in the Christian community, the notion of loving self is much more controversial since such a suggestion may be viewed as encouraging pride, self-absorption, or narcissism. Therefore, a point of clarification is in order. The *"self-love"* being suggested here is defined as *"taking steps to care for oneself emotionally, intellectually, physically and spiritually as a person of worth who is valued by God and which results in a greater ability to love God and others."*

This understanding of self-love recognizes its inherently reciprocal nature and therefore avoids the common cultural tendency to view such an undertaking as an isolated and individualistic activity. Therefore, the self-love being described here is not self-indulgence or selfishness, just as appropriate self-care is not narcissism. Healthy self-love recognizes that these activities are not ends in themselves but instead work to enable a person to love others more completely, more effectively. It is also not the same thing as self-esteem, which tends to emphasize a person's need to feel "good" about herself as a measure of how well they are doing. While healthy "self-love" certainly allows for positive feelings about self, it also recognizes that spiritual growth and the self-censorship it invites often requires the need to entertain negative appraisals of ourselves in order the see the need for change.[29]

Utilizing this understanding of "self-love" allows us to see how critically related such activities are to the resolution of the problems that we see at the Fall. We cannot be good to others if we are not good to ourselves. Like Jesus, there are times that we need to pull away from the crowd and attend to our need for food, rest, and spiritual communion with God.[30] The individual who tries to utilize an approach to ministry that disregards the need for appropriate self-care will harm not only themselves but also those that they seek to help. Such compulsive selflessness inevitably results in some form of spiritual, intellectual, emotional, and/or physical starvation that can only lead to destructive consequences for others.

While Jesus' call for self-denial[31] may certainly result in privation for the cause of Christ, we must not interpret this message to be a call to self-neglect. Isn't such an approach to life attempting to deny that which we were created to be . . . human? Wouldn't this be agreeing with Adam and Eve by saying that our humanity is something that we should flee, that there is something wrong with the way we were created, and that our inherent dependence on God reveals the flawed condition of our created state? If not, then we are left asking the question, "Just what *is* my worth as a human being before God?"[32]

Ultimately, our sense of value or worth to God can fully be realized only when we come to realize the depth of our sins and the liberation and restoration that we have been granted through the grace of Jesus Christ. Our value as God's creation is manifest most clearly in the value of the atoning sacrifice of His Son. Jesus' death on our behalf answers once and for all the question of how much God loves and values us. It also forever contradicts the shame-full message perpetuated by Satan that God's supreme creation, man, what He proclaimed to be "very good," should be held in disrepute.

As we have seen, shame and mistrust are not just personal matters but issues that have far-reaching implications for all relationships. Our ability to love others, to forgive others, to trust others is reciprocally related to our own ability to love, forgive, and trust ourselves. Therefore, we must learn to change the damaging messages, which give rise to shame and mistrust in order to prevent the cycle of distorted emotions from infecting our relationships with others. We must confront the messages of personal unacceptability and embrace the fullness of the message that we are truly new creatures in Christ.

Divine Balance: Some Necessary Distinctions

Several questions naturally emerge when we embark on the journey of cultivating healthy relationships with God, self, and others—what we have called working toward restoration of divine balance. One question invites us to ask, "Is our own unique understanding of divine balance really valid or scripturally consistent?" A related question concerns the practicality of pursuing such an abstract or nebulous goal. In other words, "Can this idea or goal be framed in such a way as to promote its practical application?" Each of these concerns will be addressed briefly in the following discussion.

We have already addressed the validity of pursuing divine balance in the previous examination of Matthew 22:36-40. However, the question being raised here is not whether the concept of divine balance is legitimate but whether our *unique* understanding and application of balance is valid. Consistent spiritual growth requires that we continually examine our ideas to test whether what we are actually pursuing or promoting is in fact consistent with a true picture of divine balance. In other words, we may know divine balance to be a legitimate goal but are our ways of pursuing or describing it accurate?

For example, our Western culture tends to promote a popular misconception that marriage should be a 50-50 proposition, quid pro quo—something for something. Such an approach seems to represent a balance between self-care and other-care. Yet, were Christians to adopt this understanding of marriage, as the ideal of divine balance, then their marriages would be destined for strife or failure. From a worldly perspective, the idea of 50-50 only seems reasonable. You get something, I get something, hence our relationship is in balance. The problem with this view, aside from scriptural evidence to the contrary, is how do we measure the "somethings?" Invariable the "somethings" never quite seem to match up because we can never agree on how to balance the relationship ledger. Most commonly, the result of this imbalance is that we end up feeling as though we didn't get something we deserved.

Let's consider another example. One common perception of balance as it pertains to an individual and his functioning is witnessed in the statement, "He sure is a balanced person." Implicit in this view of such a person is that he lacks emotional reactivity and refrains from what could be considered extremes in behavior. In other words, balanced people would never appear radical in their temperament or behavior. While the case could certainly be made that Christian spirituality enhances self-control and temperance, such a perception is far too narrow to reflect the richness of divine balance. Christ himself frequently demonstrated behavior that represented a radical departure from what his culture and setting would have understood as balanced. From driving money changers out of the temple to other challenges to both secular and religious practices of the day, Christ exhibited a counter-cultural lifestyle that was nevertheless the epitome of divine balance.

The problems posed by the previous illustrations stem from an excessive reliance upon a rationalistic, culturally informed, or otherwise worldly approach to describing balance. They represent only two ways in which balance can be misconstrued. In the divine economy, however, we discover that balance is often counter-intuitive in nature. For example, we learn that we get by giving and that whoever wishes to gain his life must first lose it. For this reason, we should be ever mindful of the limitations of appealing to reason as the primary measure of what constitutes balanced living. While reason and experience certainly inform our approach to dealing with life, nothing can take the place of allowing Scripture, illumined by the Holy Spirit, to be our ultimate guidepost in the pursuit of balanced Christian living. Furthermore, these observations remind us that while Matthew 22:36-40 reveals the very spirit and heart of this most worthy goal, we still rely upon the whole corpus of Scripture in seeking to live out this balance in our day to day lives.

The second question posed by the pursuit of divine balance represents a natural extension of the first. With such a broad and far-reaching concept as divine balance, in what ways can we best promote its useful and practical application? In other words, is there some way to further refine this idea to aid in its application? The following discussion represents an attempt to respond to this concern.

Frequently, attempts to create a model for behavior using Matthew 22:36-40 result in persons creating assorted lists of descending priorities. For example, God, as the preeminent focus of our love, always rests at the top of the list. The primacy of our love for God is followed by successively less important relational commitments. So for one individual, after God, family, church, friends, then co-workers, and so forth, might be listed as ever decreasing objects of love or concern. For another, the list would be altered somewhat to reflect her unique patterns of commitment. (Love and care for oneself, if it is mentioned at all, is usually placed at the bottom of the list.) Each person, however, with completed list in hand, would then seek to use this as their model for directing or expressing their love. Therefore, if simultaneous needs were to exist demanding attention to both family and church, then based on the previous example family would always get the nod.

The problem with this attempt to operationalize these verses is that such a linear and static approach to divine balance fails to account for its dynamic nature. For example, on any given day, spending time caring for ourselves may actually be God's perfect desire for how we should direct our caring energy at that given moment in time (for example, Elijah being fed by the angel after fleeing into the desert from Ahab [1 Kings 19]). However, according to the previous example, only when all the other needs represented earlier in the list are satisfied, can we direct energy to care for self.

The critical reader may muse that the patterns of self-interest observed in human behavior should remove any concern for rampant problems of self-neglect. However, the problem being addressed is not the human tendency of self-interest over other-interest. Rather, the problem is whether the model of balance being offered really addresses the *legitimacy* of directing love energy to objects found lower and lower on one's list. The prioritization model given earlier cannot ever really legitimize such behavior since the needs of the previous groups are never fully satisfied.

A second problem related to the prioritization approach pertains to its relationship to shame. From the time one begins to distinguish between self and mother during infancy, a child practices making separations between self and other objects and experiences in the world. This practice of ordering experiences into mutually exclusive or contradictory groups is known as dichotomous thinking. It reflects a natural proclivity in all young children to make sense and bring order to the world around them.[33] Such simplistic categorizations help them to foster a sense of competence in their ability to know and navigate the world in which they live. This form of thinking represents a necessary and efficient, albeit immature, way of perceiving the world. However, as persons grow older they are challenged to see how reality or truth is often not represented accurately by such strict mental separations.

For example, while a shovel and a spade are two separate and distinct objects, they share common features and functions. Both have wooden handles, metal blades, and are used for working soil. Or, when describing people, we discover that being accurate in our representations requires avoiding extreme terms such as good/bad, brilliant/stupid, or ravishing/

repulsive, and instead use words that allow for more shades of meaning such as nice/unkind, smart/challenged, and attractive/plain, respectively. We learn that seeing the world in terms of polar opposites limits accurate descriptions of our experiences and the people we meet—that approaching our descriptions with integrity requires that we embrace the more challenging task of finding reality somewhere in-between the polarized or unidimensional pictures of our youth. We also learn that, at times, no list of adjectives can fully capture or describe the qualities of the subject of interest. And somewhere along the way, we hopefully discover that truth can only be pointed to but never fully apprehended—that ultimately truth is discovered through faith rather than intellectual assent.

This natural progression of intellectual, ethical, and spiritual development may seem inevitable, but it is often resisted with great fervor. Dichotomous thinking is attractive in that it offers the illusion that you actually know more than you really do. There is a sense of certainty that the category into which a thing, event or person is placed captures its complete essence. After all, it's either a spade or a shovel. The person is either good/bad, smart/dumb, liberal/conservative, and so forth. With such labels, one begins to think that he or she actually knows all there is to know about the subject in question, . . . period, end of story. No complexities, only certainty. By assigning information to strict, rigid, and mutually exclusive categories, we foster the illusion that we fully know what we are describing and therefore don't have to face the limitations of our knowing. For in facing our limitations, we risk the possibility of triggering our shame, that sense of inadequacy that somehow, by not fully knowing, we are flawed.

And so we find ourselves walking lockstep with Adam and Eve toward the tree, seduced by the world into believing that somehow we can really be gods, free from the shameful limitations of our knowledge and ultimately our humanity. Therein lies the second problem in using the prioritization approach as the model exemplar for pursuing divine balance. For in the end, such lists remove God from the decision-making process. Why? Because once the list of priorities is made, we mistakenly assume that we now know how to direct our caring energy in the future, indifferent to our need for day-by-day, moment-by-moment guidance from our Lord. This is where our faith as counselors becomes particularly important. We can never know with certainty what will benefit a particular client in a particular situation at a particular point in time. Therefore, while our training helps to inform our approach to any situation, our faith ultimately enables and guides our actions.

So the second question remains, "Is it possible to describe divine balance in a way that will aid in its practical application?" While there are practical limitations to any model, another way to conceptualize this idea is to return to the picture of a pendulum. Again, God rests at the top as the focal point of our love and concern. However, rather than just "self" and "others" being listed at opposing sides of the swinging pendulum, we place our expansive lists of possible love objects randomly across the path of its arc. Now, rather than being constrained by some artificially contrived list, we find ourselves, moment by moment, having to depend on God's grace and direction as to how we invest our care. As we allow the pendulum to swing, unrestricted by the limitations previously imposed with listing, we find that at any given point the object of our love can vary, depending on Divine direction. Utilizing this understanding of divine balance allows us to remain sensitive to our priorities but not be bound by them.

The Call to Reconciliation

The invitation of the Great Commission is that we all are called to be reconcilers just as Christ was the great reconciler. Yet the problem that we all face is just how do we best accomplish this goal? Consider for a moment that the longest extant sermon we have by Jesus is the Sermon on the Mount. Interestingly, this sermon is not an elaboration of the Great Commission, at least not directly. Rather, again and again we see an "emphasis on the principles of healthy relationships."[34] Given the importance of relationships witnessed in this passage, the role that they play in spiritual, mental, relational and even physical health cannot be overemphasized.

If we are to prevent the cycle of damaging messages and emotions from hindering future generations of believers, we must understand the central role they play in perpetuating alienation and seek reconciliation in all areas of our relationships. As we have seen, the garden experience provides a rich theological foundation from which to view the emotional and relational problems experienced by people. In fact, most problems encountered in the counseling office can be understood in terms of alienation in one or more of these three relational domains. For this reason the RFC helping model was developed in order to provide a theologically consistent and pragmatically oriented conceptual framework to help guide both pastors and counselors in the helping task.

Up to this point, we have deliberately focused on only problems related to shame and mistrust. Table 1 is an attempt to outline the events leading to the six primary emotional struggles resulting from the Fall, each of which is commonly related to relational difficulties witnessed in the counseling setting. The relational repercussions and scriptural responses are also outlined.

Table 1. Primary Emotional Struggles Resulting from the Fall
[Numbers (1) – (4) are explained on page 39 below]

Precipitating Event	Unbalanced/Distorted Message(s)	Unbalanced Mood (1)(4)	Relationships Compromised (2)	Balanced/ Undistorted Messages	Balanced Mood	Spirit Empowered Reconciliation/ Balance Restored
"Did God really say . . . You will not surely die?" Gen. 3: 1, 4 ". . . she also gave some to her husband, who was with her, and he ate it." Gen. 3:6	"God must be deceiving me" "My senses are not reliable" "People are not to be trusted"	Mistrust Doubt Disbelief Paranoia Skepticism Jealousy	– Deny/Distrust God – Resist commitment in relationships – Exercise futile attempts at self-sufficiency – Unnecessarily question the intentions of others – Avoid self-disclosure – Struggle to be faith-ful in relationships	"Trust in the Lord with all your heart; and do not lean on your own under-standing." Pr. 3:5 ". . . It is not good for the man to be alone; . . ." Gen 2:18 "A friend loves at all times." Pr. 17:17	Trusting Faithfulness Jer 32:1-3 Obedient (legal, accurate) Cautious, Not Careless	Love of God, Self, and Others Mt. 22:36-40 Exercising the Ministry of Reconciliation 2 Cor. 5:11-21
". . . you will be like God . . ." Gen. 3:5 "Then the eyes of both of them were opened, and they realized they were naked;" Gen. 3:7	"I am inadequate, flawed, deficient, powerless" "Nakedness, exposure, vulnerability in relation-ships must be avoided" "I'm not lovable the way I am"	Shame Inferiority Low self-esteem Sense of being flawed Perpetually inadequate	– Engage in destructive mood-altering behaviors – Compensate by acting arrogant, prideful – Pursue power – Avoid the risk of necessary closeness – Be unaccepting of self/others – Diminish others to elevate self artificially – Avoid self-awareness	". . . you have been given fullness (i.e., made com-plete) in Christ." Col. 2:10 "Therefore, if anyone is in Christ, he is a new creation, . . ." 2 Cor. 5:17 "Therefore confess your sins to each other and pray for each other so that you may be healed. . . ." Jas. 5:16	Other –Acceptance Self-Acceptance Love Peace (Affirmed, Championed)	Love of God, Self, and Others Mt. 22:36-40 Exercising the Ministry of Reconciliation 2 Cor. 5:11-21

"... I heard you in the garden, and I was afraid because I was naked; so I hid." Gen. 3:10	"Retribution is inevitable" "Bad things are going to happen, it is just a matter of time"	Fear Worry Apprehension Dread	– Fearful of self-awareness (shame) and therefore lack feedback necessary for the improvement of social skills	"Perfect love casts out fear" 1 Jn. 4:18 "Who of you by worrying can add a single hour to his life" Lk. 12:25 "So God created man in his own image, in the image of God he created him; male and female he created them." Gen. 1:27	Faith Peace Love—Perfect love casteth out fear	Love of God, Self, and Others Mt. 22:36-40 Exercising the Ministry of Reconciliation 2 Cor. 5:11-21
"... she took some and ate it. She also gave some to her husband, who was with her, and he ate it ..., and they both realized they were naked" Gen 3:6-7	"I have committed an offense for which there is no remedy" "I feel a sense of distance or separation from God"	Guilt Regret Remorse Condemnation	– Compensate through blaming behaviors – Avoid responsibility – Disobey – Rebel	"Therefore, there is no condemnation for those who are in Christ Jesus" Rom. 8:1 "But in keeping with his promise we are looking forward to a new heaven and a new earth, the home of righteousness." 2 Pet. 3:13 "All this is from God, who reconciled us to himself through Christ and gave us the ministry of reconciliation. . . . God made him who had no sin to be sin for us, so that in him we might become the righteousness of God." 2 Cor. 5:18-21	Forgiveness Goodness	Love of God, Self, and Others Mt. 22:36-40 Exercising the Ministry of Reconciliation 2 Cor. 5:11-21

Precipitating Event	Unbalanced/Distorted Message(s)	Unbalanced Mood (1)(4)	Relationships Compromised (2)	Balanced/ Undistorted Messages	Balanced Mood	Spirit Empowered Reconciliation/ Balance Restored
"To the woman he said, 'I will greatly increase your pains in childbearing . . .' To Adam he said, '. . . Cursed is the ground because of you; through painful toil you will eat of it.' . . . So the Lord God banished him from the garden." Gen. 3: 16-17, 24	"My privileged relationship with God is gone forever." "There is no hope." "Suffering is unbearable and is going to last forever." "Life is to be endured."	Distress Anguish Suffering Loss of relationship and security Grief Crying Loneliness Estrangement from creation.	– Hopelessness – Meaninglessness – Live for today	"I have come that you might have life and have it more abundantly." Jn. 10:10 "Therefore we do not lose heart." 2 Cor. 4:16-18 "Therefore, since we have been justified through faith, we have peace with God through our Lord Jesus Christ, through whom we have gained access by faith into this grace in which we now stand." Rom. 5:1 Mt. 11:28-30; Pr. 18:10; Rom. 5:5; Zeph. 3:17	Hope Joy Peace	Love of God, Self, and Others Mt. 22:36-40 Exercising the Ministry of Reconciliation 2 Cor. 5:11-21

Then the Lord said to Cain, "Why are you angry? . . ." Gen. 4:6 "The woman you put here with me—she gave me some fruit from the tree, and I ate." Gen. 3:12	"God/life is unfair" "I must not let others get over on me" "Problems in my life are not my fault"	Anger (3) Revenge Resentment Unforgiveness	— Seek to hurt or destroy those persons or things believed to be responsible for one's struggles	"In your anger do not sin: Do not let the sun go down while you are still angry, and do not give the devil a foothold." Eph. 4:26-27 "When anxiety was great within me, your consolation brought joy to my soul.." Ps. 94:19	Love Peace Patience Kindness Gentleness Forgiveness	Love of God, Self, and Others Mt. 22:36-40 Exercising the Ministry of Reconciliation 2 Cor. 5:11-21

(1) As was stated earlier, not all negative emotions, such as mistrust, guilt, fear, etc., are bad or wrong in a world compromised by sin. It is only when they arise from distorted/unrealistic messages that they are seen as "unbalanced" and in need of correction.

(2) These are just a few of the many examples of relational maladjustment resulting from these distorted messages.

(3) It is often helpful to view anger as a secondary emotion, triggered by primary feelings such as fear, hurt, frustration, etc.

(4) All of these negative feelings contribute to a general state of anxiety. Anxiety, as understood here, is recognized as a condition of tension resulting from the merging of acute and previously differentiated emotional states. While anxiety has always been closely associated with fear, worry, dread, etc., it is more completely understood as an undifferentiated mass of emotion (both positive and negative). Especially in regard to negative emotional states, one might conceive of anxiety as an attempt to diffuse the more acute discomfort stemming from primary feeling states. By merging or blending together these intense feelings states, their respective ties with previously troubling thoughts must be loosened, inevitably decreasing the intensity of their associated feelings. The resolution of anxiety, therefore, is in part dependent on identifying and resolving the previously conflictual and often distorted thoughts inherent in feelings of guilt, fear, shame, mistrust, etc. Again, the focus of RFC is to replace previously distorted messages with spiritually balanced thinking.

Chapter 2

Reconciliation-Focused Counseling: Basic Principles

Now that we have laid the theological groundwork for our understanding of emotional and relational problems, we can begin to work toward a more holistic approach to helping people. In the following discussion, we will attempt to explain how we can appropriate these theological resources in a practical way in the counseling setting. The following principles are seen as foundational to a proper understanding and application of RFC. They serve as the "operating system" of this approach, if you will, serving to guide counselors throughout the helping task.

Principle #1: Promote the Ministry of Reconciliation

"'Love the Lord your God with all your heart and with all your soul and with all your mind.' This is the first and greatest commandment. And the second is like it: 'Love your neighbor as yourself.'" (Matthew 22:37-39)

As previously emphasized, the overarching goal of the RFC model is to work toward reconciliation between the three relational domains represented by God, others, and self. While the authors recognize that not all human struggles stem from relational malfunctioning, emotional, interpersonal, spiritual, and at times even physical problems can be understood as developing from or being maintained by various types of alienation (or disordered attachment) in one or more of these three domains. Alienation, in turn, can be understood as taking either active or passive forms. "Active alienation" is more obvious and deliberate. It might be represented by a breakdown in previously established relationships such as estrangement between marital partners or family members. If questioned, participants in this type of alienation can usually identify and accept the presence of distance or fracture in their relationship(s). "Passive alienation" is more subtle and inadvertent. It can best be understood as the underutilization or failure to utilize necessary connection or relationships with self, others, or God. As might be inferred, this form of alienation is often overlooked or denied by participants in many instances since the "presence" of necessary relationships may have never been established.

For example, a depressed woman who comes to a counselor expecting a spiritual or psychological remedy to her problem may be surprised to discover upon referral to a physician that her depression is the result of hypothyroidism. One might argue convincingly that this type of situation simply represents a lack of knowledge by the sufferer and such might well be the case. However, frequently the failure to utilize helpful "new" or "outside" relationships stems from the presence of mistrust, shame, fear, and so forth, on the part of this same individual. Some individuals resist seeing doctors due to a latent mistrust of the profession or because of the shame associated with being dependent on any type of medication. Alternatively, the family caught in a web of destructive conflict or abuse may fail to reach out for help because fear and mistrust promote disconnection or alienation from potentially restorative resources. In the course of working with a client's particular problem(s), RFC counselors should conduct a relationship inventory to help determine the presence and quality of a client's relationship with God, self, and others. (See appendix C.)

While this discussion has hopefully provided some clarity regarding the distinctions between these types of alienation, in actuality they rarely appear in such pure forms. Most people usually experience differing degrees of both active and passive alienation. Ultimately, both types can simply be understood as the need on the part of the individual for necessary connection with potentially restorative resources, irrespective of the reasons such connection may not exist. Such resources might include God, ministers, counselors, doctors, spouses, siblings, and friends.

Thus, the counselor's role is one of being a relationship builder, seeking to promote forms of connection that will promote healing in the individual, couple, or family. In fact, the overarching goal of RFC is to encourage helpers to approach the unique problems of their clients with a reconciliation-focused mind-set. Many contemporary therapies tend to view human struggles as merely isolated symptoms in need of correction. RFC proposes that we use an alienation/reconciliation framework to set each client's problems in a context that will responsibly link them with their spiritual struggle to find meaningful and satisfying connection in life. Oriented by this conceptual guide and sensitive to the roles that mistrust, shame, anger, and other damaging emotions may play in this age-old drama, the counselor can now work to promote change in the thoughts and behaviors of the counselee led by this insight into human struggles.

Given this understanding of the helping process, the overall goal of RFC is to facilitate *corrective relational experiences* in the lives of our clients. In other words, just as we have seen how a client's problems may stem from negative relational experiences involving, for example, mistrust and shame, we seek to counter these experiences with their corresponding corrective. This remedial process begins with our ability as counselors to serve as healthy relational figures to our clients, modeling a style of relating that is both affirming and trustworthy. In a real sense, the counselor is "technique" by virtue of the personal strengths he brings to the counseling relationship. Set in this context, clients are then encouraged to cultivate new or enhance existing relationships with a view to promote healthier ways of relating to self, others, and God.

This view of the helping process has very broad implications for our work as counselors and defies any attempt to reduce such efforts to "three easy steps." However, as important as contemporary techniques may be which give isolated attention to the thoughts and behaviors of the client, the centrality of maintaining a reconciliation mind-set is critical in guiding our work with others. This leads us to the next principle of helping others.

Principle #2: Prepare the Way for a Divine-Human Encounter

> " . . . *Man does not live on bread alone but on every word that comes from the mouth of the Lord.*" (Deuteronomy 8:3)

This passage reminds us of a fundamental principle, which should guide our work with others. People, all people, regardless of their presenting problems, need God. This statement may seem rather self-evident or even unnecessarily doctrinaire to a predominately Christian readership.

But the inherent risk for Christian helpers as they begin using various counseling techniques is that as symptoms begin to abate, they fail to frame these symptoms within the larger framework of a person's spiritual condition. Consequently, symptom reduction often becomes an end in itself and the techniques related to their reduction begin to take center stage. Frequently, as symptoms subside to an acceptable level, little additional obligation is assumed toward the clients since they seem to be content. Of course, secular therapists naturally assume this position unless goals involving enrichment or growth were sought initially. However, the absence of symptoms can all too easily become signposts of success for Christian counselors as well. Thus, we may find ourselves, inadvertently to be sure, joining our secular colleagues in the faulty assumption that the absence of symptoms equates with personal or relational well-being. And what Christian counselor, having fallen into such a position with a terminating client, has not wrestled with a lingering sense of tension or remorse that more should have been done?

What should be the ultimate goal of Christian counseling? Should it, as some have suggested, only take into account the explicit wishes of the client? Or should it not recognize and validate an implicit goal that is present when persons seek out their pastor or Christian counselor for help? By choosing to come to see us rather than our secular counterparts aren't they saying, "I want to somehow experience God in the process of getting help"? Even if we were to assume, for the moment, that the clients in question were already Christian, isn't the challenge of the Great Commission not only to baptize but to disciple others? Therefore I believe that an acceptable goal for all Christian counseling, not to dismiss any other unique needs that are present, is best summarized in the following definition offered by Edward Thornton. He suggests that the purpose of all pastoral ministries, including counseling, is to prepare *"the way for a divine-human encounter in which grace is communicated and reconciliation experienced"* (37).

As Deuteronomy 8:3 states and this definition affirms, our work with people needs to be guided by this overarching awareness of the deepest need of persons. Supporting this theological understanding of the counseling task is the work of Robert C. Roberts (*Limning the Psyche*, 81). Roberts actually suggests that, among other things, humans are unique by virtue of their verbivorous nature. In other words, much like describing other living creatures as carnivores or herbivores, describing humans as verbivores means that humans actually feed on or need to be fed by words.

We are by nature word-digesters, pursuing different forms of both verbal and written communication in an effort to understand ourselves better and our relationships with God and others. Interestingly, this verbivorous word-digesting nature suggests an explanation as to why counseling tends to have such an edifying effect on its participants. Through dialoging with their counselor people literally feed on the words, helping them bring order and understanding to their inner worlds. But more importantly, Roberts's observation suggests a partial explanation of our nature as God-needers. John 6:35 states, "And Jesus said unto them, 'I am the bread of life: he that cometh to me shall never hunger; and he that believeth on me shall never thirst.'" When taken together, these two observations point to the fact that the Word of God is the quintessential hunger satisfier. In a very real sense, we need to feed on the Word of God. In pondering these ideas, we begin to develop a much better appreciation and understanding of the significance of Logos or the Word, as John describes Christ at the beginning in his Gospel.

Consequently, RFC recognizes that as Christian counselors seek to minister to the multiple needs of their clients, central and integral to this process is the facilitation of a divine-human encounter for the counselee. Without an encounter with the living Word, there will be a hunger and thirst that will never be quenched by symptom resolution alone. The approaches that we use to facilitate this process are multiple. We should be mindful to resist any imperialistic attitudes regarding any "ultimate" avenue since God is never constrained to respond to any preconceived approach. Instead, we should carefully consider the needs and attitudes of each counselee and respond accordingly as the Lord gives direction. Like Paul, we should seek to "become all things to all men so that by all possible means" we might save some.[35]

One final note: given the universal and reciprocal nature of all applied theology, counselors are likewise challenged to take this Word into themselves and meditate upon it. Otherwise, we will starve ourselves *and* therefore our counselees just as surely as if we were to quit eating physical food. In other words, RFC challenges us to acknowledge that we can't take our clients further in their journey toward reconciliation with God than we have gone ourselves.

Principle #3: Acknowledge the Need
for Therapeutic Trialogue

> *"O Lord, you have searched me and you know me. You know when I sit and when I rise; you perceive my thoughts from afar. You discern my going out and my lying down; you are familiar with all my ways. Before a word is on my tongue you know it completely, O Lord." (Psalm 139:1-4)*

> *"Pray continually." (1 Thessalonians 5:17)*

These verses remind us that as we participate in the ministry of counseling there is a clear need on the part of the counselor to acknowledge the ongoing presence, workings, and leadings of God in this process. RFC seeks to do this by recognizing and validating the reality of therapeutic trialogue. In others words, rather than being merely dialogical in nature, communications during a session for the Christian counselor are really trialogical or tri-polar in nature. This reality, referred to by Wayne Oates as "the central dynamic in our dialogue with counselees," is extremely relevant in the day-to-day work of the pastoral counselor (Oates, 1986, 23). Holding an attitude acknowledging one's reliance on the Spirit's leadership is critically important in the helping process (Rom. 8:14). Only then can we be in a position to best promote the healing and reconciliation being sought by the counselee. Lacking this direction, the counselor is like a ship without a rudder, left to wander through a virtual myriad of counseling approaches and his own logic in seeking to provide direction to the counselee. Even the most disciplined effort on the part of the helper is no match for the complex problems that persons bring to a counselor's office. Certainly a more skilled and experienced helper will increase the likelihood of a favorable outcome. But knowing what to focus on, when to do an intervention, how to carry it out practically, and so forth, is not just a matter of skill and experience but also encompasses the use of judgment and intuition which must be informed by God. This is by no means intended to diminish the value of personal training and effort on the part of the helper. Ultimately however, the counselor must depend on the infinite wisdom and leading of God to provide the sensitivity, insight, and wisdom necessary to make appropriate application of any personal training resources available to the helper.

A question we might ask at this point is, "How can we integrate the notion of therapeutic trialogue into the counseling setting without letting it become an obstacle in attending properly to our clients?" By suggesting that we should "pray without ceasing," are we to assume that only conscious, purposeful, and continuous prayer is what is being suggested here? Certainly this cannot be the case. To approach life in this manner would not only be unrealistic, it would be unwise. Formal prayer requires a focusing of attention that would at times distract Christians from detailed tasks requiring undivided attention. For a brain surgeon to be consistently distracted by conscious attention to prayer might result in dire consequences for the patient. Likewise, constantly praying, even silently, throughout a session would unnecessarily distract the helper from adequately attending to the helping process. Oswald Chambers in *My Utmost for His Highest* has aptly illustrated what is being suggested in this verse.[36] He suggests that prayer at these times is like the blood flowing through our veins or the breath in our lungs. We are not always conscious of these processes but they continue nonetheless. Prayer therefore is not just a conscious exercise but an ongoing attitude in the life of an obedient believer. This attitude holds that the presence of God is a moment-by-moment reality in the helping process, without which we struggle in vain.

Principle #4: Maintain a Redemptive/ Hopeful Attitude

"Finally, brothers, whatever is true, whatever is noble, whatever is right, whatever is pure, whatever is lovely, whatever is admirable, if anything is excellent or praiseworthy, think about such things."
(Philippians 4:8)

Quick, . . . try to think of five things you like about yourself or that represent your personal strengths. Now, try to think of five things that you don't like about yourself or which you would consider to be your personal weaknesses. Which was easier? Chances are, coming up with the negative rather than the positive characteristics was the answer. We live in a culture dominated by a general approach to problem-solving that encourages a search for causes, damage, and deficits as a necessary prerequisite in finding a remedy to many of life's problems. This problem-solving focus stems, in part, from the widespread acceptance of the medical model (sometimes called the "damage model") and the misapplication of mechanistic approaches to solving social problems. Because of this mindset, people have become so problem focused that they automatically assume that these same principles should be helpful in finding solutions to an individual's emotional or relational difficulties. Now it is certainly true that identifying symptoms related to such issues holds merit when seeking to arrive at an accurate picture of a person's problems. It is also true that accurate assessments, as we will discuss later, are a critical component in helping people since these same assessments serve to guide our interventions. However, the question now becomes, "Should this method of observation dominate our approach to helping people with emotional and relational struggles?"

The Tyranny of Regressive Thinking

The difficulties associated with becoming too problem oriented or negatively focused were first highlighted in my inpatient work with sexual trauma survivors. Inpatient sexual recovery groups are by necessity "open." By this I mean that, unlike closed groups, which start and proceed with a fixed number of original members, open groups allow for new members to be admitted on an "as needed" basis. Understandably, trauma survivors need to talk about their ordeals in a warm and supportive atmosphere to allow for the expression of painful and often long repressed feelings. Such a process is common to helping people with most any troubling experience. It also gives the counselor an opportunity to gather important information about a counselee's particular problem and to help build rapport. However, a complication can arise from this natural need to share painful experiences. When the original group members were given sufficient opportunities to process their painful emotions, the next natural step in their healing process would have been to move toward a more solution or goal-focused approach to addressing their problems. However, when new members were admitted to the group, there was again the need for that individual to share her pain. Not surprisingly, the painful disclosures of the new client would invite the original members to re-visit their painful experiences. Eventually, such groups often would digress to the point that they would actually reinforce a sort of victim orientation, with people endlessly rehearsing their pain and their problems. The patients literally would get stuck in their pain.

Counselors working with either groups or individuals may unwittingly encourage this process when they themselves fall into the trap of believing that problem resolution will naturally emerge through the repeated examination of the problem. This mind-set is not surprising when you factor in that most people have been socialized in a culture that has embraced a view of therapy largely shaped by the influence of psychoanalysis. Throughout the first half of the last century this approach encouraged therapists so trained to use free association to assist clients in exploring repressed memories and feelings from their past. While this description is a drastic simplification of the process, the psychoanalytic method is not without some foundation. Clients who are given the opportunity to express powerful, pent-up emotions often show improvement initially. The problem, as analytic thinkers were to discover, is that such improvement tends to be only temporary if catharsis is not followed with a more solution or goal oriented focus.

Helpers Can't Afford the Luxury of Hopelessness

Another difficulty with seeking solutions to human struggles using approaches that emphasize regressive and/or extended examinations of the problem, rests in the fact that such methods tend to diminish rather than cultivate an attitude of hope. Rare is the counselor who has not witnessed an individual or family leave a session more disillusioned than when they first arrived after spending the entire session rehearsing their problem(s). In fact, it is difficult during such encounters for the helper not to get caught up in the clients' view of the problem and become as pessimistic about the future as they are.

At times like these there are several important things we need to remember. Christian counselors cannot afford the luxury of a negative or hopeless attitude when seeking to help others. As Wayne Oates and Andrew Lester remind us,

> The pastor represents hope to persons who face the unalterable, the unknown, or the frightening. . . . In an age when despair, discouragement, and disillusionment are the predominant emotional dynamics, it becomes increasingly necessary for the Christian faith to unmask, refurbish, and communicate its belief in hope. (Oates and Lester, *Pastoral Care in Crucial Human Situations*, 18)

The apostle Paul reflected the potential for Christians to maintain an attitude of hope in the midst of very trying circumstances. Few Christians have experienced the trials that Paul had to endure. Yet in spite of his many hardships, Paul was able to maintain an unwavering spirit of optimism. How did he do that? 2 Corinthians 4:16-18 provides some clues when he states:

Therefore we do not lose heart. Though outwardly we are wasting away, yet inwardly we are being renewed day by day. For our light and momentary troubles are achieving for us an eternal glory that far outweighs them all. So we fix our eyes not on what is seen, but on what is unseen. For what is seen is temporary, but what is unseen is eternal.

Clearly, Paul challenges us to consider the ultimate realities of life and our need to remain focused on our eternal destiny in Christ. We, of all people, have reason to find hope in the midst of even the most troubling of circumstances. Paul was not suggesting that we embrace some groundless hope or some Pollyanna version of positive thinking. He was not suggesting, as some have claimed, that people should use religion as some opiate to deny facts or to distort the harsh realities of our finite existence. On the contrary, he is suggesting that we be careful not place our hope in the transient and passing securities offered in our material and finite world. He is highlighting the dangers of attaching our hope for the future to fantasies and illusions which will ultimately only disappoint. Frequently, the mental illness witnessed in our midst is only a reflection of what happens when hope attaches itself to unreality. Hope based on empty and distorted expectations is in fact false hope and will only lead to despair, emotional distress, and at times psychic decompensation. As theologian William Lynch has aptly stated, "Reality is healing for those who are without hope and it is the separation from reality that causes despair" (Lynch, *Images of Hope: Imagination as Healer of the Hopeless,* 171).

One should never underestimate the healing power of Christ-centered hope. A number of years ago, a family called me to request counseling for one of their family members who had recently been released from a psychiatric hospital. Having only sketchy information about the client prior to the appointment, I was somewhat surprised by the level of emotional disablement when we first met. Accompanied by a number of family members, Janet presented as plainly dressed, overweight, and expressionless. As I began to ask about the circumstances leading up to her recent hospital admission, her brief, monotone responses, protruding tongue movements, and obviously dry mouth suggested that this individual was on a substantial amount of psychotropic medication. Indeed, further investigation revealed that she was on fairly high doses of both anti-psychotics and major tranquilizers. Her medical records also revealed a sobering observation regarding this individual. She had been diagnosed with schizophrenia. Every clinician knows that this is one of the most dreaded psychiatric disorders. There is no known cure, only the hope that with early intervention, proper medical and stress management, and family education the individual may be spared the onset of another psychotic episode and live a fairly normal life. Even so, individuals may continue to decline in overall functioning over time or never regain their level of adaptive functioning prior to the onset of their illness. Judging by her initial presentation, the prognosis for this client appeared to be very bleak. In true cases of schizophrenia, it is unfair to talk to the client about cure since such a suggestion breeds unrealistic optimism. My impression was that the family understandably harbored no such notions and was ready to accept a goal of improved management of the symptoms.

However, despite such dire initial presentations, I believe that it is still realistic to suggest to clients that they can experience a better life . . . that circumstances don't have to determine their sense of well-being (Phil. 4:11). And as was true in Janet's case, she communicated a deep faith in God that further bolstered my sense of optimism. Little did I know, however, how much that optimism would influence her life for the better.

The next several years of work together brought some profound changes for Janet, some of which again challenged the depth of her resources. However, slowly but surely she began to improve as new diagnoses were considered, medications were altered, lifestyles and relationships were adjusted, and her undying commitment to faith in God persisted. Initially, there was an alleviation of her profound depression, which had earlier led to the psychotic episodes, followed by the return of her previously bright personality. Other symptoms of her depression likewise began to fade. She lost much of the weight she had previously added. Her energy returned and many of her compulsive habits began to subside. After several years of increasingly infrequent sessions, months would often go by without word from Janet. Periodically, however, I would receive a card, letter, or well-visit from her updating me on her progress. First, there was a return to part-time and then full-time employment. Then there were relationship adjustments and better job opportunities. Eight years have now passed and Janet is quite different from the person who initially seemed so lifeless and without hope. Even though she continues to struggle at times with her mental health, she has progressed even beyond my expectations. There have been many factors that have been instrumental in her recovery but if you were to ask her, hope stands out as central.

One of her favorite hobbies is writing poetry, and I have been fortunate enough to be the recipient of her writing. At our last meeting prior to her move out of town, she presented me with the following poem which now hangs on my wall reminding me of the vital role of hope in counseling. At the risk of sounding vain, I wanted to share it with you since it so accurately communicates the centrality of Christ-centered hope in the process of healing.

A Seed of Hope
By Janet M.

In everyone's life there comes a time to face despair. Fiery trials may be so great, you wonder does anyone really care? It looks like your whole world is just caving in. Can someone rescue you from the turmoil that is within? Where is your hope? You feel that all hope is gone. You reach for help but you feel so all alone.

Yes, I know because this describes where I was for some time. My joy was all gone, no peace I could find. All I needed was just a seed of hope. Something or someone to help me to cope. I needed someone to believe in me and not to count me out in life. God sent that someone during this most trying time of strife.

A man was sent with a calling to build up those that are torn down. God used a brother in ministry who knew where the peace of God could be found. That seed of hope was planted inside of me and it has remained.

I will never forget these words he said to me. "You can lead a productive life again." I've held on to these words for years. With faith in God and belief that I could achieve again, that has calmed my fears. I'm ever grateful to Asa R. Sphar III, whom God chose to inspire me by planting that special seed of hope. May God receive all praise, for that seed has flourished.

What About Sin?

One argument often raised by some Christians in defense of a more problem-focused approach is based on the concern that clients need to be more aware of the "sin problem" that exists in their lives. "Don't we need," the argument goes, "to highlight the sin in people's lives so that they can repent and be challenged to take responsibility for changing their behavior?" At times this is the case. Christian counselors must never forget that we are more than just emotional and relational consultants; we are also moral consultants as well. There remains a risk, even among Christian counselors, of omitting the language of sin from our dialogue with counselees. A broad examination of this pervasive cultural tendency has been well documented in Dr. Karl Menninger's highly acclaimed book *Whatever Became of Sin* (1973).

However, experience suggests that most counselees who come to see their pastor or Christian counselor are well aware of the sin that exists in their lives. In fact, many persons who come to their pastor or pastoral counselor for help are already Christians. Most are more than willing to take responsibility for seeking to change their sinful behaviors. The problem for such clients is that simply acknowledging their sin or even praying about their sin has not been sufficient to bring about a desired change in their behavior. For us to use challenge or confrontation as our exclusive approach to helping these people may only duplicate their own failed attempts to find healing through what has often become self-flagellation. In such cases, by attempting to use a solution that excessively emphasizes sin (the problem) rather than the grace of Christ (the answer), the solution can itself become the problem.

What clients need is to experience the healing grace of Jesus Christ within the context of the helping relationship, to find Christ incarnate in the counselor, which is unfortunately what they have often failed to find in other Christian encounters. There are five Greek verbs used in the New Testament to describe various approaches to the counseling task, all of which may be found in 1 Thessalonians 5:14.[37] Each has its place depending on the circumstances or challenges being faced by the counselor. A counselor's ability to apply flexibly these various approaches to the helping task will insure that his counseling remains balanced and maximally effective. The example set by Christ, our supreme model for Christian living as well as counseling, reflects a posture that seems to be most consistent with this approach.

Hope: A Central Dynamic in the
Healing Process

Not only is an approach emphasizing hope and redemptive thinking theologically correct but it is empirically sound. In a review of forty years of outcome research, Matthews and Edgette made a rather startling discovery regarding their investigation into the differences in clinical efficacy of various counseling approaches. "No model, method, or package of techniques was demonstrated to be more reliable than any other (Matthews and Edgette, *Current Thinking and Research in Brief Therapy: Solutions, Strategies, Narratives*, 204). What they found instead were "four common curative elements" (206) that were reflected in a wide variety of helping models. Of the four factors identified, the factor of hope/expectancy/placebo was the third most significant, contributing 15% to positive counseling outcomes.[38] Clearly, the positive role that hope plays in counseling outcomes has been well established.

In Summary

Focusing on the positive or exceptions to the problem facilitates change in the positive direction. Philippians 4:8-9 suggests that rather than focusing on the negative we seek instead to identify positive ways of thinking and behaving and attempt to follow those patterns. RFC believes that this principle should permeate and shape the way we approach the helping process. We do this by looking for the positives in our clients' lives, taking careful note of exceptions to their problems, encouraging them to draw on their God-given resources, and in general attempting to be ministers of grace in their lives.

Principle #5: Make the Most Efficient Use of Time

> *"As long as it is day, we must do the work of him who sent me. Night is coming, when no one can work. While I am in the world, I am the light of the world." (John 9:4-5 NIV)*

As we have already indicated, the management of time is a critical issue for the contemporary pastor/counselor. The multiple demands of ministry make extended counseling situations unrealistic. As a rule, we think that it is wise for helpers to limit most counseling opportunities to four to six sessions. This guideline is in keeping with the previously cited data concerning the average length of time that counselees participate in counseling. And for those who have not been specifically trained as counselors, it also serves to acknowledge that the counseling skills necessary to go beyond this point have often not been sufficiently developed. Therefore extended involvement may bring the risk of being ineffective or even detrimental.

Certain key ideas will be helpful in preventing counseling opportunities from becoming unnecessarily lengthy:

1. Approach each session as if it might be your last. What can you do for the counselee today that might offer the best opportunity to provide help should you never have the opportunity to see this person again?
2. Be sure to clarify with the individual, couple, or family that you generally work with clients up to a maximum of 4-6 sessions. This will help to motivate both you and the client to work quickly toward solving the presenting problem.
3. Attempt to follow, as closely as possible, the steps outlined in the RFC helping model.
4. Remember that one of the biggest reasons for ineffectiveness in counseling is the failure on the part of the counselor to get carefully defined goals from the counselees. (See the following section on "Characteristics of Redemptive Goals.")
5. Be sure you understand what the counselee wants from therapy. You must be going in the direction desired by the client for counseling to be both efficient and effective.

Principle #6: Emphasize Change in the Thoughts and Behaviors of the Counselee

> *"Finally, brothers, whatever is true, whatever is noble, whatever is right, whatever is pure, whatever is lovely, whatever is admirable—if anything is excellent or praiseworthy—think about such things. Whatever you have learned or received or heard from me, or seen in me—put it into practice. And the God of peace will be with you." (Phil. 4:8-9)*[39]

While the verbalization of feelings by the client is an important part of the counseling process, wise counselors recognize that the focus of attention and change rests on the thoughts and behaviors of the counselee.[40] Notice this emphasis in Philippians 4:8-9 where after being encouraged by the apostle Paul to "think" and "act" differently, or in carefully directed ways, we are told that the feeling of "peace" will then follow. In other words, changes in the counselees' thoughts and behaviors will often lead to the desired changes in their emotions. However, at the risk of sounding too dismissive of the counselees' feelings, several points of clarification should be made.

First, clients need for the helper to respect as well as reflect their feelings in order to experience their counselor as a caring and understanding individual. Second, feelings serve as critical linchpins in the counseling process by helping clients make necessary connections with troubling thoughts and behaviors. Most clients initially find it easier to identify troubling feelings rather than problem thoughts or behaviors. This is due to a number of factors. We all tend to be more aware of our feelings rather than our thoughts since feelings exercise such a powerful influence upon our moment-to-moment experience. We live in very feeling laden worlds. Feelings punctuate our life experiences and serve as strong motivators of behavior.

Furthermore, the prevalence of feelings in our moment-to-moment experience helps to explain what has come to be called "state conditioned memory." Our memories of past behaviors or thoughts tend to be tied to some degree to the feeling states that we were experiencing when those memories or thoughts took shape. For example, if I were to ask a client, "What kind of thoughts do you have when you are depressed?" she would likely have difficulty answering this question unless she is currently in a depressed state. However, if we ask her to go back to a time when the depression was strong and then to use her senses and imagination to recreate the circumstances around her previously depressed state, the chances are much better that her corresponding thoughts would be accessible. This is due to the fact that a slight return of those depressed feelings would naturally accompany this exercise. Consequently, these same feelings would now serve as triggers or springboards to thoughts and behaviors related to those feelings.

What we find is that the relationship between feeling states and thoughts can have both positive and negative ramifications for counselors attempting to help others. For example, a husband who has had an affair or who has used pornography in the past may find that old troubling thoughts or memories begin to emerge during current sexual experiences with his wife even after he recommits to a relationship of fidelity. This is not necessarily an indication of his continued latent waywardness. It is more likely an illustration of how feelings of sexual arousal have triggered recent memories associated with that arousal. The irony of this drama is that those same feelings can and do serve as triggers to memories of thoughts and behaviors that can be of benefit in the counseling task. Therefore, while feelings do not constitute good goal material given their abstract and transitory nature, they nevertheless can be used as springboards to help identify thoughts and behaviors which need to be changed.

Principle #7: Be Both Collaborative and Directive

"The eye cannot say to the hand, 'I don't need you!' And the head cannot say to the feet, 'I don't need you!' On the contrary, those parts of the body that seem to be weaker are indispensable." (1 Corinthians 12:21-23)

We are God's workers, working together; . . . (1 Cor. 3:9a New Century Version)

In 1 Corinthians 12, Paul reflects a deep concern about the attitudes represented among some members of the Corinthian congregation. Evidently these individuals tended to look down upon other church members whose gifts were not seemingly as important or impressive as their own. However, contrary to their exaggerated notions of self-importance, Paul wanted to communicate that such attitudes were not only unloving and prideful but also demonstrated a failure by these persons to recognize the absolute necessity of seemingly unnecessary members of the body. In fact, without each and every member serving in its appropriate role, the functioning of the entire body is compromised. This is a principle that should be emphasized in the counseling enterprise. The fact that someone comes to us seeking our help does not mean that they "cease to be a part of the body."[41] We still need to recognize that effective counseling is very much a collaborative enterprise. We collaborate because it is respectful of clients and because in many ways we need them as much as they need us. Every client brings information and resources that vitally inform the counseling task and serve to promote the understanding and resolution of the problem.

Take, for example, a client who feels her husband should be more "attentive and affectionate." Just what does she mean? Without more specific feedback, we are simply left to wonder what kinds of attitudes and behaviors would have this *meaning* to this *client*. We may think we know the "attentive and affectionate" behaviors to which she is referring, but these may only have meaning to us, not necessarily this particular client. This distinction is critical. Just because one's wife likes to have coffee brought to her in bed does not mean that all other wives will find this consideration that important. We need the client to tell her husband and us, in detail, what behaviors communicate attention and affection to her. One can guess all day long but never know exactly what she specifically desires.

However, there are also times when we need to be directive. The efficient use of time requires that we remain active during the counseling session. We simply can't allow sessions to become too bogged down in excessive problem exploration or a preoccupation with any single stage in the helping process. RFC promotes this end by facilitating the structured examination of the problems, goals, and strategies in a manner that will move clients toward their desired outcomes. How do we manage to do both? Maintaining a balance between a collaborative and directive orientation is aided by both the spiritual sensitivity and experience of the counselor. The Scriptures outline many directives that seek to guide people toward redemptive behaviors. They serve as critical signposts in helping counselors provide direction to their counselees. On the other hand, the saying "There's no substitute for experience" finds no greater example than in one's work with people. Solomon's words in Ecclesiastes 3:7 that there is "a time to tear and a time to mend, a time to be silent and a time to speak" highlight how experience has informed the king's approach to life and people. Likewise experience, coupled with super-vision from a trained helper, will provide a critical framework for deter-mining whether the counseling process is staying on task. When it is not, collaboration may need to give way to direction as we seek to redirect the client toward more productive thoughts and behaviors.

A point of caution should be offered at this point. A common mistake made by beginning counselors is to assume that being directive necessarily means that they are to engage in giving advice. Advice giving is basically telling someone what we think they should do. Being directive may occa-sionally involve such a role if the client's choice-making abilities are severely compromised by physical, intellectual, or emotional distress. However, by-and-large being directive simply means attempting to lead counselees to consider other possible courses of action. In the former, we are assuming a broad responsibility for a client's life and choices that often can lead to less-than-desirable consequences for both the client and the counselor. In the latter, we are encouraging the client to move in a direction that will facilitate better choice-making . . . choices that we hope the client will necessarily assume. In the end, RFC encourages helpers to recognize that the ability to carry out both of these functions effectively is strongly related to the quality of the relationship we have with our clients.

Principle #8: Encourage Clients to Exercise
Their Choice-Making Abilities

"But if serving the LORD seems undesirable to you, then choose for yourselves this day whom you will serve, whether the gods your forefathers served beyond the River, or the gods of the Amorites, in whose land you are living. But as for me and my household, we will serve the LORD." (Joshua 24:15)

We live in a day and age that tends to minimize a person's "freedom to choose." To listen to some people, it would seem that after the effects of genetics, family history, culture, environment, and so forth, are all considered, we are all hopelessly determined by forces that lie beyond our control. In other words, we have no freedom to choose at all. In fact, many tend to embrace a view of humanity's agency or choice making that would allow little or no freedom for self-determination.

As previously indicated, RFC encourages clients to validate and exercise their choice-making abilities. The Scriptures defend and experience demonstrates that even under some of the direst circumstances, people retain a certain degree of choice-making ability that can be used redemptively. This choice-making is certainly not unlimited. The denial of determinism does not mean that there are no boundaries to human behavior. Just as Adam and Eve learned that one cannot choose to be God, we likewise cannot, for example, choose to defy the forces of gravity. Similarly, we must be careful not to ascribe more freedom to the client than is realistically present. For example, telling a seriously depressed client to "pull yourself together" or the alcoholic to "stop drinking" fails to recognize the serious limitations to choice making that are imposed by their conditions.

However, one central task of the Christian counselor is to look for continued areas of freedom in our clients' lives and ways that they can use this freedom productively. We begin to do this by recognizing that actions vary in type. In other words, actions can involve behavior (such as choosing to exercise for five minutes a day) or be purely mental (such as working out in one's head which A.A. meeting to attend on a given night). Given this understanding of actions, we then must identify the amount of exertion that the client must utilize to accomplish the given task. Some tasks, of course, involve more exertion than others. Therefore, helpers must be sensitive to how much perseverance a client can engender toward a give task. Finally, the actions and exertion levels available to the client are all subject to the empowering presence of the Holy Spirit in a believer's life. Paul's statement "I can do all things through Christ which strengtheneth me" (Philippians 4:13 KJV) is a powerful reminder of the spiritual resources available to counselor and client alike. Rather than exercising our agency in isolation, we actually are co-agents with God, choosing to allow him to help us overcome the limitations we experience as temporal and finite human beings.

Taken together, this information challenges the helper to evaluate carefully the choice making abilities of a client at any particular time. Such judgments are critical in counseling. Placing excessive expectations on clients who are severely disabled by their current circumstances not only reflects a lack of empathy, but also sets them up for failure. Conversely, underestimating our clients' abilities will compromise their ultimate potential. The point being encouraged here is that appropriating the resources of the client is a delicate matter requiring great sensitivity from the counselor. Wise counselors will continue to look for points of freedom in their clients' lives that can be used for benefit. Paul could have easily allowed the difficulties encountered during his missionary journeys to "determine" his attitude in a very negative direction. However, as we see from his letter to the Corinthians, such was not the case:

> Therefore we do not lose heart. Though outwardly we are wasting away, yet inwardly we are being renewed day by day. For our light and momentary troubles are achieving for us an eternal glory that far outweighs them all. So we fix our eyes not on what is seen, but on what is unseen. For what is seen is temporary, but what is unseen is eternal. (2 Corinthians 4:16-18)

Principle #9: Recognize the Role of the Counselor as Moral Consultant

> *"Come back to your senses as you ought, and stop sinning; for there are some who are ignorant of God—I say this to your shame."*
> *(1 Corinthians 15:34)*

Until recent years, most therapists have embraced a morally neutral position in the counseling setting. In other words, they felt that introducing one's own values into the context of counseling was inappropriate. Such an approach has been defended on a number of grounds, including that failing to be value neutral exerts an unfair influence on necessarily dependent clients, limits the client's right to self-determination, reflects a disrespect for the individual, and often indicates a judgmental and superior attitude toward the client. Unfortunately, even some Christian counselors have adopted this view, resulting in the need for such individuals to perform a sort of moral lobotomy before approaching the counseling task. Increasingly, however, the wisdom of "value-neutral counseling" has come into question, for a variety of reasons.

First, the assumption that one can take a completely value-neutral position in the counseling setting has been largely dismissed by communications researchers. Everything we do and say tends to communicate a sort of value orientation. Second, the basic wisdom of attempting to be value neutral has also been questioned. Even many secular counselors are beginning to recognize that using their influence to increase the moral sensitivity of their clients will ultimately promote their clients' best interest. While this also highlights a long-standing problem in the profession of excessively and exclusively promoting the self-interest of clients (often to the neglect of any responsibility they should feel toward others), the net result has been an increased openness to discussions of a moral nature.

The purpose in emphasizing this role for those involved in the ministry of Christian counseling takes at least two forms. First, there is a need to encourage such helpers to validate the language of moral concern in the counseling setting and to embrace their roles as moral consultants. While such a position for Christian counselors may seem self-evident, the cultural forces calling for value-neutral counseling continue to be felt in this arena. Second, counselors need to recognize that there are actually a variety of levels of moral consultation. Introducing a greater moral awareness into discussions with counselees can vary from very direct to very subtle. Both extremes, as well as various positions in between, can be appropriate depending on the circumstances and needs of the clients. For example, Paul's statement above demonstrates a very direct confrontation. Evidently, certain members of the Corinthian congregation had become very lax with regard to a variety of sins. In this case believers were beginning to allow false teachers to undermine their belief in the resurrection. Such false teachings were judged by the apostle to need sharp rebuke. However, most moral issues in therapy reflect a need for a more subtle challenge or confrontation.

While the approach used by Paul is needed occasionally, helpers would do well to remember that the more direct the confrontation, the greater the risk of jeopardizing positive counseling outcomes. Such approaches, for example, run the risk of alienating a client who has not yet come to trust the intentions of the helper. They also carry a greater risk of causing the helper to appear judgmental or moralistic, possibly damaging rather than helping the client in the process. Counseling can be morally sensitive without being moralistic. Moralistic counselors communicate a sense of superiority in their challenges to counselees. Morally sensitive counselors recognize that they must earn the right to confront in such a direct manner. Paul had spent months investing in the lives and welfare of his readers, often humbling himself by the type of servant leadership he assumed. Morally sensitive counselors recognize that for challenges to be effective, clients must be convinced that the helper holds a deep concern for their welfare, a concern that often needs to be demonstrated over time. They also attempt to utilize the subtlest form of challenges that will still serve to meet the moral needs of the client. At times, simply stopping and attending to certain subjects introduced by the client will promote this end.

Take for example a man whose wife has committed adultery and who is considering divorce. In discussing this choice with the helper, the client states, "I realize that my decision to stay or leave may adversely affect my children." Rather than simply acknowledging this statement, the counselor may stop here and encourage the client to explore this idea in an effort to heighten the client's sensitivity to a very vital subject. At other times, counselors may choose to voice their own concerns about various choices being consider by a client; give their own position on a subject; begin to use more explicitly moral language; cite research supporting the appropriate moral position; and/or encourage clients to explore the implications of any decisions they are contemplating (Doherty, *Soul Searching*, 42-46). Any or all of these may lead clients to productive discussions involving the moral implications of their decision making.

Principle #10: Take a Multi-Generational and Contextual View of the Client

> ". . . for I, the LORD your God, am a jealous God, punishing the children for the sin of the fathers to the third and fourth generation of those who hate me, but showing love to a thousand generations of those who love me and keep my commandments." (Exodus 20:5)

> "For the Christian wife brings holiness to her marriage, and the Christian husband brings holiness to his marriage. Otherwise, your children would not have a godly influence, but now they are set apart for him." (1 Corinthians 7:14 New Living Translation)

For us to understand clients' problems sufficiently, much less help them to move toward the solution to their problem, we must consider both the immediate and the inter-generational context in which this problem arises. Exodus 20:5 indicates that the influence of past generations continues to be felt in successive generations, both in positive and negative ways. Other Scriptures demonstrate how current relationships and situations can work to assist (1 Corinthians 7:14) or hinder (1 Corinthians 15:33) clients in their efforts to experience or move toward wholeness. Therefore, by investigating the nature and types of relationships that exist or have existed between a client and his family of origin, the counselor not only can gain an increased understanding of the problem but with this information also can identify ways that alterations in the environment and relationships may promote a more redemptive outcome.

For example, we gain valuable information about the nature of humankind and the struggles we face by looking at the nature of relationships that existed in the garden. Likewise, an investigation of the nature and types of relationships that existed in more recent generations can yield valuable insights into clients and their problems. RFC encourages helpers to become familiar with constructing genograms and/or lifemaps (Richardson, *Family Ties That Bind*, 90-94), both of which can serve as valuable resources in this regard. They are also encouraged to ask about significant stressors or life changes that clients are currently facing or have faced over the past year as a way of further evaluating the contextual forces operating in their lives. Ultimately, taking a contextual or "systemic" view of a client's situation means that counselors recognize the emotional, financial, relational, intellectual, and physical forces that are operating on and in a client's life at any given time. By understanding these forces, they can seek to respond to or influence these in ways that will promote the client's well-being.

Principle #11: Recognize the Holistic Nature of Man

> *"When I kept silent about my sin, my body wasted away through my groaning all day long. For day and night Thy hand was heavy upon me; My vitality was drained away as with the fever-heat of summer. I acknow ledged my sin to Thee, And my iniquity I did not hide; I said, 'I will confess my transgressions to the Lord'; And Thou didst forgive the guilt of my sin." (Psalm 32:3-5 New American Standard Version)*

RFC joins other Christian approaches to counseling in that it seeks to address the needs of the whole person. As the above Scripture implies, the physical, genetic, psychological, and spiritual aspects of humanity are all intricately related. In this case, David's choice to hide his sin regarding Bathsheba and Nathan had direct consequences on his physical and spiritual well-being. Likewise, a person's physical condition has a direct bearing on her emotional condition, and so forth. For example, a woman who comes to her pastor for help in dealing with depression may in fact need to visit her medical doctor instead. Apart from the emotionally draining effects of chronic illnesses in general, there are literally dozens of medical conditions, such as hypothyroidism, that may initially present with symptoms of depression. A failure to recognize the interrelated and interdependent nature of humankind can lead to overly simplistic and damaging consequences for the client. The problem, which is shared by most all disciplines, is one of reductionism. Most people who attempt to specialize in various people helping professions tend to see the problems that people bring to them as reflecting issues addressed in their discipline. Medical professionals tend to reduce problems in human functioning to medical problems. Theologians tend to trace these same problems to spiritual sources, and so forth. RFC seeks to caution Christian counselors against becoming too reductionistic in their views of clients problems, and be willing to refer or work in a multidisciplinary way in order to promote the welfare of the people they seek to help.

**Principle #12: Recognize That If What You
Are Doing Is Not Working for You, by
All Means Do Something Different**

> *"If something is crooked, you can't make it straight. If something is missing, you can't say it is here." (Ecclesiastes 1:15 New Century Version)*

Most of us have heard the admonition, "If at first you don't succeed, try, try, again." The problem with this idea is that most people interpret it to mean that we should continue to do what we have previously been doing, but just do *more* of it. Unfortunately, this is notoriously bad advice. If you are figuratively "hitting your head against the wall" in trying to solve a problem in a certain way, it only makes sense to try something different. Otherwise, it's just like continuing to hit your head against the wall and foolishly thinking that it will stop hurting if you do it long enough.

Unfortunately, it often takes us a long time before we recognize what we are doing is not working. I am reminded of an Aggie joke about the two hunters who got lost in the woods. Seeking a solution to their predicament, one of the hunters said that he had heard that if you shoot your weapon in the air three times in a row it is a sign to other hunters in the area that you are lost. When other hunters hear the shots they will in turn shoot three times and then both will continue this process until the lost hunters follow the sounds back to safety. Sensing this was a good idea, they proceeded to shoot three times and then listen for a response. When none came they decided to try again. But again there was no response. They tried a third time but again heard no reply. Finally, one of them said, "I am afraid this is not going to work," to which the other responded, "Yeah, and we are almost out of arrows too."

Far too often counselors find themselves in the embarrassing situation of encouraging clients to continue to try things that have already been tried and found to be ineffective or insufficient. Experienced helpers are careful to ask what their clients have already attempted in their efforts to solve their problem and avoid suggesting a course of action that already has been demonstrated as ineffective.

Summary

While a number of the preceding counseling principles are found in other helping models, this unique constellation of principles is distinctive to the RFC approach. We certainly are indebted to the developers of interpersonal, cognitive-behavioral, solution-focused, and various other approaches for their insights into the helping process. However, as useful as these counseling models may be, they lack the relational emphasis and theological foundation necessary to promote a truly holistic approach to the helping process. As we have seen, an appreciation for the relational dimensions of the helping process is critical in order to address the deeper needs of those seeking our help. The following chapter will now continue laying the groundwork for the three-stage RFC model by exploring the qualities of effective helpers and the characteristics of good goals.

Chapter 3

Reconciliation-Focused Counseling: Counselor Qualities/Redemptive Goals

Christianity is often proudly described as not being a religion but a relationship—vertical with God, horizontal with others. However, it is here, as they say, that we often witness a "slip between the cup and the lip." Unfortunately, persons preparing for ministry often receive a great deal of theological and technical training but very little training and/or feedback regarding how to cultivate positive interpersonal relationships. But without a strong set of people skills, it is difficult if not impossible to be effective in virtually any area of ministry. Therefore, working to establish the following personal qualities will greatly enhance the possibility of counselors offering what might be called a "faithful presence" to those who seek their help. The following discussion draws from the many contributions of Gerard Egan (1975, 1977, 1982, 1994, 1997) and Robert Carkhuff (1969a, 1969b, 1979, 1983, 2000).

Qualities That Define the "Faithful Presence" Counselor

Good Listener

Helpers need to recognize that we all are to some degree hearing impaired. In other words, like persons with cotton in their ears we all struggle with "filters" to our listening. The Bible illustrates the reality of "spiritual filters" in that without Christ, people cannot hear the truth of God's Word (i.e., Mark 4:9 "let him who has ears . . ."). It's not that they don't literally hear the words; they do. They just don't hear the message. Commenting on this risk for counselors, Douglas Anderson encourages helpers to listen "attentively for the inbreaking of the grace of God in the lives of clients and in the counseling hour . . . remembering that God is the Source of all healing and growth" (Burton, *Religion and the Family*, 94). Building on this idea, Gerald May observes that pastoral counselors are unique in that they manifest " . . . a radical willingness to be nothing but an instrument through which God's healing and growth can happen" (May, *Will and Spirit*, 295). By carefully listening for God, helpers can serve as potential channels rather than obstacles of God's grace in the lives of their counselees.

Other potential types of listening filters exist as well. Emotional, physical, and intellectual filters also hinder our ability to hear accurately what our clients are attempting to communicate. To further complicate the matter, spoken messages involve both verbal content and nonverbal components making the potential for misunderstanding even greater. Considering only the verbal components of communication for a moment, Egan (1982) highlights that the meaning of the messages we ultimately give one another are influenced to varying degrees by the speaker's particular choice of words, tone of voice, voice level, pitch, intensity, inflection, spacing of words, emphases, pauses, silences, and fluency. Add to this Mehrabian's research (Egan 1982b, 63-64) which suggests that only 7% of messages are determined by the speaker's selected words while 38% are determined by the vocal clues offered by the individual. (Accordingly, 55% of the messages we receive are determined by nonverbal cues.) With so many ways for potential misunderstandings to occur, helpers are encouraged to recognize the multifaceted task of effective listening and consider consulting some of the resources listed at the end of this section.

Skilled Observer

While listening primarily involves attempting to hear both the speaker's words and manner of speaking, there are additional messages being communicated by the client that are communicated through their bodies. Specifically, a client communicates nonverbally using changes in body posture, facial expression, movement, focus, and overall reactions. In fact, these nonverbal aspects of a client's communication exert a dominant influence over the ultimate meaning of the messages received by the listener. Again, the research previously cited indicates that a stunning 55% of the message received by the listener is determined by such nonverbal behaviors, with the impact of one's facial expression having the greatest impact overall.

Relevant to this discussion on the importance of observation skills is the familiar story of Jesus and Zaccheus. The reader will recall that Jesus spotted the despised chief tax collector in a sycamore tree, perched there in order to see over the throng of people gathered around Him. Among the numerous lessons present in this story, one that sheds light on this discussion is the fact that Jesus would attend to someone perched in a tree when so many others in more immediate proximity clamored for His attention. Aside from the spiritual issues involved, one facet of what stands out about Christ's recognition of Zaccheus is not so much the demonstration of His visual acuity, per se, but His keen sensitivity to unique visual cues in His environment. Likewise, astute observers will, with disciplined effort and practice, develop a sensitivity to the critical visual cues offered by their clients therefore furthering a better understanding and approach to their clients' problems.

Positive Positioning Skills

In addition to becoming more aware of the client's nonverbal communications, helpers also need to be aware of their own nonverbal communications. A counselor's nonverbal communications, like those of the clients, can work to enhance or diminish the faithful presence we seek to offer counselees. Specifically, Egan (1982b, 60-61) has identified five aspects of physical positioning that counselors need to consider when seeking to enhance their therapeutic leverage with clients. While the flexible application of these guidelines is encouraged due to both the individual and cultural differences represented among clients, counselors will do well to use these guidelines as a basic framework for their positioning behaviors during the session. Following the use of the acronym **SOLER**, Egan suggests that helpers

S – Sit *squarely* in front of the client
O – Use an *open* stance, avoiding the use of crossed arms and legs
L – *Lean* forward about 30 degrees
E – Maintain good *eye* contact
R – Try to remain *relaxed*

Minister of Acceptance (Grace)

If we want people to experience divine grace in their lives, then certainly they need to find it in the context of the helping relationship. If, as we have contended, shame is a primary culprit in the emotional and relational problems experienced by humankind, then we need to allow the accepting, healing grace of Jesus Christ to flow freely in the counseling enterprise. Understandably, many people have difficulty understanding the grace of our Lord due to the fact that grace has been experienced as conditional in their experience with others. Grace is by definition the unmerited favor of one individual toward another. It is unconditional by virtue of the fact that there is nothing we can do to earn it. It is freely granted and therefore not dependent on the behaviors of the individual to whom it is given.

However, a person who reflects a positive, accepting attitude toward individuals may still remain opposed to their behaviors. Like the familiar refrain to "condemn the sin and not the sinner," Jesus was able to challenge the behaviors of the woman caught in adultery ("go and sin no more") while at the same time reflecting an attitude of acceptance of her as a person ("neither do I condemn you"). Holding both censoring and accepting positions with people is enabled when the individual reflecting grace remains aware of her own need of and experience with the grace of Jesus Christ. As Luke 7:47 so clearly communicates, the degree to which we are aware of how much we have been forgiven is the degree to which we will reflect the love and therefore the acceptance of Christ to others.

Self-Aware

Alexander Bruce once said, "One who knows his weakness may become strong even at the weak point; but he who knows not his weak points cannot be strong at any point" (Bruce, *The Training of the Twelve*, 12). Self-awareness is a critical precursor to effective ministry in any form. Numerous Scriptures encourage Christians to pursue a greater level of self-knowledge. For example, consider Christ's words to us in Matthew 7:3-5:

> Why do you look at the speck of sawdust in your brother's eye and pay no attention to the plank in your own eye? How can you say to your brother, 'Let me take the speck out of your eye,' when all the time there is a plank in your own eye? You hypocrite, first take the plank out of your own eye, and then you will see clearly to remove the speck from your brother's eye.

Or consider the Psalmist's words in Psalm 139:23-24: "Search me, O God, and know my heart; test me and know my anxious thoughts. See if there is any offensive way in me, and lead me in the way everlasting."

The Scriptures are filled with such illustrations of how vital self-knowledge is to anyone wishing to engage in redemptive ministry. These illustrations also remind us of the tragic consequences which may result from a lack of self- knowledge, especially when a lack of insight into our own weaknesses is involved. When Christ warned that all those present at the Last Supper would desert Him, Peter responded by saying, "Even if all fall away on account of you, I never will" (Matthew 26:33). Was Peter consciously lying? Hardly. He just lacked an awareness of how subject he was to the fear of man. One can only imagine how Peter's denials must have compounded Christ's pain of being betrayed. Or consider how King David, who seemingly at the height of personal and spiritual success, found himself engaging in the rape of another man's wife and ultimately the murder of her husband. No doubt David, a man of established char-acter, must have been surprised to discover that he would end up the willing participant in such decadent acts. Sadly, most participants in such dramas have at some previous juncture thought, "It will never happen to me." Therefore, lest we be tempted to think that such tragic circumstances, stemming in part from deficient levels of self-awareness, are limited only to others, we should be reminded that history proves otherwise. And since a counselor who lacks self-awareness may be subject to many damaging behaviors, he would be well advised to seek out supervision of his work and to pursue relationships that promote honesty, integrity, and accountability.

Compassionate/Loving/Empathic

It has been said that "people don't care how much you know until they know how much you care." Helpers should recognize that regardless of how technically proficient they become at the counseling task, they must first convince the client of their care[42] and concern if they hope to be helpful. One way counselors can communicate their concern for clients is through the use of empathy. Empathy or empathic reflection, as a counseling skill, is a two-part process. First, the helper attempts to *understand* the current story or problem from the client's perspective. However, having come to this awareness is only half of the process. The second part involves communicating or *reflecting* that understanding back to the counselee. Both understanding and reflecting must take place if empathy is to have its desired effect. One might say that clients need to see their emotional reflection in the therapeutic mirror provided by the counselor. Our ability to demonstrate care and concern for clients will be significantly enhanced as we grow in our ability to understand and reflect *accurately* their communications. However, the beneficial effects of empathy don't necessarily hinge on our ability to hear and reflect the messages of our clients. Even when our understanding of their problems is somewhat lacking, clients benefit from knowing that we cared enough to try to understand their struggles and pain. Aspiring counselors would do well to practice their empathic reflection skills with their clients using the following frequently cited format. "You feel _____ when _____ occurs in your life." The first blank is filled in using a feeling word that best describes what the counselor believes the client is feeling. The second blank represents the experiences the counselor believes that the client associates with that feeling. If counselors wish to emphasize the experience rather than the feelings, they may choose to reverse the format as follows: "Because of _____ you feel _____." Over time, helpers can vary the format of these statements to avoid seeming too mechanical.

Spiritual Disciple

While this book is about helping counselors and other ministers become more proficient in their helping skills, no amount of training or technical expertise will ever take the place of the helper being a spiritual disciple of Jesus Christ. As the ultimate source of all healing, our connection to the supreme counselor (John 14:26; 16:2-3) allows us the unique opportunity to serve as the conduit through which "grace is communicated and reconciliation experienced" (Thornton, 37). Helpers who wish to occupy this privileged role need to be involved in regular individual and corporate Bible study, prayer, and worship. As we will see, seeking inspiration, wisdom, and discernment represent integral and ongoing activities in the RFC model. Those who are serious about the role God plays in the counseling process recognize that such activities are not merely a form of spirituality based only in abstract and ethereal meditation. Rather, they must be informed by the disciplined pursuit of God. The Psalmist's proclamation "Your word is a lamp to my feet and a light for my path" (Psalm 119:105) reveals a practice of spirituality that is centered around the Word of God as being the primary point of reference for these activities. *(See spiritual discipleship resources listed separately below.)*

Hope Engendering

As emphasized earlier, helpers cannot afford the luxury of being hopeless with their clients. In spite of what often appear to be overwhelming and intractable circumstances, effective helpers should always attempt to communicate an attitude of Christ-centered hope. As we are reminded in 1 Peter 3:15b, "If you are asked about your Christian hope, always be ready to explain it." Andrew Lester draws on this injunction when he states,

> Since despair is so painful and debilitating, and because hope is so basic to living joyfully, I am convinced that we need to be more explicit about our commitment to a God who is out in front of us calling us into an open-ended future. . . . Indeed we represent to our parishioners (as pastors), clients (as pastoral counselors), or patients (as chaplains) a hope based on the promises of God that a new future is always available to us, that numerous possibilities exist in every present circumstance. (Lester, *Hope in Pastoral Care and Counseling*, 15)

Perceptive counselors, aware of these realities, can always find a legitimate way to interject an attitude of hope into the troubled lives of their clients. You might say that our Christian hope provides the fertile ground from which substantive and lasting change can emerge.

Ethical/Good Boundaries

Just because someone is a Christian counselor doesn't mean she will be an ethical counselor, even if she is well intentioned. A helper can be sincere and hold pure motives yet still hurt her counselee due to a lack of awareness of what constitutes ethical counseling protocol. One of the most common areas of ethical violation for beginning counselors is that of confidentiality. Confidentiality is an absolutely essential practice in the counseling arena. Aside from the possible legal ramifications for helpers who violate the confidentiality of their clients rests the fact that people will avoid seeking help from those who fail to follow this practice. However, this gives rise to another potential ethical complication for uninformed helpers. There are legal limitations to confidentiality in every state, including some limitations for pastors. Therefore, appropriate counseling practice requires that helpers remain aware of these limitations and inform clients of these before they begin the counseling process. Other areas requiring ethical awareness and practice from those who wish to counsel include issues such as child abuse, elder abuse, suicidality, dual relationships, the representation of credentials and abilities, just to name a few. The more helpers study the subject of ethics, the more they begins to see how ethical counseling involves the process of identifying and pursuing appropriate emotional, physical, relational and intellectual boundaries with their clients. All relationships are governed by rules or boundaries that regulate the way people interact. In casual relationships, these rules, while consciously held, are seldom committed to writing. The field of professional ethics really represents an attempt by persons in the profession to commit to writing those rules or boundaries that are considered appropriate for the occupation under consideration. Ministers may wish to enhance their ethical readiness for counseling by reading the ethics statement developed by the American Association of Christian Counselors (AACC). A copy of this statement can be found online at http://www.aacc.net.

Genuineness/Integrity

Again, just because a person is a Christian counselor doesn't necessarily mean that he will reflect integrity or genuineness in his work with others. Integrity, as it is being used here, is not meant to be limited to a person's level of honesty, moral virtue, honorableness, uprightness, and so forth. Understandably, these characteristics are important for any

Christian to reflect. For our purposes, integrity or genuineness is also understood to include the need for counselors to avoid duplicity in their personalities. In other words, a person of integrity is also a person who says what he means and means what he says, who is the same on the inside as he is on the outside, a what-you-see-is-what-you-get kind of person. Why is this important? Well first, the Scriptures discourage hypocrisy as can be seen in Jesus rebuke of the Pharisees:

> Woe to you, teachers of the law and Pharisees, you hypocrites! You are like whitewashed tombs, which look beautiful on the outside but on the inside are full of dead men's bones and everything unclean. In the same way, on the outside you appear to people as righteous but on the inside you are full of hypocrisy and wickedness. (Mathew 23:27-28)

Second, a lack of genuineness or integrity in a counselor will invariably promote, among others things, a lack of trust in the counseling relationship. People almost always sense a lack of genuineness in others when such incongruity exists. They simply intuit it. And when clients sense this inconsistency in their counselors, they will withhold their trust and limit their disclosures given the uncertainties of dealing with someone who is guarded, duplicitous, deceitful or simply unaware. Tragically, a counselor's perceived duality results in promoting the same type of duality in our clients, modeling a behavior which is the very opposite of what they need. Given our previous understanding of the crucial nature of promoting trust as a way of restoring healthy relationships, we simply cannot afford to compromise our dedication to an open, honest relationship with clients. Guided by the illuminating insight and direction of the Holy Spirit, counselors should continually be circumspect about any inconsistencies in their interactions with others and make appropriate adjustments as needed.

Non-Anxious Presence

In numerous places throughout the Scriptures believers are encouraged to resist anxiety and enjoy the benefits of having peace with God. In Philippians 4:6-7 Paul challenges readers,

> Do not be anxious about anything, but in everything, by prayer and petition, with thanksgiving, present your requests to God. And the peace of God, which transcends all understanding, will guard your hearts and your minds in Christ Jesus.

While the benefits of enjoying reduced levels of anxiety remain fairly obvious to the believer, these benefits find increased importance for the counselor. The importance of effective self-regulation for the counselor is magnified is due to the inherent relationship between effective helping and the counselor's ability to manage tension. Stress researchers have long recognized that everyone experiences some degree of anxiety and that in modest levels it tends to enhance a person's performance. However, when anxiety exceeds a certain level, personal performance begins to decline. Ultimately, a high level of anxiety will lead to more impulsive and feeling-laden behavior as rationality gives way to a persons rising emotionality. Consequently, previously held principles and goals may be compromised or abandoned during these points of stress.

A counselor's ability to remain objective and controlled, manage stress, facilitate rapport, and even utilize humor are all influenced by his anxiety level. Helpers who find anxiety or reactivity with others to be a continual point of concern would do well to reflect on the ideas presented by Murray Bowen, Michael Kerr, and others regarding a person's need to be differentiated (Kerr and Bowen, *Family Evaluation*, 1988; Richardson, *Family Ties That Bind*, 1995). A differentiated person, according to this view, is someone who by virtue of working through issues of attachment and detachment with his family of origin has now become less reactive (i.e., anxious). For counselors, this lowered level of anxiety benefits not only them but also the clients with whom they work. Less anxious counselors are better able to think creatively, effectively utilize humor, avoid positions of over-responsibility and/or damaging alignments, and demonstrate more self-control than their more anxious counterparts.

However, while acknowledging the significant contributions of Bowen's innovative model for understanding and modifying the impact of anxiety on human behavior, Christians have even greater resources. Christian counselors recognize that Christ's and therefore the helper's resources for dealing with troubling levels of anxiety extend far beyond this limited view. Christ's peace was ultimately derived from His intimacy with the Father and the abiding presence of the Holy Spirit, the same peace Adam and Eve originally experienced in the garden. We too may experience the intimacy and peace of such divine communion by committing to draw close to the ultimate Author of all true and lasting peace.

Additional Counselor Preparation Resources

- *Listening and Caring Skills in Ministry: A Guide for Pastors, Counselors, and Small Groups* by John S. Savage, 1996.
- *The Skilled Pastor: Counseling as the Practice of Theology* by Charles W. Taylor, 1991.
- *Christian Counseling Ethics: A Handbook for Therapists, Pastors & Counselors* by Randolph K. Sanders (Editor), 1997.
- *The Art of Christian Listening* by Thomas N. Hart, 1981.
- *Excellence and Ethics in Counseling* by Mark R. McMinn, 1991.
- *Building Basic Therapeutic Skills: A Practical Guide for Current Mental Health Practice* by Jeanne Albronda Heaton, 1998.
- *Hope in Pastoral Care and Counseling* by Andrew D. Lester, 1995.

Spiritual Discipleship Resources

- *Into Abba's Arms* (AACC Library) by Sandra Wilson and Larry Crabb, 1998.
- *Abba's Child: The Cry of the Heart for Intimate Belonging* by Brennan Manning, 1994.
- *Lion and Lamb/the Relentless Tenderness of Jesus* by Brennan Manning, 1986.
- *The Ragamuffin Gospel: Embracing the Unconditional Love of God* by Brennan Manning, 2000.
- *Reflections for Ragamuffins: Daily Devotions from the Writings of Brennan Manning* by Brennan Manning and Ann McMath Weinheimer (Editor), 1998.
- *Homesick for Eden: A Soul's Journey to Joy* by Gary Moon, 1997.
- *The Sacred Romance: Drawing Closer to the Heart of God* by Brent Curtis & John Eldredge, 1997.

Characteristics of Redemptive Goals

One of the most difficult tasks for any counselor is helping clients to set well-formed goals. This distinction cannot be overemphasized. Setting goals is easy. The task for effective helpers lies not in just setting goals but setting *well-formed* goals. This goal is more daunting than most aspiring counselors first realize. What may initially appear to be a "good" goal may in fact be a very poor goal when compared to some well-established goal screening criteria. To illustrate the necessary considerations involved in establishing redemptive goals, consider the following actual counseling situation.

Mary and Bill were a middle-aged couple who initially came requesting counseling for what they described as a "communication problem." For most of their twenty-year marriage, both had held separate full-time jobs, reared two sons, and participated in numerous activities in their local church. The last son, David, had recently gone to college, resulting in the couple being back together alone at home, much like the situation that existed for the first two years of their marriage. As is common for many dual-career couples, Mary spent more time with the boys growing up, putting additional schooling and potential career advancements on hold to allow more time for their care. Bill's job had required him to work long hours and travel extensively, often resulting in little extra time for the family or his marriage. The recent changes in the family's structure and Bill's work situation resulted in more time together as a couple and highlighted how emotionally distant and out of touch they had become.

For several months prior to their first session, Mary and Bill's interactions had become increasingly conflictual. With Bill's job now providing more income for the family and with less time being required to manage the lives of her two sons, Mary was now ready to quit her secretarial job and return to college and finish her degree. Bill, on the other hand, was enjoying the benefits of his recent promotion. For the first time in years he was beginning to feel less financial pressure and have more time away from work. Ready to relish their new situation, he saw Mary's plans as a threat to their new-found financial freedom and time together. While Bill acknowledged that years earlier they had discussed the possibility of Mary returning to school, he failed to see the financial benefit of her decision and was therefore resistant to this choice. Mary, on the other hand, had become increasingly disillusioned with their relationship and with what she described as Bill's lack of attentiveness and "failure to honor" the career sacrifices she had made all those years. She wanted a "more loving" relationship but wondered if it was still with Bill. The week before, she had brought up the possibility of a separation, which prompted Bill to call for the initial appointment.

The following criteria were utilized in helping Bill and Mary to establish redemptive, well-formed goals.

1. Positive in orientation. Working toward the presence of something is easier than working toward the absence of something. In other words, effective goals are stated in positive terms, working toward *initiating or increasing* **desirable** thoughts and behaviors rather than seeking to *eliminate or decrease* **undesirable** thoughts and behaviors. The reason for such a position can best be demonstrated by a consideration of the following. Pick a sound in your current environment and then try to imagine that it is getting softer. Try to imagine for a moment that the sound is becoming less and less noticeable. Now switch gears. Rather than trying to diminish the sound, pick another sound in your environment and imagine trying to increase it by selectively focusing your attention in that direction. Consciously focus all of your listening ability on its source. Which was easier? Imagining the first sound decreasing in intensity or imagining the second sound increasing in intensity. The chances are, increasing the new sound through selective attention was the answer. What happened to the original sound as you focused on the new sound? Chances are that it became less noticeable. Why? Because in the first half of this exercise, in attempting to use your imagination to diminish the sound, didn't you *first* have to recall the sound before attempting to imagine its absence? In other words, you first had to recall the problem (the sound) before attempting to remove it. A negative goal is like this in that you first have to recall the problem before working toward its absence. This process of first remembering the problem indirectly tends to reinforce the problem. In the second half of this illustration, by using your imagination to try to increase a different sound (which for our purposes we'll call the solution) your focus on the second sound naturally reduced your awareness of the first. Positive goals are like this in that rather than even thinking about the problem, we now only think about the solution, avoiding the risk of reinforcing the problem often experienced in pursuing negative goals.

In going back to our case, when the counselor asked Bill and Mary what they meant by "communicate better," they responded by saying that they would not argue as much. While this may sound like an admirable goal, it is stated in negative terms since it seeks to eliminate or decrease the arguing behaviors. As we have seen, this type of goal will be more difficult to pursue than one stated in positive terms. Therefore, the counselor responded to their statement by saying, "That's a good idea. When you are no longer arguing with one another, what will you be doing *instead?*" The response was now, "We would be nicer to one another, be more self-controlled and show a willingness to compromise." Notice how by simply using the word "instead," the counselor helped this couple move in a more positive direction. They can now begin to identify specific thoughts and behaviors that will start or increase when progress is made in pursuing the agreed-upon goal. Occasionally, clients will respond to this question by saying, "I don't know." In these times, the counselor can respond by saying, "If you did know, what thoughts and behaviors would you be using?" or "Imagine the thoughts and behaviors that are present when your relationship is going well." By invoking their imagination, clients can now think freely about any number of possible thoughts and behaviors they would like to utilize to approach their current problem. Interestingly, after listing these "possible" thoughts and behaviors clients will often recognize how they have already utilized some of these in the past. However, it was not until they were guided to discover them in this fashion that they could be recalled. Identifying a client's experience with previously positive behaviors is a very desirable discovery for the counselor since this greatly enhances the likelihood that these behaviors will be repeated.

2. Specific and measurable. While "feeling words" (i.e., "more loving") and "wishes" (i.e., "communicate better") are most commonly used by counselees to describe their objectives, these types of goals are far too subjective in nature to be very helpful in measuring progress in counseling. However, since feelings and wishes are by nature the closest point of contact that clients have to their problem, they serve as critical springboards to the thoughts and behaviors related to those same problems. For example, when Bill described wanting better communication in the relationship, the counselor might have responded by saying, "When you are practicing better communication with Mary, *specifically* how will you be thinking and acting differently?" The reader will immediately notice that the counselor purposely imbedded the words "specifically" and "thinking and acting" into Bill's question. This is due to the need for goals to relate to actions and thoughts that are specific enough to be readily identifiable by the client when they occur. As previously discussed, RFC assumes that a change in the thoughts and behaviors of the client will naturally result in a change in the way they feel. Additionally, thoughts and behaviors can be measured. Therefore, clients can better relate to their progress from one session to the next.

Note that making such a direct leap from problem feelings to positive thoughts and behaviors might not always flow easily for the client. Negative feelings naturally tend to limit positive perspectives. Therefore, it may first be necessary for the client to access the negative thoughts and behaviors related to their negative feelings and then ask themselves "What will I be doing or thinking *instead?*" Once again, feelings serve as linchpins not only to negative thoughts and behaviors but also to positive thoughts and behaviors. Consequently, it may be necessary at times to recall negative thoughts and behaviors first before their positive counterparts can come into focus. In Bill's case, building resentment along with his recent experience with negative communication patterns may result in the answer "I don't really know" when responding to the counselor's request for thoughts and behaviors associated with improved communication. To circumvent this, the helper should inquire about the specific thoughts and behaviors that are present when the problem is occurring and then ask the client what the opposite thoughts and behaviors would be or what the client would be doing "instead." For example, on further questioning, Bill stated that when Mary started to cry during an argument, he would think "how selfish and manipulative" she was being and would retaliate by yelling insults at her. Upon reflecting on the opposite of these thoughts and behaviors, he was then able to see how Mary's behavior was not simply reflecting self-interest but showed the "sensitivity he originally found so attractive" in her personality. He was also better able to identify and challenge his damaging retaliatory behaviors.

3. Reasonably attainable. The idea of reasonably attainable goals encompasses several areas of consideration. First, does the goal reflect changes in the thoughts and behaviors of the counselee or does it somehow expect changes in someone else? Clearly, as we will discuss in more detail under #7 of this section, clients must choose goals that they themselves can accomplish. Second, goals must be realistic given the limitations of our humanity, the leading and guidance of the Holy Spirit, and the particular circumstances and challenges unique to the counselee's situation. Paul's statement that "I can do everything through him who gives me strength" (Philippians 4:13) should not be interpreted to mean that if a person has enough faith he can go jump off of a building and expect to be unhurt when he hits the ground. Setting goals that are excessively "lofty" may sound attractive at first but may only set the client up for disappointment and failure. A common mistake for helpers is setting goals that require almost complete perfection in a given area or that do not allow for sufficient flexibility. For example, Bill and Mary's idea of better communication may be never to raise their voices to one another. While seemingly an admirable attitude, setting the bar at this level inevitably would result in disillusionment.

4. Desired by the client. While setting goals desired by the client may seem rather self-evident at first, it is amazing how subtly the goals of the counselor can replace a client's goals. Counselors cannot help but bring preconceived notions of what they think would be best for the counselee. However, attempting to pursue anything other than what is truly desired by the client (except when the goal compromises the counselor's Christian ethic) is a sure formula for ineffective counseling. Counselors should be careful to avoid assuming that simply because clients agree to a goal that this is truly what they want to accomplish. Often clients, if not encouraged to explore sufficiently what they really want or because the counselor is so convincing, will agree to goals that they don't really want. Therefore, in the long run clients will lack sufficient motivation to accomplish the goals. To minimize this possibility, helpers should listen closely for the presence of ambivalence in the client. Ambivalence is when the client feels divided over whether or not to go in a particular direction. Part of the client may favor a given course of action while the other part resists. There are many reasons why clients feel divided over goals. Additionally, most clients will reflect some degree of ambivalence. What is important to consider is just how much ambivalence do clients feel toward the particular goal at hand? Do both their verbal and nonverbal responses suggest that they favor the identified direction? Nonverbal feedback suggesting reluctance usually means that they will not follow through with even verbally agreed-upon goals until the reluctance is addressed and resolved. For example, Mary's explicit and implicit communications regarding her disillusionment with the marriage coupled with her recent suggestion of separation certainly suggest more than a little ambivalence. In order to increase her desire to work on the marriage, the counselor must directly address this issue. Just because she showed up in the counselor's office does not mean that she actually wants to work on the relationship. Therefore, further questioning should be done to explore her willingness to go in this direction.

5. In the client's language. Counselors should be mindful of attempting to use the client's language to describe goals when ever possible. This counseling principle has evolved because of repeated observations that clients already have an emotional attachment to the words they use to describe their goals. Therefore, clients are more motivated to pursue them. To help use this idea to counseling advantage, counselors should consider writing down the exact words used by the client. Further discussions involving the goal may result in the client choosing to reword it based on points of clarification and improved understanding. However, the final goal should be written reflecting language that the client volunteers or in language with which the client is thoroughly comfortable. For example, when Bill indicated that he wanted to work on "better communication" in his marriage, the counselor, recognizing that this language is in fact too imprecise, may be tempted to correct the client's use of vague language. However, working to improve the specificity of the goal while still building on Bill's use of language can still be accomplished without having to correct him or in some other way show disapproval of his selected vocabulary. This objective is accomplished by simply complimenting Bill on his initial goal of "better communication" and then proceeding to get more specifics regarding what the goal actually means. So, rather than saying something like "words like communication really are not specific enough," the helper could again say "that's really great. When you are practicing better communication with one another, how will you know this based on how you are acting or thinking differently."

6. Related to the here and now. Well-formed goals will always be related to thoughts and behaviors that can be accomplished or performed in the present. Often clients come in with goals that imply the occurrence of some future event in order to determine whether the goal has been met. For example, if someone comes saying that her goal for counseling is to decide whether or not to pursue marriage with a particular man, the attentive helper will immediately recognize that such a goal cannot *presently* occur since by necessity the decision looms somewhere in the future. In fact, agreeing to such a goal might result in a failure to identify progress in the client's journey toward a decision regardless of whether the final decision about marriage is ever reached (i.e., completing a premarital seminar). In another example, if a client came to counseling desiring to lose 20 pounds, and the counselor accepted this proposal, would this mean that if the client lost only 15 pounds that she had not met her goal or had no sense of accomplishment? Wouldn't stating the goal in this way undermine progress along the way and unnecessarily diminish the value of the final outcome? For this reason, counselors should attempt to identify goals that reflect thoughts and behaviors that can occur *presently*, even within or shortly after the session concludes. In Bill and Mary's case, the counselor might ask, "If you were *on your way* to practicing better communication when you leave here today, how would you know this based on how you were thinking or behaving differently toward one another?" The key idea here is for the counselor to highlight for clients goals that reflect thoughts and behaviors in which they can *currently* engage. While practicing some new or strengthened thoughts and behaviors will by necessity require certain contexts (i.e., the next disagreement) before they can be utilized, facets of the goal should be something that can occur in the present.

7. In the client's control. The idea of goals being in the client's control is closely related to Stage 1, Step 3 of the RFC Helping Model presented in the following chapter. Clients must be "customers" of the counseling process in order for helping efforts to be effective. In other words, they must want something for *themselves* that involves a willingness to change how *they* act or think in order to reach their goal. However, clients often come with goals that, at least in part, require changes in the behaviors of others. When this is the case, helpers should work toward redirecting a client's attention to changes that are within their control and emphasize the futile nature of attempting to change another person's behavior. For example, Mary revealed that she wanted her relationship with Bill to be "more loving." Further inquiry into this statement would likely reveal that Mary's idea of "more loving" would focus mainly on changes that Bill would make, not her. While it may be reasonable to expect Bill to change in order to improve the relationship, goals for Mary must pertain to changes in the ways that she will think or behave in the relationship.

What is interesting to observe, from a relational perspective, is that significant changes in the client inevitably lead to changes in the behaviors and attitudes of those with whom they are intimately connected. This related or systemic change in the lives of significant others may or may not result in greater satisfaction for the client due the inherent unpredictability regarding the direction of such change. However, the case can be made that if the desired positive change in the lives of significant others is to be even a possibility, then it may occur only if clients are willing to risk their own change.

Chapter 4

Reconciliation-Focused Counseling:
A Three-Stage Model

The following discussion provides an overview of the RFC counseling model. It should be noted that any effort to outline a counseling approach in a systematic, stepwise fashion is inherently limited since in reality it is rarely such a linear process. In actuality, counseling is much more recursive or circular, often revisiting earlier "stages" in an effort to clarify goals and objectives or redefine problems. You might say that it is "two steps forward and then one back" as we struggle together with those we seek to assist. Therefore, the RFC Model uses triangular-shaped lines moving in a somewhat counter-clockwise fashion around each stage of the helping process to depict the "circling back" tendency characteristic of most counseling experiences. Using a triangular shape was seen as helpful for two reasons. *First*, this form helps to highlight that each stage of the helping process is comprised of three steps. *Second*, the reader will notice that at points the lines actually move in a backward direction, indicating that there are times that helpers will need to step backward in the model. This may be due to any number of factors. Sometimes new information emerges that indicates the need to repeat earlier steps. For example, at times counselors may discover the need to refer a client, even after several sessions, when they realize that in spite of their initial best efforts to evaluate their abilities to handle the problem that they are really in over their heads. Alternatively, the helper may discover that an omission took place that can be remedied only by revisiting earlier steps in the process. Whatever the reason, helpers need to exercise a degree of flexibility in their desire to work their way through the model.

Readers will also note how the guiding theme of reconciliation with God, self, and others is highlighted by the pendulum figure within each triangle. The RFC approach to helping recognizes that *symptom resolution and enhanced levels of reconciliation are corollary and reciprocally-related processes.* Therefore, with each unfolding stage in the model, the lines between God, self, and others in these figures become increasingly defined as reconciliation is experienced and relationships are restored.

A graphic illustration of the RFC Model is given below (figure 2). This diagram is followed by a written depiction of both the model *and* the steps involved in counseling session preparation. The end of this chapter will include a discussion of the four facilitative processes (EARS—bottom of figure 2) which serve to enhance and further the counseling enterprise.

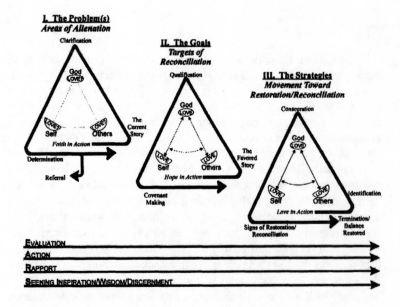

Fig. 2. RFC Model

Outline of the RFC Model

Counseling Preparation

    A. Session Preparation
        1) Make Initial Telephone/Outside Contact
        2) Engage in Focused Prayer
        3) Investigate Possible Referral Sources and Supportive
            Services
    B. Personal Preparation
        1) Offer a "Faithful Presence"
        2) Recognize a "Compromised Presence"

Counseling Process[43] (Ongoing Activities: Evaluation, Action, Rapport, and Seeking Inspiration)

    I. The Problems—Areas of Alienation
        1) The Current Story
        2) Clarification
        3) Determination
            Referral

    II. The Goals—Targets of Reconciliation
        1) The Favored Story
        2) Qualification
        3) Covenant Making

    III. The Strategies—Movement Toward Restoration/Reconciliation
        1) Identification
        2) Consecration
        3) Signs of Restoration/ 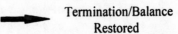 Termination/Balance
            Reconciliation   Restored

For those who are curious about the theoretical leanings represented within the model, it might best be described as a compilation of several approaches, beginning with a sort of problem-solving design and moving toward a more interpersonal/solution-focused/cognitive-behavioral format. An appreciation of the need for an intergenerational and systemic framework for understanding human problems is emphasized throughout. Sophisticates within the counseling field may find objection with such blending, claiming that stark theoretical inconsistencies exist for example between problem-solving and cognitive-behavioral approaches that give detailed attention to the problem and solution-focused approaches that usually give only incidental attention to such matters. My experience suggests that such differences occur more frequently in theory than in practice. What usually happens, even among strict solution-focused practitioners, is that prior experience with problem-solving models continues to exert an influence on their thinking while practicing their chosen approach. In other words, while solution-focused counselors give less formal attention to describing the problem functionally, my observation has been that they still give mental attention to the client's verbal distinctions around the problem for later use in measuring progress. In other words, much like the behaviorist, but much less obvious, they tend to engage mentally in a type of functional analysis of the problem. Therefore, I would suggest that such approaches remain complementary, even if not simultaneously compatible.

Discussion of the RFC Model

Counseling Preparation

Successful counseling experiences begin with giving consideration to the task of counseling preparation. Before we examine the stages and steps of the RFC model, we will first think about the importance of session and personal preparation.

1. Session preparation. Given their need to make the most efficient use of time, helpers need to expand their often-limited awareness of the ways that interventions can be utilized. Traditional forms of counseling tend to encourage the view which says that attempts to promote change by the helper are primarily restricted to the formal 45-50 minute counseling hour. However, in reality, a lot of positive things can be done to facilitate change prior to formal meetings with the client.

A. Make initial telephone/outside contact. Use this time to gather critical information related to the person's call for assistance. Some helpful questions to consider might be, Can you *briefly* describe your problem? What has prompted you to seek counseling at this time? In other words, Why now? Or between now and next time identify specifically what you would like to accomplish by coming to counseling. What are some things that you would like to see continue in your life/relationships?

B. Pray a focused prayer. We have discussed the limitations of conscious prayer during the actual course of the counseling session. However, praying before a session can be of great benefit, especially when the helper has received information during the initial client contact, which can now serve as a point or focus to guide her prayers.

C. Investigate possible referral services and supplemental services. Given the information that was garnered during the initial contact, the helper should begin to investigate the availability of both referral sources and supplemental services. While the need for a referral may have been ruled out during the initial contact, not uncommonly the first session will reveal problems far more complex or deserving of specialized care than the helper can provide. Additionally, appropriate ancillary services such as twelve-step groups or supplemental reading resources (often referred to as bibliotherapy) should be identified prior to the first meeting with the client. During the course of the first session, the helper may decide not to use any of this information. However, people in crisis will be greatly assisted by not having to wait for this information or uncover it for themselves.

2. Personal preparation. Many approaches to counseling give little if any attention to personal preparation on the part of the counselor. They either assume the presence of an emotional/spiritual/physical readiness to counsel on the part of the counselor or view these issues as largely insignificant or irrelevant to the helping process. However, persons using the RFC Model should recognize the need to be intentional about such matters.

A. Offer a faithful presence. To begin with, helpers must give careful consideration to their ability at any point in time to offer a "faithful presence" to their counselees. By emphasizing the idea of a "faithful presence," we hope to highlight the intrinsic relationship that exists between the personal and professional lives of helpers and emphasize the need to be all we can be for our clients emotionally, physically, spiritually, and intellectually. When situations exist that compromise our ability to offer this presence, our faithfulness to the counselee demands that we must remedy our limitation or refer our client. Basically, the more people have to work to get around any limitations we bring to the counseling setting, the more we become inhibitors rather than facilitators of relational and emotional healing. Therefore, we must monitor these areas to be sure they remain sources of liberation and not limitation.

While I am proposing that counselors bring a level of bio-psycho-spiritual wellness to their counselees, this is not to suggest that persons who counsel are not themselves wounded in some way. In fact, this woundedness, be it emotional, spiritual, or even physical, may be a significant asset in the helping process. Our own personal struggles can give us a depth of understanding uncommon among counselors not so challenged. The question should not be whether one has been wounded, but whether this same person has taken steps to deal appropriately with that woundedness. Henri J. M. Nouwen in his classic *The Wounded Healer* (87) argues convincingly that our journey in dealing with our own woundedness can provide a healing framework, which can guide our work with others. And assuming the satisfactory resolution of our woundedness, we now have a roadmap which may serve to help others seeking similar destinations. We can further identify with all clients as being fellow strugglers in the inevitable challenges we all encounter in this life. However, despite Nouwen's position, he offers the following point of clarification: "Making one's own wounds a source of healing, therefore, does not call for a sharing of superficial personal pains but for a constant willingness to see one's own pain and suffering as rising from the depth of the human condition which all men share" (Nouwen, 88).

   B. Recognize a compromised presence. It should be noted that personal preparation entails remaining sensitive to issues, both past and present, which may interfere with the counselor's readiness to counsel. For example, counselors unhindered by unresolved issues from their past may still need to question their ability to provide counseling due to any number of current stressors in their lives. The presence of any of the following may compromise an individual's ability to provide a faithful presence:

- Current conflictual or distant relationships with one's wife, husband, family, in-laws, and/or children
- Excessive job stress, number of hours worked, and/or scheduling demands
- Physical illness, injury, or chronic fatigue
- Depressed or anxious mood
- Poor peer relationships
- Lack of a social support or accountability network
- Failure to cultivate one's relationship with God through regular Bible study, prayer, etc.
- Recent personal losses (i.e. death of a loved one, natural disaster, divorce, etc.)
- A recent change in jobs or a move to another city
- Current legal or financial troubles
- Changes in the family unit such as family members moving out, moving in, pregnancy, birth, and so forth

Each of these stressors, individually or in combination, may result in the need for the helper to refer all or selected portions of their client populations. Having addressed the need for session and personal preparation, we will now walk together, step-by-step, through each of the each of the three stages of the RFC Model.

Counseling Process

Evaluation   Action   Rapport   Seeking

I.   **The Problems—**
     Areas of Alienation

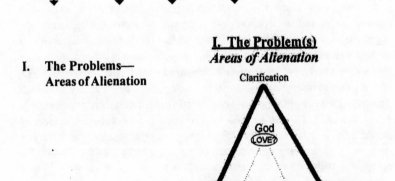

I. **The Problem(s)**
Areas of Alienation

Clarification

God LOVE?

LOVE? Self   LOVE? Others

The Current Story

Faith in Action

Determination

Referral

1. The current story. Every client needs to be given an opportunity to ventilate and tell his or her story. This is a critical step in the helping process. Most of us can probably remember numerous times when simply having someone listen attentively to our struggles seemed to help, even if the listener offered no specific feedback or guidance in the matter. Clients likewise can benefit immensely from having someone with whom to share their pain. The encouragement to "confess your sins to one another and pray for one another so that you may be healed" (James 5:16) is but one reminder of the benefit of confession as well as prayer. Throughout the Psalms, David demonstrates how the sharing of his sorrows, fears, and even frustrations helps him to move through these painful experiences, leading to greater insights and a general receptivity to God. While it is unlikely that simply allowing clients to share their pain will result in a satisfactory resolution of most problems, it will nevertheless help to begin the healing process. During this time the counselor can work to build rapport and explore the client's feelings, thoughts, and behaviors to get a clearer understanding of the problems or missed opportunities.

*RFC Emphases: Care should be taken to listening carefully for how the problems being shared represent areas of alienation that may exist between God, self, and others (see appendix N). Estrangement can take many forms. How does the identified problem relate to distance in any of these three relational domains? Does the distance involve **negative or counterproductive thoughts and behaviors** toward God, self, or others or is the person simply out of touch in one or more of these areas? What **opportunities for more meaningful relationships exist** that are currently being missed? Alienation may be reflected in the underutilization of potentially helpful relationships, even if these relationships have not previously existed (i.e., reluctance in going to see a medical doctor for tests or failing to reach out to establish new friendships). These observations will vitally inform the helping process.*

   2. Clarification. It has been said, "Action is no substitute for clarification." Nowhere is this statement more appropriate than in the helping task. Good actions proceed from well-defined and clarified problems. I can distinctly remember one of my doctoral professors coming into a counseling seminar one day and opening our discussion with the following question: "What is the first thing you do in a counseling session aside from working to establish rapport?" Well, our studious group had spent weeks reading and discussing a wide variety of counseling theories, each with its own unique spin on what to do "first." Somewhat puzzled by his question and not wanting to show our ignorance, we waited, knowing he was looking for a particular response and also knowing we didn't have it. "Assessment," he said with a grin. Obviously, I have never forgotten this lesson. Neither have I failed to develop an appreciation for just how important this step of counseling can be. If counselors are not careful, we can be like our confused group that fateful day and lose sight of the forest for the trees.

When I first started my counseling career, I mistakenly assumed that clients would come to counseling with a fairly good understanding of their problems and what they wanted from counseling. Reality has long since taught me otherwise. Clients most commonly present with only a vague understanding of what is wrong. And when asked what they would like to accomplish from the counseling sessions, they likewise tend to respond in very general terms. In retrospect, it was unrealistic for me to expect otherwise. Clients have not been trained to think of their problems in functional or objective terms. They therefore tend to use less than concrete terms to describe their difficulties. These problems are often bound up in descriptions such as "I just don't look forward to anything anymore" or "My husband and I just can't communicate." While both of statements tell us that the client has a problem, they actually tell us little more.

While I am sympathetic with approaches to counseling that consider additional details regarding the problems as unnecessary and even counterproductive to the helping enterprise, I still believe that a certain amount of information regarding clients' concerns can be quite useful. This information generally falls into four categories.

A. Duration. Specifically, how long has the problem been occurring? When the problem occurs, how long does it last? Using the above example with the client who reports that he no longer looks forward to the future or experiences any pleasure in life, the helper needs to know how long the client has been feeling this way and what exceptions to this feeling have occurred during this time. Furthermore, given that feeling words are used so frequently by clients to describe their problems, they can serve as critical linchpins to identifying the associated problem thoughts and behaviors. For example, a very helpful response to a client who has just used a feeling word like "depressed" to describe their problem might be, "This must be very difficult for you to endure. Can you tell me the kind of thoughts and behaviors that go along with your feelings of depression?" Depression usually prompts us to have excessively negative thoughts about our experiences, other people, the future, and ourselves. A careful examination of these thoughts usually reveals areas of alienation in one or more of the relational domains. Therefore, using feelings as a springboard to these thoughts, the counselor might also ask the client to complete sentences like "I feel depressed because _____." If they were to say, "I don't know," simply respond by saying "If you did know, what would you say?" This will usually elicit a helpful response. Once helpers have assisted clients in identifying the thoughts and behaviors associated with the problem (in the above case, depression), then they can more easily transition to the thoughts and behaviors that occur when the problem no longer occurs (when he is happy). Again, using duration as our focal concern here, the helper could ask, "How many hours a day do you suppose you spend thinking this way?"

B. *Intensity.* When the problem occurs, just how intense is it. For example, in dealing with the wife who said that she and her husband couldn't communicate, if from further discussions she disclosed that "not communicating" actually involved frequent arguments, it would be important to know specifically, the thoughts, feelings, and behaviors that occur during this time. Attempts should be made to mentally if not literally record the content and level (intensity) of troubled thoughts and behaviors. Do the arguments involve shouting, cursing, throwing things, hitting one another, and so forth? What specific thoughts does each partner have during these events? What thoughts are involved that reveal the inferred motivations that each partner ascribes to the other?

C. *Frequency.* Just how frequently does the problem occur? Several times a day? Weekly? Monthly?

D. *Antecedents/consequences.* Behaviorists have long recognized the value of evaluating situational factors that may precede or follow the problem behavior. What precipitating events tend to serve as triggers to the problem? Do they involve particular people or settings? What are some typical patterns of behavior that occur in others following the behaviors? Are there predictable environmental changes that occur following the problem? Do these involve expected changes in the behaviors of others? How might changes in either the antecedents and/or consequences of the behavior contribute to the solution to the problem?

All this information can then be used to help the client identify alternative desirable behaviors that can then be used as goals. It can also help to identify when progress in counseling takes place. Clients who are not taught to look for improvement in terms of changes in the duration, intensity, and/or frequency of the problems will often fail to notice when these changes occur. Needless to say, important changes can be overlooked and even undermined if the counselor does not teach the client to notice and validate this progress.

Another critical question that needs to be asked at this stage of the process is "Why now?" What specifically prompted the client to pick up the phone or approach the helper to ask for help? The answer to this question can provide vital help in the process of clarifying the problem. Furthermore, a survey for identifying potential problems and their level of severity has been provided in appendix D. Additionally, there are also a variety of scales that can be used to help measure the levels of anxiety and/or sadness in clients presenting with these difficulties. They should be used for general assessment purposes only and not relied on for accurate evaluation purposes since they are not empirically validated testing instruments. Finally, it should be noted that most helpers using this model would not be sufficiently trained to engage in definitive clinical mental health assessment or diagnosis. However, even lay counselors need some assistance in making judgments as to whether clients should be seen or referred. They also need help evaluating the initial degree of distress being experienced by the client as well as a tool for monitoring progress and improvement.

3. Determination. The step of "determination" really involves a combination of three separate tasks for the counselor to accomplish. Each one is vitally important to the success of the counseling enterprise.

A. Determination of client status. Solution-focused counselors several years ago helped to alert the counseling community to the critical importance of *determining* whether the client who presents for help is actually a visitor, complainant, or customer. Generally speaking, *visitors* are typically people who come for counseling due to the influence of another (spouse, court system, etc.) and are not motivated to seek help on their own. *Complainants* are persons who, as the term implies, come complaining about the behavior of another or their situation but who fail to takes responsibility for changing their own behavior. Finally, *customers* are people who recognize that they are part of the problem, or at least part of the solution, and are therefore motivated to take responsibility for personal change. Making this determination early on is very important since it is only when people assume a *customer role* that counseling can be effective. Therefore, for clients who reflect either of the first two positions, counselors should make efforts to help them shift their position by encouraging them to take personal responsibility for either their contribution to the problem and/or the contribution they can make to the solution to the problem. Clients should be challenged with the notion that while they may not be to blame for the problem, that they almost always can share some responsibility for fixing it (de Shazer, *Clues: Investigating Solutions in Brief Therapy*, 87-89).

B. Determination of central concerns. Clients usually don't come to counseling with one problem but many. Therefore, counselors must help guide clients in selecting the problems or concerns that, when remedied, will make the biggest difference in their lives. Problem selection also involves evaluating which problems are actually changeable by the client, which may need third-party assistance of some type (i.e., involvement of a spouse in therapy, medication referral, etc.), and which may need to be broken into smaller, more workable units. As we have indicated, problems need to be described discretely by evaluating a client's thoughts and behaviors according to their duration, intensity, and frequency. This information can then be used to guide the client in addressing a *piece* of the problem. Ultimately, clients should be allowed to lead helpers in determining which problem areas they actually want to address.

C. Determination of referral needs. From the beginning of the helping process, counselors should be considering the advisability of referral. This is more than a "yes" or "no" decision since there are actually a variety of referral types. These may be loosely grouped into the following categories:

(a) Referrals resulting in termination: Counselors using the RFC approach should ask themselves the question, "Can I reasonably expect to help this client in 4-6 sessions?" If the answer is "no," then the appropriate referral sources (hopefully those which were identified earlier will be helpful here) should be suggested. A guideline for assisting helpers in making determinations regarding "termination referrals" can be found in appendix N.

(b) Referrals resulting in supplementation: Even though a counselor may choose to work with a particular person she may still recognize that the best interests of her client dictate utilizing a multidisciplinary approach to treating the problem.

- **Intermittent**—Not infrequently, clients may need to be referred for medical checkups or supplemental medications. For example, a client presenting with a mood disturbance such as excessive sadness or anxiety *and* who has not had a medical checkup within the past year should be referred for a physical examination and blood work. Or a grief-stricken client who has not slept for the last three nights may require a temporary sleep medication to get necessary rest. These types of referrals are considered intermittent since the client does not continue to consult with the referral agent on a continuous basis.

- **Continuous**—At other times, clients may need ongoing contact with a specialized form of support to help supplement the counseling they are receiving. Types of referrals resulting in a continuous supplemental activity may include the client's participation in any of the more than 140 twelve-step recovery groups now in operation; government agencies, including the welfare department or the unemployment bureau; private employment agencies; drug prevention centers; shelters of various types; food pantries; vocational rehabilitation centers; financial advisement centers; and so forth.

Readers will notice that the line circling the first stage of the counseling process is preceded by the statement "*Faith in Action.*" The RFC Model reflects the idea that clients in the first stage of the counseling process are predominately reflecting a choice to exercise their God-given faith potential. Even though they often have no objective reason on which to base their optimism, their attitude of positive expectation actually represents the latent faith potential within the individual. Counselors will do well to validate and champion this choice on the part of the client. It can serve as a vital reminder of not only their spiritual nature and longing, but also how God is already at work bringing about a redemptive response to their situation. Such spiritually sensitive counseling will help to increase a client's awareness of God's faithful presence in their lives. Also, punctuating the faith potential of the client provides a useful way to introduce the discussion of how clients can consciously direct their faith toward God, the focal point around which attempts at personal change find their most productive and satisfying expression.

II. The Goals—Targets of Reconciliation

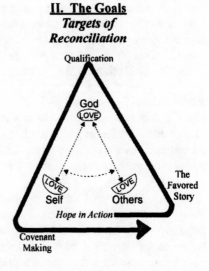

II. The Goals
Targets of Reconciliation

Qualification

God
(LOVE)

(LOVE) (LOVE)
Self Others

The Favored Story

Hope in Action

Covenant Making

1. The favored story/cultivating a vision of hope. In Luke 18:35-42 we have the story of Jesus healing the blind man on the road to Jericho. What is fascinating about this story, aside from the miracle of the healing itself, is the question that Jesus felt led to ask this man. When the blind man was told by the crowd that "Jesus of Nazareth is passing by," he immediately began to shout, no doubt in the hope that Jesus would ultimately respond to his cries and heal his blindness. However, after asking that the man be brought to him, Jesus inquired, *"What do you want?"*

A. Find out what the client really wants. Our initial reaction to this question may well be one of perplexity since it would seem clear by nature of the circumstances what the man desired from Jesus. Could this be a reflection of insensitivity on Jesus' part or simply a glaring case of overlooking the obvious? Of course, neither of these scenarios would accurately reflect what the Scriptures have come to reveal about Jesus. In addition, the more we become involved in the process of counseling others, the more wisdom we tend to see reflected in the question that He poses to this man. *First,* counselors learn early on to "Be careful not to assume that you already know what the client wants." Rare is the counselor who, having been given just a little information about a client's problem, has not rushed down the primrose path of seeking a particular goal only to later find out that this is not really what the client wanted. *Second,* just because a client presents for counseling doesn't actually mean he actually wants something from the counselor. As we have seen, visitors come because they feel as if they have to and complainants come to complain about others in the futile hope that somehow the counselor can make the other person or their circumstances change. Neither of these individuals really wants help with changing something about themselves. *Finally,* finding out what the client wants is critical to insuring that he is motivated to pursue his goals. Finding the motivation that clients need to pursue their goals is critically related to tapping into what they really want. As we have seen, we can't assume that we always know what this is; we need to ask them.

It should be noted that in requesting that clients tell us what they would "like to accomplish" as a result of coming to therapy, we are actually asking for them to begin to share their vision of hope for the future. Before the blind man could literally see, he had to allow hope to give life to a belief that he could actually see again. At this point in the counseling process, we can begin to see how faith and hope are beginning to work together in tandem to help promote a redemptive outcome.

B. Be specific. As we have mentioned, there are times when clients come to counseling with less than a clear understanding of *specifically* what they want from the counseling process. They just know that they want to feel better, or communicate better, and so forth. Effective counselors help counselees facilitate a vision of hope that serves to objectify their often abstract visions of the future. Specifically, helpers guide counselees to identify the thoughts and behaviors that will accompany their renewed visions of what they would like to change. For example, if a client says that she wants to "feel better," the helper should immediately respond by asking, "When you are feeling better, *specifically* how will you know that based on how you are *thinking* or *acting* differently?" If the client says, "I don't know," simply respond with, "If you did know, what do you suppose you would be thinking of doing differently than you are doing now?" Such a response often helps to get the counselee unstuck by inviting her to view an imagined hypothetical rather than a view of redemption or restoration that often has become blurred by the vision-limiting weight of the problem. The value of "hypotheticals" will be considered in more detail below.

C. Look for exceptions. An additional way to get clients outside of what have often become excessively negative views of their situations is to ask them, "What are some *exceptions* to the problem that are already occurring in your life or your relationships." Similarly, "When does the problem *not* occur." Again, this approach to establishing well-formed goals is developed to great advantage by Solution-Focused therapists like Walter and Peller (Walter and Peller, *Becoming Solution-Focused in Brief Therapy*, 91-105). When an exception to a problem is identified, it suggests that the client is doing or thinking something differently during this time that results in some improvement in the problem. Rarely does a problem exist when exceptions to the problem cannot be uncovered or when a reduction in the severity of the problem cannot be detected. By focusing on these exceptions, we help clients to discover how they are already engaged in redemptive behaviors that may just need to be validated and expanded in the future. While at times clients may dismiss these exceptions as being insignificant, the wise counselor will find great benefit by attending to these exceptions since they may offer valuable insights regarding thoughts and behaviors that the client has already learned to use. At other times, exceptions to the problem are identified by the client as being spontaneous rather than deliberate, implying therefore that the improvement noted in the problem during this time was *not* under voluntary control. Helpers can counteract this tendency to minimize personal control by making several suggestions to the client. For example, when an exception is identified, the counselor may say, "How did you do that?" to help embed more perceived control. If the response is "I don't know," you may again respond with "If you did know, what do you suppose you were thinking or doing differently during this time that accounted for an improvement in the problem?"

As helpers work to highlight the exceptions and encourage a view of personal control, clients begin to experience more hope as they begin to see their problems in a more redemptive light. Whereas clients initially may have seen very little to commend about the way they handled their problems in the past, they now can see that not everything they were doing was without merit. Additionally, they feel empowered because they may begin to sense that they have more control over their problems than they initially realized. Finally, care should be taken to connect these thoughts and behaviors to the overall goals of seeking restoration in the three relational domains. The counselor should be mindful that the overarching goal of RFC is to maintain a focus on goals that establish or enhance the client's ability to demonstrate "love" in his or her relationships to God, self, and others. Such a view helps both the counselor and counselee maintain the spiritual framework necessary to promote lasting and meaningful change.

D. Consider using "hypotheticals" to facilitate specific goals. Finally, one of the best ways to help clients who are having difficulty identifying specific thoughts/behaviors related to their goals or for those who have failed to find meaningful exceptions to their problems is for counselors to employ what in solution-focused therapy is referred to as the "miracle question" (de Shazer, 5). By capitalizing on what is already part of our clients' Christian vocabulary and belief system, helpers will find great benefit in using this question to assist clients in developing well-formed goals. After all, don't most clients who present for therapy really want a miracle to occur? The question is introduced like this. Suppose that one night, while you were asleep, there was a miracle and this problem was solved. How would you know? What would be different? How will your husband know without your saying a word to him about it? (de Shazer, 5).

Interestingly, counselees' responses to this question usually reveal thoughts and behaviors that meet many if not all of the qualifications for well-formed goals. This is due in part to the fact that we are now asking them to create a *hypothetical* situation reflecting desired goals rather than working to identify goals through examining just *exceptions* to the problem (Walter and Peller, 63-75). As a result, clients are free to consider all imaginable solutions they believe to be appropriate for the problem being considered, not just those that they have been accustomed to using. A limitation to using goals derived from hypothetical situations is that they may involve behaviors or thoughts that have never been attempted before. Behaviors that have never been attempted are by nature less likely to be produced than are previously enacted behaviors identified by examining exceptions to the problem. This is due to both the novelty of new behaviors and their perceived or real difficulty to initiate. However, often once hypothetical situations and related behaviors are identified, clients often realize that these situations reveal behaviors they have already utilized in the past but could not see without first creating a hypothetical.

RFC Emphases: Additional questions that should be considered at this point include: How do the goals that have been identified help to address the areas of alienation and needs for reconciliation initially highlighted in the client's story? In what ways do the goals address the need for more loving, caring, or affirming behavior in any of the three relational domains? Are opportunities for more meaningful, potentially restorative relationships being pursued? How are the spiritual needs of the client being addressed? Do the goals reflect morally responsible behavior? Do they reflect an appreciation for relational commitments, honesty, justice, mutual caring, trustworthiness, social obligations, and/or a general appreciation of a Christian ethic? Difficulty in answering any of these questions may indicate a need to review whether the identified goals are appropriate or sufficiently meaningful to warrant their pursuit.

2. Qualification. The qualification stage of the goal setting process is designed to remind the helper to make sure that the goals identified above satisfy the seven criteria for "Redemptive Goals" outlined earlier. In other words, the second step in the goal setting process is to compare any ideas, exceptions, or hypothetical solutions to the problem with these criteria to determine the advisability of continuing to pursue a certain direction. Once again, redemptive goals are

- Positive in orientation
- Specific and measurable
- Reasonably attainable
- Desired by the client
- In the client's language
- Related to the here and now
- In the client's control

Failure to satisfy these criteria should necessarily prevent the helper from allowing the client to proceed until the goal can be redefined in a way that satisfies these areas. Again, disregarding this component of the counseling process has been identified as one of the most prominent errors leading to poor counseling outcomes by investigators. Therefore, helpers would do well to give adequate attention to this stage of the goal setting process.

3. Covenant making. Even when goals have been sufficiently identified and qualified by the counselee, there is still a need for them to make a commitment to pursue such goals. RFC likes to utilize the concept of "covenant making" in describing this process. Viewing commitments as covenants draws upon biblical language that encourages counselees to embrace a needed awareness of the spiritual implications of such decisions. Jesus' admonition to "Simply let your 'Yes' be 'Yes,' and your 'No,' 'No'" (Matthew 5:37a) is a clear reminder that commitments made by Christians ought not to be taken lightly. Evidently the Pharisees were notorious for the making of oaths by "heaven" or "earth" or "Jerusalem" and then breaking them, claiming that God had not been a part of the oath. Likewise, our culture promotes a very superficial view of commitments that makes their violation little more that an inconvenience, and certainly not a reflection of the lack of moral character represented by the covenant breaker. Therefore, emphasizing the importance of commitments invites a spiritual awakening on the part of our clients and further encourages their spiritual development.

A further component of the covenant-making stage of the helping process involves identifying which goals the client would most like to pursue. After considering the various possibilities, clients must select from a list of possibly goals those, which are viewed as being the most meaningful and/or relevant. This narrowing of focus usually means reducing the list down to the top two or three goals since attempting more than this at any given time usually results in setting clients up for failure. Such failures are due to several factors. First, clients are generally able to remember only two or three points or goals within 24-hours of any given counseling session. Unless the counselor writes down the goals (a useful practice regardless of the number of goals agreed to), it is unlikely that clients will remember with sufficient clarity the ones that they agreed to pursue. Second, having numerous goals may so overwhelm clients or divide their "recovery energy" that little significant gain is experienced in any one area. Therefore, disillusionment rather than hope may well be the final outcome.

III. The Strategies—
Movement Toward
Restoration/
Reconciliation

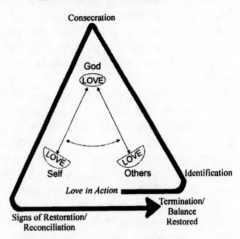

III. The Strategies
Movement Toward
Restoration/Reconciliation

Consecration

God
LOVE

LOVE
Self

LOVE
Others

Identification

Love in Action

Termination/
Balance
Restored

Signs of Restoration/
Reconciliation

1. Identification/strategies for getting there. Proverbs 21:5 reads, "The plans of the diligent lead to profit as surely as haste leads to poverty." There is an old saying that goes, "I would rather build a fence at the top of the hill than a hospital at the bottom." Much like the idea that an "ounce of prevention is worth a pound of cure," it is important to recognize that even the best goals can be rendered useless if helpers are too hasty in encouraging their pursuit. At this stage of the helping process, it is important to ask the question, "What possible obstacles exist that might prevent clients from achieving their goals? How can these obstacles be avoided? What are some creative ways to get from where the clients are now to where they want to be? How can we involve naturally occurring resources and relationships to assist clients in pursuing their goal(s)?"

A. Brainstorming sessions. At times, the strategies needed to achieve the identified goals seem to emerge naturally from discussions about the goal itself. At other times, the counselor and client may need to engage in open and/or structured forms of brainstorming in an effort to discover creative ways to reach the client's desired destination. A lot of people know what they want; it is just getting there that presents the problem. However, before beginning the brainstorming process, helpers are encouraged to ask questions such as "In what ways have you already attempted to deal with your problem in the past?" Most people coming for counseling have already attempted a number of different strategies to solve their problem prior to seeking formal help. Therefore, asking about these efforts will often elicit critical information regarding strategies that may have already been demonstrated to be less than effective. Knowing this history will help to guide future brainstorming efforts and save the counselor the embarrassment of suggesting the "same old thing."

Once the helper has investigated previous attempts to solve the problem, then formal efforts at brainstorming can take place. One of the reasons that clients find themselves stuck in their problem situations is that they have literally run out of ideas on different ways that the problem could be approached. Therefore, part of the helper's job is to work with the client to stimulate creative thinking that will hopefully lead to a host of new alternative strategies. There are a number of ways to help clients engage in this process. One way is for the counselor to make some tentative initial strategy suggestions as a way of encouraging the client to begin to "color outside the lines." Where does the counselor come up with these suggestions? As the RFC model emphasizes, throughout the helping process the counselor needs to be in prayerful pursuit of divine inspiration as a prerequisite to any helping efforts. With this in mind, the counselor should begin to consider what resources and relationships exist in the client's environment that could be used in strategy formation.

For example, Brenda is a 34-year-old single mother who wants to learn how to be a better parent. Specifically, she desires to set up a structured behavior management plan for her 4-year-old son. However, after working out the details of what she would like to implement with her son, her fatigue and frustration after a long day at work often undermine her positive parenting efforts. In particular, she often finds herself screaming and yelling when attempting to manage her son's behavior in spite of her awareness that this only aggravates the problem. Previous attempts to manage her anger have included "counting to 10" or just "gritting her teeth." However, these have been of limited usefulness. The counselor has already come up with some strategy suggestions from carefully considering exceptions to the problem from her past as well as future hypothetical scenarios. However, a further analysis of her environment and relationships might yield additional strategy resources. For instance, the counselor might ask, "What **people** might provide personal support (i.e., other single parents), model self-control (past or present significant others), or trade off baby-sitting responsibilities to give regular breaks from parenting?" Or "What **organizations** in your area have support services for single parents? Does your church offer mother's day out or evening out child care?" Finally, "What **programs** exist in the community that might regularly offer parenting skills training?" These represent but a few of the areas worthy of investigation by the helper working to expand the number of possible strategies to be considered with the client.

B. *Structured strategies.* Other possible approaches to strategy development may include more structured approaches to establishing new thoughts and behaviors in the life of the client. For example, when working with problematic moods, helpers should consider using the *"Thought Journal"* (appendix A) and/or *"Activity Log"* (appendix B) to guide their counselees in identifying redemptive forms of thinking and behaving. Building on RFC Principle #5 and the work of Beck (1979), Thurman (1989), Greenberger (1995), et al., clients struggling with depression, anxiety, anger, shame, and so forth, can find great benefit in utilizing these approaches to identify problem thoughts and behaviors first, then modify and practice more redemptive forms of acting and thinking. The use of these forms will be examined in more detail under chapters related to these issues.

Once again the reader will notice that like each stage before it, this stage of the helping process is encircled by and emphasizes an action orientation, in this case the tangible action of love. Just as James 2:14 reminds us that faith without works is dead, so too 1 Corinthians 13:1 reminds us that love without an attitude of care is like a "noisy gong or a clanging symbol." While the best goals will remain useless unless they are put into action, such actions should be characterized by the balanced exercise of love toward God, self, and others. If we are to reclaim the divine balance demonstrated in our pre-fallen world, then all our helping efforts must strive to promote reconciliation in all three relational domains through the greater expression of Christ-centered love.

2. Consecration/commitment to a plan. Proverbs 16:3 says, "Commit to the LORD whatever you do, and your plans will succeed." Committing our plans to the Lord is essential for success. After the careful consideration of as many alternative strategies as seems advisable, the helper should then lead the counselee to select prayerfully the most appropriate strategy and then to ask God's blessing upon its pursuit. This verse should not be interpreted to mean that God guarantees divine assistance for all our efforts. Proverbs 1:32 and 6:9-11 remind us that the ways of the "fool" and the "sluggard" will come to undesirable ends. However, even clients with the best strategies and wholesome intentions are dependent on the Lord's assistance for their success. Proverbs 16:9 affirms this position where it states that "In his heart a man plans his course, but the LORD determines his steps." The spiritual life of one who desires to follow Christ cannot be turned on and off at will. Rather, being a disciple of Christ represents the consistent intention of a heart turned toward Him.

3. Signs of restoration/reconciliation. Even the first session is not too early to begin looking for signs of improvement in the life of the client. It may be helpful for the counselor to determine when the changes begin to occur.

A. Identifying pre-session change. Research suggests that in 20-30% of the cases, the problems that prompted clients to first contact the helper have improved by the time of their initial appointment. The reasons for this are many. Often, just the knowledge that help is on the way prompts some improvement. This "knowledge of help" represents a positive change in the client's thoughts or expectations leading to an enhanced attitude of hope. Highlighting how this change in thoughts has led to an improved sense of well-being provides the helper with a vital teaching opportunity regarding the role that thoughts play in personal change.

Another reason for improvement is that when clients know they will be sharing their problem with another individual, especially when this sharing involves discussing their actions involving another individual, they work especially hard to be on their best behavior. This is not to be taken too lightly. Remember that times of improvement or interruptions in the problem are exceptions and exceptions imply that there are thoughts and behaviors that the client is already using that are to some degree working. The helper not only will find future grist for the mill by attending to this improvement but also will begin to empower clients to see how they already have some of the skills that will be needed to promote a solution to their problem.

B. Between-session change. Having considered pre-session change, the helper now must begin to evaluate the occurrence of between-session change. In others words, from the second session forward, the initial part of each meeting should be devoted to investigating what improvements have occurred in the client's problems. A good way to initiate conversations with clients in an effort to uncover these changes is to ask a question similar to the following: "Tell me how things have improved, even slightly, since our last meeting." The assumption of improvement embedded in this statement is important, even if clients initially respond with "bad news," since it challenges an often overly negativistic evaluation of their situation. Additionally, what the helper is doing by initially focusing on the positive is to train the client to search for signs of improvement, even if the problem is still present. Such an approach again reflects an extension of RFC Principle #3 and the value of maintaining a redemptive and hope-engendering position with clients.

C. Scaling questions. Another versatile technique that is helpful for highlighting and promoting positive change is to utilize what are known as scaling questions. Scaling questions can be used in a variety of ways to help quantify and encourage change. They involve asking questions such as "On a scale from 1-10, with 1 being where you started when you first picked up the phone to request help and 10 being when you have completely resolved the issues that bring you to therapy, where are you on this scale today?" What is interesting about this question is that the most frequent response given by clients, regardless of the problem being treated or the seeming progress or lack of progress, is a 3 or 4. In other words, this question tends to invite clients to see progress in their situation by their natural resistance to seeing their situation as still being a "1." This is not simply a form of "mind over matter" thinking since in most every situation true positive change can be noted if only the counselee and counselor can find it. Therefore, the question that should immediately follow this initial inquiry is "How did you get to be a 3 or a 4 based on how you were thinking or acting differently?" This usually leads to the discovery or validation of positive between-session changes. Additionally, the helper can then follow up this approach with questions such as "Given that you are a 4 today on the scale, how will you get to be a 5 this coming week based on how you will be acting or thinking differently?" Again, the momentum-engendering qualities of this scale coupled with the way that it structures and quantifies change or progress serves a valuable role in the process of attempting to identify signs of restoration and reconciliation.

Four Facilitative Processes

Having examined the main body of the three-stage RFC Model, we will now take the opportunity to examine carefully four facilitative processes that simultaneously occur throughout the helping task. **EARS** or Evaluation, Action, Rapport, and Seeking Inspiration represent ongoing activities that take place throughout each stage of the helping process. Each of these processes serves as a point of reference to guide counselors in their attempts to promote effective counseling outcomes. Counselors might find it helpful to imagine dividing these four processes into two sets of parallel lines marking opposite sides of the counseling highway. By staying within these lines, the helper is insured that the counseling process will stay on track and avoid becoming sidetracked or ineffective. The centerline on the highway is represented by the centrality of humanity's need for reconciliation as described in chapter 2 (see figure 2). As the overarching goal of counseling, these guiding principles help to insure that counselors reach the appropriate destination.

Evaluation

Evaluation involves two separate but overlapping tasks. The *first*, which we will cover in more detail in Stage I under "Clarification," involves making a careful initial assessment of the client's presenting problem, current emotional state, possible involvement with drugs, history or emotional, relational, or legal problems, and any potential danger that the client may pose to self or others. The *second* task of evaluation involves asking ongoing questions that more directly address the current state and progress of therapy. An example of some questions that counselors might ask themselves and possibly their clients during the helping process might be: "Is the counseling process contributing substantially to achieving the desired goals of the client? Are the initial goals of counseling still realistic and/or desirable given what has been revealed so far? Have new areas of concern emerged that should take precedence over those initially presented by the client?"

Action

Action serves to highlight a fundamental principle of effective counseling as well as Christian living (James 2:17). For us to say that we have really been helpful to the client, what takes place in the counseling setting must somehow translate into effective action outside the helper's office. You might say that clients should give counselors a greater appreciation of the statement that "actions speak louder than words." The two critical forms of action highlighted as a focus for attention in the RFC Model are the *thoughts* and *behaviors* of the client. Therefore, some questions the counselor might consider asking throughout the helping process are: "Is the client reflecting new or increased thoughts and/or behaviors that serve to promote goal attainment? If not, then "What different actions do I need to take to promote these changes?"

Furthermore, "action" serves to inform the counseling approach utilized by the helper. Counselors cannot afford to be too passive in the counseling setting without running the risk of allowing the process to become bogged down or ineffective. As previously noted, counselors must strive to maintain a balance between a collaborative and a directive orientation. Neglecting either position over a long period will compromise our efforts to help others.

Rapport

Rapport is defined differently by various people depending on which aspects of this idea they wish to stress. However, at its core rapport describes *a warm relationship of mutual trust*. Given the central role that trust initially played in the garden in promoting and maintaining healthy relationships, the need for counselors to attend to this aspect of their work with clients cannot be overemphasized. While chapters in books are devoted to the subject of how to build and maintain rapport, a helper's ability to reflect the redemptive counselor qualities outlined earlier should go a long way to achieving rapport in the counseling relationship. A good principle to remember for helpers wishing to cultivate more rapport in the counseling relationship is to use more "reflecting" responses with their clients. By "giving back"[44] or reflecting to clients what we hear them saying to us, both their verbal and non-verbal communications, they sense that we really care about their concerns and are trying to understand their problems. A point of caution should be noted with regard to rapport. People often assume that since trust can only be developed over time, that rapport requires a long time to develop. Clients understandably come to helpers with high levels of anxiety and awkwardness about talking to a stranger regarding their problems. However, skilled helpers can often build effective levels of rapport in a very short period, even with the most anxious clients. Therefore, rather than thinking we should spend extensive periods of time building rapport, we can serve our clients better if we work to improve the efficiency of our relationship-building skills.

Seeking Inspiration/Wisdom/Discernment

This process is fairly self-explanatory in that throughout the counseling enterprise helpers should seek the guidance and leading of the Holy Spirit. Such seeking can be both active and passive. As discussed earlier under the principle of "therapeutic trialogue," there are times when counselors may wish to pray purposefully for direction during a session, silently or with the client. This is obviously a more specific "seeking activity" in that the thoughts and/or behaviors of the helpers are being consciously directed toward the seeking enterprise. At other times, seeking inspiration may be more passive. As we have noted, conscious attention to prayer may momentarily distract the helper from critical listening or attending activities, which could hinder the helping process. Therefore, the helper should cultivate an attitude of openness so that the guiding influence of God's Spirit can be experienced and followed. Describing how this openness is to be accomplished can be somewhat elusive, given that the process of cultivating spiritual awareness is not an exact science. However, various Scriptures such as "Be still, and know that I am God" (Psalm 46:10a) affirm that there is a conscious choosing on the part of the believer to be open. Such openness may best be understood as the listening side of prayer. Unfortunately, prayer is often viewed as a monologue or one-way process in which an individual is simply talking to God. Even the acrostics that are used to guide prayer, such as ACTS or Adoration, Confession, Thanksgiving, and Supplication, fail to emphasize the listening side of prayer. Therefore, listening for God's response or word for the moment may go overlooked or unacknowledged. In actuality, prayer is intended to be more dialogical in nature, pausing at times to sense God's presence and listen with our spiritual ears for feedback and direction.

To illustrate the type of spiritual listening being suggested here, try for a moment to listen for small, incidental sounds wherever you are at this minute. If you are outside, do you hear some soft or even distinct sounds of nature? If you are inside, do you hear sounds coming from some mechanical device, the humming of fluorescent lights or the rush of air coming through the air conditioning or heating vents? In light of this discussion, what sounds do you hear now that previously represented noises that you would have dismissed? Now, if you had not consciously chosen to be open to these sounds *and* were later asked, after you changed locations, whether such sounds were present, you probably would have responded that you did not notice them or that they simply did not exist. However, by consciously focusing your ears to be open to sounds that are normally and summarily dismissed, your awareness of this information is now acknowledged and recorded. Likewise, we need to choose to pause at times in the counseling process, not to talk but to listen with our spiritual ears for God's direction in the moment.

It should also be noted early on that the RFC Model is a *generalist* model by design. By this I mean that it attempts to offer the counselor a broad, all-encompassing framework for conceptualizing emotional and relational problems in and between people. It also offers a general framework for guiding the helper in effecting interventions. However, attempting to paint with such a broad stroke by necessity precludes the necessary specificity required to address adequately any number of problems seen in the ministry setting. Persons utilizing this model should always seek to be mindful of these limitations and not attempt to treat problems beyond the intended scope of the model and/or their level of training. Obviously, making such judgments is not always clear-cut, even to the skilled counselor. Therefore, it is generally recommended that helpers, without formal counseling training, utilize a 4-6 session time frame as a guide for determining which problems they will agree to address. In other words, when initially approached for help, counselors should ask themselves if they believe that they can be of assistance within this time frame. If not, then referral may be the appropriate alternative. For more detailed guidelines regarding referral, see appendix C.

Part II

Applying the RFC Model

Chapter 5

Applying RFC in Pastoral Counseling

Before We Begin

The following case studies examine the application of the RFC model to specific counseling concerns. The problems presented here will only indirectly address the *problem definition* and *goal setting* portions of the model in an effort to provide more detailed information on *strategy formation.* Specifically, the use of "structured" strategies demonstrated to be effective in resolving such problems will be highlighted. These approaches are offered as fresh ideas only and should not be utilized in any cookie cutter fashion nor understood as contradicting the collaborative nature of the helping process. Instead, they are provided in an effort to address the frequent need among helpers for practical approaches to commonly faced problems. Having said this, many of the strategies provided in the following pages originally relied on assessment procedures utilizing the RFC Relationship Inventory (appendix C). This inventory can be used to help highlight a client's relational deficits. As we have seen, RFC assumes that correcting these deficits is critically related to solving the problem at hand.

Furthermore, it should be noted that issues related to shame and mistrust tend to permeate each of the highlighted problems. However, readers will notice that no single case study isolated these troubling issues as the focal problem of concern. The reason for this seeming omission is that rarely do people come to counseling requesting help specifically for shame, mistrust, and so forth. Rather, these problems naturally emerge in the course of dealing with more readily identifiable difficulties. Therefore, rather than a separate case study which might infer a distinction between issues related to shame and mistrust as opposed to all others, readers are encouraged to remember the pervasive nature of such concerns and approach each situation accordingly.

Each case presentation will highlight interventions which either explicitly or implicitly address these problems. The reader will also notice that an attempt has been made to identify or match each intervention with its corresponding RFC principle. While every problem situation might reflect the need to utilize all of the 12 RFC principles in some fashion, only those deemed most relevant to identified problem will be highlighted.

Depression: A Case Study–
Barbara

> *"Have mercy on me, LORD, for I am in distress. My sight is blurred because of my tears. My body and soul are withering away. I am dying from grief; my years are shortened by sadness. Misery has drained my strength; I am wasting away from within." (Psalm 31:9-10 New Living Translation)*

Barbara was one of those clients who impresses you just for showing up. Both of her preadolescent sons were stricken with cystic fibrosis, an incurable and often fatal illness that affects the pancreas, respiratory system, and sweat glands. Her oldest son, Kenny, had died from this illness six months prior to her calling to request an appointment. Her younger son Brian was in the latter stages of the illness. Short of a miracle or breakthrough in treatment, he also would soon die from this condition.

Grief resulting from the death of a child is one of the most difficult losses a parent can experience. Aside from the obvious reasons, such losses are complicated by their disjointed and premature nature. They break the chronological sequence of the parent's expectations regarding death. Understandably, Barbara had good reason for being overwhelmed by her grief and subsequent depression that registered as severe (38) on the RFC Sadness Scale. She reported struggling with a depressed mood, weight loss, crying spells, disturbed sleep, excessive guilt and lack of energy, for at least the last six months. Currently, getting through the average day of childcare activities took all the energy she could muster. Finally, the initial examination of her problem also revealed another significant complication regarding her grief. Given the likely outcome of her younger son's illness, Barbara stated she would have little reason to go on living.

The consideration of suicide under such circumstances is fairly common, given the nature and degree of the losses involved. Losses occurring simultaneously and/or in numerous relational domains can rob individuals of their motivation to live. For Barbara, not only might she ultimately lose her relationship with both of her sons but other relationships had been compromised as well. Her relationship with God was being shaken to its very foundation. Her husband had started drinking a year earlier in his failed attempts to cope and was therefore in no position to provide her with desperately needed emotional and functional support. She was also questioning her own attempts to provide care and proper medical help for her children, and even felt guilty at times for having had children since there had been a family history of cystic fibrosis. By the time Barbara presented for counseling, she was in desperate need of support and direction.

An examination of Barbara's case reveals multiple areas of *alienation* that had complicated an already difficult situation. Her previously supportive and soothing relationships with both God and her husband had been compromised by the stress of dealing with her son's chronic illness and the poor coping choices of her husband. Also, burdened by the demands of caregiving, Barbara had withdrawn from friends who had previously been supportive, stating "I don't want to burden them with my problems." Finally, her unreasonable guilt around providing "deficient" childcare and "irresponsibility" for having children given her family's medical history had resulted in destructive self-condemnation.

The Application of Structured Strategies to Depression

The outline below illustrates the various strategies or interventions that were utilized with Barbara. During the process of her counseling, she was encouraged to take the following actions.

1. Obtain a medical evaluation—RFC Principle #10.[45] Any time counselors seek to help someone with a significant mood problem, especially depression, they should ask that person how long it has been since they have had a *physical with blood work*. If more than a year has passed, they should be encouraged to consult with their physician to check for literally dozens of physiological mimickers of depression. Conditions such as hypothyroidism may bring with it symptoms like secondary depression (Gold, *Good News About Depression*, 145-50). Even for people like Barbara whose circumstances would help to explain their depressed mood, preexisting or coexisting physical conditions can underlie and aggravate a counselor's attempts to provide relief. The choice to encourage medical attention is currently mandated by most state counseling licensure boards and therefore reflects the standard of care expected in competent mental health counseling. While blood tests failed to show any complicating physical problems, the doctor did offer a two-week supply of a sleep medication to help Barbara reestablish a healthy sleep pattern. Disturbed sleep is common in depression and is widely knows to aggravate, or in some cases, cause this condition. Therefore, correcting a disturbed sleep cycle often helps to promote a more rapid recovery from grief or depression.

2. Engage in more physical activity—RFC Principle #6. Persons like Barbara who are depressed commonly have become very sedentary, isolative, and/or avoidant of previously pleasurable activities. Understandably, they often "just don't feel like" getting out and doing things given their current condition. However, such inactivity only serves to complicate their already depressed mood for several reasons. First, vigorous physical activity helps to keep our bodies healthy and stimulate the release of chemicals called endorphins, both of which serve to enhance mental well-being. Second, when we become sedentary, especially in conjunction with being depressed, we are more prone to worry and focus on our problems. Activities, especially those associated with increased pleasure, serve to counteract the negative influence of inactivity and, if for no other reason, serve as a vehicle of distraction. While not an end in itself, distraction helps to break the cycle of negative thinking and allow for the introduction of more redemptive forms of thinking. Therefore, Barbara was encouraged to use the activity log provided in appendix B to begin identifying those activities each hour throughout her week that are associated with an improved sense of pleasure and rate each activity of the day on a scale of 1-5. Activities that were identified as being more pleasurable during the week, such as coffee with friends, relaxing bubble baths in the evening, reading the Psalms, and setting aside time to watch her favorite television program, were regularly built into her schedule in subsequent weeks. In addition, she agreed to add some form of aerobic exercise each day.

3. Challenge and modify counterproductive thought patterns —RFC Principle #6. As emphasized earlier, the RFC model also encourages a careful examination of a client's thoughts in an effort to discover ultimately those forms of thinking that will best facilitate a redemptive outcome. Of particular value in this regard is the "Thought Journal" provided in appendix A. Utilizing this format, Barbara was able to identify the troubling thought patterns that were contributing to her sad and depressed state. Most depressed individuals reflect negatively biased thoughts due to the presence of their depressed mood. The counselor's task is to help the client discover unrealistically negative thoughts and replace them with more realistic and redemptive thinking. Aaron Beck (Beck, 1987) provides helpful direction in this regard by dividing a depressed person's thinking errors into three general areas: overly negative views of self (thoughts often resulting from feelings of inadequacy [shame] and guilt), of the future, and of their experiences (understood here as including experiences with God and others). Christian counselors likewise can use this framework for examining the thought life of the client. (The first and last of these three categories highlight the importance of RFC principle #1 and how the initiation or maintenance of problems often stems from alienation with God, others, and self.)

In Barbara's case, she was able to begin to recognize how extreme and fatalistic her thinking had become. A sample of such troubling thoughts included "my husband doesn't love me anymore" and "I'm a failure as a mother" (representing feelings of shame and inadequacy), "God is punishing me" (unrealistic guilt and mistrust), "I will never be able to get over these losses" (despair and hopelessness), and so on. However, with help, Barbara discovered that such negative attributions were based in large degree on how she felt, not on facts. In examining her interactions with her husband over the past several months, she found a number of exceptions to the belief that he didn't love her anymore including frequent attempts to encourage her to get out of the house while he watched over their son. She also was able to challenge her view that God was somehow punishing her. In fact, she slowly began to see how he was instead sustaining them both in the midst of all of the losses they were experiencing. Punitive thoughts regarding her own perceived inadequacies were largely dispelled as her counselor joined her in discovering long-overlooked personal qualities. Over a period of several weeks, Barbara's successful efforts at retraining her overly pessimistic thought patterns allowed her to see more clearly the relationship between the way she thought and the way she felt. Passages such as Proverbs 6:7 and Philippians 4:8 were instrumental in this regard. These verses took on a whole new meaning in the light of her recent struggles. She discovered that by memorizing these verses that they would help to refocus her thinking when she was tempted to dwell in the negative. A more detailed discussion of how to work with clients in developing more positive and realistic forms of thinking can be found in the suggested reading resources for counselors given at the end of this section.

4. Address feelings of self-harm—RFC Principle #8. Utilizing the "Suicide Assessment Checklist" provided in appendix G, Barbara's feelings and thoughts of suicide were explored. As it turned out, while Barbara often felt like she "could not go on living" after the anticipated death of her second child, she nevertheless felt that she would never be able to carry out such an act. For one thing, in exploring the reasons why she would not choose this option, she stated, "I know God does not approve of suicide" and "I don't know for sure if I could be forgiven." Additionally, she felt that she "could never do this to her husband" after all that they had both been through. Finally, she had never formally considered how she would go about killing herself and therefore had no plan. While this information along with other facts gleaned from the assessment of her suicidality helped to alleviate any immediate concerns regarding her risk of self-harm, she continued to be monitored for any changes in this regard.

5. Seek reconciliation in significant relationships—RFC Principle #1. In the course of counseling with Barbara, it became apparent that meeting together with her husband Don would be productive for a number of reasons. Prior to the illnesses of their children, they had experienced a warm, affectionate, and mutually supportive relationship. However, over time, the stress of the children's illnesses coupled with Don's drinking behavior had compromised this critical relationship. Fortunately, Don was willing to work toward improving their marriage but was reluctant, at first, to address his drinking behavior. However, when confronted by his supervisor about potentially losing his job due to his compromised work performance, he realized that his drinking really had become a problem. Even though he bristled against the notion that he might really be an alcoholic, he nevertheless agreed to attend A.A. meetings and ultimately found them very beneficial.

As previously mentioned, Barbara's relationship with God had become strained under the pressures and confusion that resulted from her children's illnesses. However, it was clear that she was not comfortable with the anger that she felt with God and longed for the relationship that she once enjoyed. The question she asked was, "How do I work toward a reconciling with God when I feel so angry with Him today?" In response to her question, she was asked to identify the Scripture passages or stories that came to mind or that seemed relevant given her circumstances. She immediately mentioned how she "identified with Job's struggles and losses" and the "anger that Jeremiah had felt toward God" when things did not go well. At which point, she was encouraged to go back and read those Scriptures with the question, "How did these people get through these difficult times?" What she discovered was immensely helpful in resolving the tensions she was experiencing. First, she concluded that Job never did get an answer as to "why" so many troubles came his way but that the question "why" had become less important when he was confronted with the awesome nature of God. Second, Jeremiah helped her to see how the open expression of our anger toward God can actually be a turning point that allows reconciliation and forward movement to proceed. Once Jeremiah expressed his anger, he continued his role as a prophet and God did not leave him or punish him for his anger. These and other reflections on the struggles of God's people continued to be helpful for Barbara as she replaced her thoughts of anger and mistrust with those reflecting her renewed appreciation of God's faithfulness. Fortunately, she had a good working knowledge of the Bible. This made it easier for such stories to be identified and then used as vehicles of restoration.

6. Change routines/environment—RFC Principle #10. Research indicates that changing a person's environment often can help to alleviate symptoms of depression. For example, in the course of identifying more pleasurable activities mentioned in item #2 above, Barbara began to notice that aerobic activities performed outside, such as walking or jogging, were more refreshing than staying inside to exercise. She also noticed that certain friends tended to be more positive and upbeat while others tended to pull her down with their stories of woe. In order to limit her stress, she decided to spend more time outside when the weather permitted and to limit the time spent with certain negative individuals. She also worked to modify her routines to allow more opportunities for her and her husband to go on weekend vacations and have regular date nights. Ultimately, five weeks after first coming for counseling, Barbara scored a 19 on the RFC Sadness Scale, indicating that her mood and accompanying grief had significantly improved since her initial evaluation.

Suggested Reading Resources

Client: Dennis Greenberger, Christine A. Padesky, et al., *Mind Over Mood: Change How You Feel by Changing the Way You Think*, 1995.

Richard A. Heckler, *Waking Up, ALIVE: The Descent, The Suicide Attempt & The Return to Life*, 1994.

Tim R. LaHaye, *How to Win Over Depression*, 1996.

Robert S. McGee, *The Search for Significance*, 1998.

Chris Thurman, *The Lies We Believe*, 1989.

Reading Resources Specifically Designed
to Address Grief

Granger E. Westberg, *Good Grief: A Constructive Approach to the Problem of Loss*, 1971. (for all types of losses)

James R. White, *Grieving: Our Path Back to Peace*, 1997. (for the loss of a loved one)

Counselor: Aaron T. Beck, *Cognitive Therapy of Depression*, 1987.

David Burns, *Feeling Good: The New Mood Therapy*, 1999.

Gary Collins, *The Biblical Basis of Christian Counseling for People Helpers*, 2001.

Binford W. Gilbert, *The Pastoral Care of Depression: A Guidebook*, 1998.

Mark Gold, M.D., *Good News About Depression: Cures and Treatments in the New Age of Psychiatry*, 1995.

Dennis Greenberger, Christine A. Padesky, et al., *Mind Over Mood: Change How You Feel by Changing the Way You Think*, 1995.

Archibald Hart, *Counseling the Depressed*, 1987.

Finley H. Sizemore, *Suicide: The Signs and Solutions*, 1988.

Siang-Yang Tan, *Understanding Depression*, 1995.

Chris Thurman, *The Lies We Believe*, 1991.

Selected Scriptures Offering Consolation/
Encouragement to Grieving, Sad, or
Depressed Persons

Job 5:8-27; 11:16-19; 16:5; 29:25; **Psalms** 9:9, 10; 23:4; 27:5, 6; 30:5; 31:7; 34:4, 19, 20; 37:23, 24, 32, 33; 41:3; 42:5; 46:1; 50:15; 55:22; 56:8-10; 62:1, 2, 5-8, 11, 12; 68:6; 69:20, 33; 71:20; 73:26; 94:17-19; 103:13, 14; 112:4; 119:50, 52, 54, 92, 143; 138:3, 7, 8; 140:12; 145:14; 147:3; **Proverbs** 12:13; **Ecclesiastes** 4:1; **Isaiah** 4:6; 14:31, 32; 25:4; 30:19, 20; 40:1, 2, 29; 41:10, 13, 14, 17; 42:3; 43:2; 49:13; 50:4, 7-10; 51:3, 12 with vv. 3-13; 54:4, 11; 58:10; 61:1-3; 63:9; 66:5, 13, 14; **Jeremiah** 31:13, 25; 39:17, 18; **Lamentations** 3:31, 33, 57; **Ezekiel** 11:16; **Hosea** 2:14, 15; 6:1-3; **Nahum** 1:7; **Zephaniah** 3:18; **Matthew** 5:4, 10-12; 10:29, 30; 10:31; 11:28; 14:27; 25:34, 36, 40; 28:5, 9, 10; **Mark** 6:15; **Luke** 6:21-23; 7:13; 12:6, 7; 21:18; **John** 14:1, 16, 18, 27; 15:18, 20; 16:20, 22, 33; Acts 12:5; 23:11; **Romans** 8:28, 35-39; 12:12, 15; 15:4; **2 Corinthians** 1:3-5, 7; 4:8-10, 16, 17; 7:6; 12:9; **Galatians** 6:2; **Philippians** 1:19; **1 Thessalonians** 4:13, 16-18; **2 Thessalonians** 1:7; 2:16, 17; **2 Timothy** 2:12; 4:17; **Hebrews** 2:14, 15, 18; 4:15, 16; 6:18; 12:1-4; 13:3, 5, 6; **James** 1:12, 27; 5:8, 10; **1 Peter** 2:21-24; 4:12-14; 5:7, 9; **Revelation** 2:9, 10; 3:2, 10; 7:14-17

Worry, Anxiety, Fear: A
Case Study–Alex

> [40]*But Martha was distracted by all the preparations that had to be made. She came to him and asked, "Lord, don't you care that my sister has left me to do the work by myself? Tell her to help me!"* [41]*"Martha, Martha," the Lord answered, "you are worried and upset about many things,* [42]*but only one thing is needed. Mary has chosen what is better, and it will not be taken away from her." (Luke 10:40-42)*

> [28]*Besides everything else, I face daily the pressure of my concern for all the churches. (2 Corinthians 11:28)*

> [3]*I came to you in weakness and fear, and with much trembling. (1 Corinthians 2:3)*

Alex first requested counseling after struggling for a number of years with various forms of tension and anxiety. Working as a systems manager in a large local technology company, he stated that recently "the pressure of my job has just gotten to be unbearable." Upon further questioning, Alex revealed that during a recent board meeting he was asked to give his usual update regarding the status of the firm's computer system, and that he just started to "wig out." "All of a sudden, the roomed seemed like it was starting to spin. I was having a hard time catching my breath, I wondered if I was going to pass out, and I had this overwhelming feeling that I just had to flee from the room." He reported that at 38 years of age, this was the first time he had ever experienced such intense nervous discomfort and was concerned that he was "going crazy." However, Alex did state that he had always been a sort of "nervous and tense person," and that at under pressure his hands and legs might shake and the palms of his hands would sweat. He also reported that his wife called him a "worrier" and that his job stress often left him feeling edgy and "keyed up." In general, he found it difficult to relax and commonly found it challenging to "unwind and get to sleep." All of this had left him feeling frustrated and guilty that he was not able to cope with this problem without help. In fact, he stated that he had always felt like going to a counselor was a sign of weakness and presently felt ashamed for having to ask for help. Alex scored a 69 on the RFC Anxiety Scale, confirming the presence of a significant level of anxiety. (*As with other forms of chronic emotional distress, anxiety can be caused by any number of factors. Wise counselors will want to read as much as possible regarding this problem so as to avoid becoming too simplistic in their assumptions or approaches.*) During the course of working with persons suffering from anxiety, worry, or fear, helpers are encouraged to address the following areas.

The Application of Structured Strategies
to Anxiety, Worry, and Fear

1. Address physiological sources of anxiety—RFC Principle #11. As with a depressed mood, problems with tension and anxiety can stem from or be aggravated by physical conditions such as hypoglycemia, hyper-tension, hyperthyroidism, and so forth (Gold, *Good News About Anxiety, Panic, and Phobias*, 10-30). In fact, many symptoms of a panic attack including lightheadedness, anxiety, trembling, feelings of unsteadiness, irritability, palpitations, and so forth, are also present in the untreated phase of many physiological disorders. Furthermore, a person's diet, lack of sleep, or use of caffeine or nicotine may adversely affect a person's level of nervous tension. Therefore, Alex was referred to his family doctor to check on the possible presence of any of these conditions. Additionally, his diet was discussed and his consumption of caffeine, which had been as high as five soft drinks a day, was altered. Aside from the benefits of removing caffeine from his diet, avoiding soft drinks also helped to reduce the simple sugars he consumed, thus helping to regulate his body's sugar metabolism. This, in turn, reduced the tendency for his sugar levels to rapidly rise then fall and therefore to avoid the nervous symptoms found in hypoglycemia. Fortunately, Alex stated that he didn't smoke or use any stimulant medications (or substances such as cocaine) that negatively affect a person's nervous system. Finally, given that during times of stress a person's body tends to deplete rapidly its stores of vitamin C and B vitamins, both vitamins were added to his diet. *(Research indicates that a person's tendency toward nervousness or reactivity, like the tendency to have a subdued or depressed mood, may be to some degree hereditary and predispositional.)*

   2. Engage in a regular program of physical exercise—RFC Principle #6. One of the most effective methods of reducing generalized anxiety is to engage in a regular pattern of vigorous exercise. Anxiety sufferers in general report a significant drop in both the onset and intensity of anxiety episodes following the initiation of a regular schedule of exercise. The reasons for this are many but include reducing skeletal muscle tension that tends to be responsible for feelings of being edgy or keyed up; increasing the metabolism of excess adrenaline and thyroxin, which promote a state of arousal; discharging frustration, which tends to aggravate anxiety; and stimulating the release of endorphins, which help to promote a sense of well-being. While Alex previously had been very active early in his marriage and work career, lately he had given up playing basketball with friends due to his busy work schedule. (Such inactivity reflects a form of physical alienation in that such persons are neglecting the necessary relationship that they need with their bodies to keep them healthy.) However, by discussing the benefits of such activities, he again determined to make time for physical exercise. Not surprisingly, after he resumed his exercise routine his difficulties with insomnia began to improve as well. Finally, he was encouraged to practice a structured form of relaxation each day for 10-15 minutes. While such exercises can take many forms (Bourne, *The Anxiety and Phobia Reduction Workbook*, 65-82), this simply involved allowing 15 minutes after lunch to sit alone in his darkened office with his feet propped up, shutting his eyes, breathing deeply and slowly, and imaging sitting in the woods. Within a number of weeks, he found that such relaxation activities helped to reduce pent-up tension from his morning's activities and improve his overall ability to relax that day.

3. Identify and modify counterproductive thought patterns—RFC Principle #6. Through counseling, Alex learned to identify and address various forms of thinking errors that aggravated his anxiety. First, he learned that phobic and anxiety-prone people have a tendency to avoid, hide, or suppress negative feelings and their associated experiences in an effort to reduce their overall tension levels. Therefore, rather than learning to deal in a straightforward manner with these uncomfortable feelings, they instead engage in a pattern of avoidance resulting in "self-alienation." While avoidance behaviors may help reduce tension in the short run, they fail to offer a lasting solution. As a result, over time anxious people often find themselves struggling with high levels of tension but find themselves unable to say why. Such excessive anxiety is really not surprising given how automatic and efficient these ingrained patterns of avoidance become over time.

To understand anxious individuals better and their tendency to avoid negative emotions, we should consider a number of common patterns observed in their background. One pattern which often emerges in persons suffering from anxiety is their strong need for control. Strong negative emotions promote feelings of being out of control and are especially difficult for anxious people to manage. Consequently, they must be avoided if at all possible. Another common pattern observed among anxious people is that they often come from families that set excessively high expectations for their behavior. When as children they failed to live up to expectations, these individuals often would respond in a number of predictable ways. One response would be to simply try harder to reach these unrealistic goals, thereby establishing perfectionistic patterns of behavior. Another response would witness the child, already subject to the parents disapproval and criticism, become both excessively angry and self-critical. However, since parental approval is so important for children, developing children will often suppress their natural tendencies to express their anger in favor of maintaining that approval. Not surprisingly, anger is one of the most common emotions that get suppressed in anxious individuals. In Alex's case, he first began to recognize how various sources of anger existed in his life that needed recognition and resolution. This involved not only learning to allow himself to be more assertive with his contemporaries, but also dealing with his need to release his anger by forgiving his parents, against whom he harbored bitter resentments. Second, he learned to overcome his longstanding pattern of self-rejection and related thoughts of inadequacy by identifying and resisting a number of common thinking errors. Some of these erroneous thinking patterns included problems with overestimating, overgeneralizing, catastrophizing, emotional reasoning, filtering, and the use of "should" statements (Burns, *Feeling Good: The New Mood Therapy*, 40-41). These errors tended to aggravate his problems with guilt and perfectionism and therefore promote a sense of self-contempt or alienation from self. While selected Scriptures affirming his worth were eventually of benefit in helping Alex overcome his sense of worthlessness, years of spiritual self-neglect had lessened the sense of authority they wielded in his life (a matter that will be addressed in more detail in the next section). He also benefitted from isolating his negative thoughts on paper and then learning to talk back to his internal critic by refuting the messages related to his thinking errors outlined above. Finally, Alex's home life involved not only unrealistic expectations but also expectations that would change unpredictably. Such inconsistent, unpredictable environments lead children to be hypervigilant, always trying to anticipate but never quite knowing what might happen next. Chronic anxiety and difficulty trusting people are two common difficulties encountered by adults who come from this background. Again, Alex had to identify and confront distorted thinking patterns related to these problems to help himself reconnect with people and God in a more productive way.

4. Examine spiritual resources for stress reduction—RFC Principle #2. Since initial questioning about his faith and its current significance in his life had seemed to cause noticeable apprehension in Alex, it was not addressed again until the third session to allow for greater rapport and trust to be established. At his point he revealed that while his wife frequently took the children to church and attended regularly herself, he had not gone in some time, stating that "sometimes I work six days a week and Sunday is the only day that I have to sleep late." He did agree, however, that he was not necessarily happy with this fact and stated that he would like to get "back into the routine" of going to church with his family.

Alex reflects a common pattern among many adults today who view faith involvement as being more of an activity than a relationship. As a result, they are left without the most essential resources for coping with life's inevitable difficulties. For Alex, his spiritual alienation had left him vulnerable to a debilitating level of anxiety. Reversing this condition and view of religion is never easy in a culture that has come to view God as something that we tack onto the rest of life when time permits. But with sensitivity and prayer, the counseling setting provides a rich opportunity to encourage a person's spiritual development. When a counselor reflects the values of Christ and therefore communicates a sense of acceptance and valuing of the client, these attitudes go a long way toward gaining the attention of persons who may be riding the fence with their faith. For Alex, the help and support he received in counseling paved the way for fruitful discussions and more openness toward a personal and living faith. In fact, after beginning to attend church with his family, not only did he feel less alienated and more connected to his wife and children, but this marked the beginning of a journey that resulted in his recommitting his life to Jesus Christ. Witnessing such a process for the Christian counselor is not unusual. In fact, the Christian counseling setting provides one of the greatest opportunities to encourage the spiritual development of others because of the strong and meaningful relationships that form there. The unique position that we occupy as helpers punctuates the critical role we can play in helping people to find the complete restoration they seek but, that in the beginning, may only vaguely apprehend. As a result of the spiritual encouragement from his counselor, Alex began to utilize Scriptures more actively in dealing with his anxiety. He found great comfort in passages like Philippians 4:6-8 and ultimately discovered how cultivating his spiritual life ultimately enhanced all aspects and areas of his relationships. While this spiritual awakening evolved over several months, it should be noted that he attended a total of just five counseling sessions. This case study should remind us that sometimes all we need to do is to help facilitate the beginning of change, and allow the Lord to continue this process.

Suggested Reading Resources

Client: William Backus, *Good News About Worry*, 1991.
Edmund J. Bourne, *Anxiety and Phobia Workbook*, 1997.
David Burns, *Feeling Good: The New Mood Therapy*, 1999.
Richard L. Flournoy, Frank Minirth, and Paul Meier, *100 Ways to Obtain Peace: Overcome Anxiety*, 1993.
Dennis Greenberger, Christine A. Padesky, et al., *Mind Over Mood: Change How You Feel by Changing the Way You Think*, 1995.
John R. Marshall, M.D., *Social Phobia: From Shyness to Stage Fright*, 1994.
Robert S. McGee, *The Search for Significance*, 1998.
Chris Thurman, *The Lies We Believe*, 1991.

Counselor: Aaron Beck and G. Emery, *Anxiety Disorders and Phobias: A Cognitive Perspective*, 1985.

Edmund J. Bourne, *Anxiety and Phobia Workbook*, 1997.

Mark Gold, M.D., *Good News About Panic Anxiety and Phobias*, 1991.

Chris Thurman, *The Lies We Believe*, 1991.

Dennis Greenberger, Christine A. Padesky, et al., *Mind Over Mood: Change How You Feel by Changing the Way You Think*, 1995.

David Sheehan, *The Anxiety Disease*, 1983.

Selected Scriptural Remedies for
Worry, Anxiety, Fear

Psalms 4:8; 29:11; 37:5, 23-26; 55:22; 94:18-19; 119:165; **Proverbs** 16:3; **Jeremiah** 17:7, 8; **Matthew** 6:26-34; **Luke** 12:22-32; **John** 14:27; 16:33; **Acts** 10:36; **Romans** 5:1-5; 8:31; 15:13; **Galatians** 5:22; **Ephesians** 2:14-17; **Philippians** 4:7, 9; **2 Thessalonians** 3:16; **2 Timothy** 1:7; **Philemon** 4:6, 7; **Hebrews** 13:5; **1 Peter** 5:6, 7

Marriage Problems: A Case Study—Lori and Tom

For this reason a man will leave his father and mother and be united to his wife, and they will become one flesh. (Genesis 2:24)

Strengthen me with raisins, refresh me with apples, for I am faint with love. (Song of Songs 2:5)

Lori (27) and Tom (35) first called for couple counseling following six months of increasing conflict. Having been married for almost two years, the first year of their marriage was relatively uneventful. However, the following months had seen growing tensions that had resulted in almost daily arguing. Their most recent fight was so heated that Tom had rushed out of their home, which was owned by Lori's parents, and refused to return for three days. By the time they first showed up for counseling, they had been back together for two weeks, had called a truce in their fighting, but had a laundry list of complaints about how their partner needed to improve. Questions about the family background and past experiences were initially treated as irrelevant by the couple. However, they quickly came to see how many of their interactions could be explained and improved by an examination of this vital area.

As is common for families with only children, Lori had received a great deal of attention from her parents through the years, especially from her mother. An attractive girl, she also had been very popular throughout her grade and high school years and was both a cheerleader and class president during her senior year. Following high school, she briefly attended a local university before deciding that she did not really need to go to college since she "was going to work in her father's wholesale furniture business anyway." From the time she was 18 years of age until she met Tom at age 25 she had several different relationships with men, all of them at least 6 years her senior. Her relationships with her parents were warm and affectionate; but since her father had worked long hours in the furniture business when she was younger, she had "always felt closer to mom." In fact, even after she was married, Lori continued to call her mother each day, which was a point of bitter division between her and Tom. Lori's family was Baptist and only moderately involved in the church during her years at home. However, when Lori was eight years of age she had made a profession of faith and regularly attended Sunday school until she graduated from high school.

Tom, on the other hand, was from a large Catholic family and was the second oldest of six children growing up, with the youngest sibling being a sister 11 years his junior. Contrary to Lori's rather calm childhood years, Tom had been "fairly wild" growing up and had experienced a stormy relationship with his parents during high school. Following this time, Tom spent a great deal of time partying and hanging out with friends. Even though his parents had wanted him to go to college, Tom's poor grades had jeopardized this opportunity and consequently he decided to go to work in his uncle's plumbing supply store. Tom was a good-looking Italian man with a sleek muscular build. At a party one night held by some joint friends, Tom and Lori met and were immediately attracted to one another. After 4 months of dating they decided to marry.

Lori's initial complaints about Tom were that he was not motivated to move beyond the job he held with his uncle and that she made almost as much money as he did working for her father part-time. Even though her father willingly provided a house in which to live, she wanted a house of their own and a commitment from Tom to start a family. However, Lori also realized that both of these dreams would take more money than Tom was earning in his present job. Also, she complained that he still wanted to go out with friends on the town, did not really spend "quality" time with her, and seemed to take no interest in coming to church with her on

Sundays. Tom complained that Lori spent too much time talking with her mother, and he resented the fact that she would often share details of their relationship with her. He also resented the way that Lori viewed his job and how she would mention the fact that her dad was providing their house whenever they had an argument. Finally, he stated that, contrary to the first year when sex had been by both accounts "very good," it had during recent months become infrequent and monotonous. Tom stated that his relationship with has parents was better since he had moved out of the house at age 19 and quickly stated that "I would never consider telling my parents the things that Lori tells her mom." When asked what they would like to accomplish as a result of coming to counseling, they both agreed that they would like to learn to "communicate better." As counseling progressed, the counselor worked to accomplish the following goals with this couple.

The Application of Structured Strategies to Marriage

1. Increase personal accountability—RFC Principle #9. Conflicted couples like Lori and Tom commonly bring a list of complaints about their spouses and the belief that if only *their partner* would change, things would be fine. Therefore, it is critically important that counselors discourage this assumption early on and work toward moving these individuals into more of a "customer" orientation. Previously, this difference in client status was reviewed under the "Determination" step of stage one in the RFC model. Clients who present with only complaints are recognized as "complainants." On the other hand, clients who recognize they are contributing to the problem (or potential contributors to the solution of the problem) and are willing to assume responsibility for personal change are seen as "customers." Only when a client assumes a customer orientation can positive change begin to take place. Therefore, "complainants" need to be challenged to recognize that not only are they the only ones over which they have control but that blaming their partners for their problems while denying their own contribution to their predicament is at best counterproductive and at worst a rejection of personal accountability.

Generally, moving couples into a "customer" orientation is relatively straightforward. First, counselors should make the observation that in their experience, they have "never seen a marriage in which each partner didn't share at least some of the responsibility for the problems that they were facing." Second, as if to drive home the point, the counselor might add, "I don't know. Maybe you guys will be the first exception to this observation. What do you think?" Couples quickly pick up on the implied meaning in such a statement and readily acknowledge that they know that they have contributed to the problem in some way. Finally, the counselor states, "Given this reality, I have found that one of the most helpful questions that each of you can ask yourselves as we go along is 'How am I contributing to the problem and what can I do to contribute to the solution?'" Having laid this groundwork the counselor can redirect couples toward looking for ways *they* can improve rather than fruitlessly trying to convince the counselor how their partner needs to improve. It should be noted, however, that many couples shift back and forth between complainant and customer positions and therefore need to be reminded periodically of their need to maintain ownership of their share of the problem.

2. **Decrease conflict and increase need satisfaction—RFC Principle #1.** Couples who engage in frequent arguing immediately need tools to limit their level of conflict. The reasons are obvious. While most couples argue periodically and even beneficially at times, frequent conflict only serves to drain couples of potentially productive energy and limit the process of reciprocal need satisfaction witnessed in healthy relationships. Therefore, Tom and Lori were challenged to adopt the position that during the coming four weeks, they "could not afford the luxury of an argument." In order to make this possible, each agreed to call "time-out" if they felt either they or their partner were about to start arguing. Regardless of the reasons, if one partner felt the need for a time-out, they each agreed to separate and go to previously identified parts of the house for 10-15 minutes until they had a chance to cool off. The ground rules included that neither mate could follow the other one around and continue to try to talk if the other person felt the need to take a break. After that time, they were permitted to make one more attempt to discuss the matter; but if voices could not remain calm, they were to set the matter aside until it could be discussed together with the counselor.

Once these sorts of damage control steps had been taken, they were each asked what they would "like to accomplish as a result of coming to counseling." Also, how would they know that they had received what they needed from counseling when it concluded, based on how they were each going to be thinking and acting differently. In keeping with the qualities of well-defined goals, care was taken to make sure that the goals they identified involved *new* or *increased* thoughts and behaviors that *they* could control rather than working just to decrease problem behaviors or focusing on the behaviors of the other person. Such questions often seem to stump couples. They have spent so much time thinking about how they would like the other person to change that they have no specific idea on what they need to be doing differently. To address this problem, you can ask them to explore when the "problem" they are having is not occurring (or when they expect the problem to develop but it never does), and then ask them how they are each acting or thinking differently. Often this is done by simply asking the question, "How do you do that?" (Notice the imbedded assumption that they have control over these experiences and therefore can repeat them if they choose.) These exceptions to the problem often provide rich examples of behaviors that they are already using that are helpful in their relationship. For example, both Tom and Lori were able to identify behaviors that helped them to avoid arguing. Lori might *think* for example that "Tom has had a rough day at work. Now would not be a good time to ask for help with the bills." Similarly, Tom would often choose to *act* preventively by going to jog, for example, when he felt frustrated by Lori's mother. In this way, each was asked individually to identify as many exceptions to the problem as they could and then identify how their own thoughts and behaviors made those exceptions possible. This time of looking for exceptions was followed-up by asking each of them to identify additional times in the recent past where they witnessed behavior in their partner that they would like to see continue. Throughout this time, the counselor needs to be making a mental or written note of each of these "solution-focused" behaviors for use in homework assignments.

Finally, the "miracle day" question was used. While both Tom and Lori had identified exceptions to the problem and corresponding solution-focused thoughts and behaviors, asking them to utilize these hypothetical days identified even more specific positive behaviors. As discussed previously under step one of stage two in the RFC model, the notion of "miracle days" is a powerful way to invite individuals into a more redemptive mode of acting and thinking. For example, Tom and Lori were each asked to pick two days over the coming week when they would be willing to pretend that while they were sleeping a miracle had occurred and made them the best mate possible. Then they were asked, "Given that this miracle happened to you and not necessarily your partner, how would you discover that it had occurred based on how you would be *thinking* and *acting* differently when you woke the next day?" Responses included items such as "I would wake up and smile and give Tom a kiss" or "I would make Lori a cup of coffee and bring it to her in bed." Such positive actions are often a reflection of early dating or marriage behaviors that initially made the relationship so satisfying but that, after the passage of time, started to fade from the relationship. The Christians at Ephesus in Revelation 2:2-5 were guilty of the same loss of relational priorities when they were told, *"I know your deeds, your hard work and your perseverance.... Yet I hold this against you: You have forsaken your first love. Remember the height from which you have fallen! Repent **and do the things you did at first**. If you do not repent, I will come to you and remove your lampstand from its place. (Emphasis added.)*

Before concluding the session, both Lori and Tom were each asked to keep the days that they had picked a secret from their partner. They were then told that when they returned the next week they would each be asked to identify which two days their partner had picked. This requirement creates a sort of "game-like" atmosphere that not only promotes mutual accountability but also enhances the tendency for each partner to look for their mate's positive rather than negative behaviors. Typically, couples become so negatively focused that they fail to recognize the positive behaviors that continue to take place in the relationship.

3. Explore the meaning of "leaving and cleaving" and its impact on marriage—RFC Principle #10. At some point, most of us physically leave the families that we grew up in as we move on to new stages of development in our lives. However, leaving our families emotionally is another matter entirely. Even if we put great distances between ourselves and our families, we often continue to re-enact the dynamics that were operating in our families growing up in any new family units or relationships that we form later in life (Richardson, *Family Ties That Bind*, 1). Such observations help us to have a greater understanding of the full meaning and importance of the biblical admonition to newly married couples in Matthew 19:4 to "leave" their families and "cleave" to their mate. Most problems in marriage can be traced, in part, to some failure on the part of individuals to separate properly from unhealthy forms of emotional connectedness with their families of origin. Therefore, counselors who begin their work with couples (as well as with individuals) by constructing their genograms will find this activity very helpful in understanding and intervening in the problems that couples face.

With the guidance of the counselor, Tom and Lori were assisted in making a number of helpful changes in their relationship by looking at their genograms. Lori came to recognize how her relationship with her mother, for all its warmth and closeness, was in fact interfering with her ability to bond properly and prioritize her relationship with Tom. As part of this understanding, she came to see how her father's involvement with the business growing up had resulted in her mother looking to her to help fill this relational void. She also learned how as an only child with an emotionally distant father, she had been influenced to date older men to remedy this deficit, often resulting in excessive expectations being placed on these relationships.

Tom, on the other hand, discovered that in his attempts to be different from his high-achieving oldest brother growing up, his tendency to go the other way had unnecessarily put limitations on his true potential. As a result, he decided to begin to take night classes in college with a view toward a new vocation as an engineer. He also learned that his distant relationship with his parents had aggravated the jealousy he felt toward Lori and the closeness they experienced. While he could not necessarily control the outcome, he purposed to work toward having more contact with his parents in the hopes that their relationship could become more affirming. A closer relationship with his family also would also be important as children came along since they would benefit from this involvement.

In addition, Tom and Lori both began to recognize how their financial dependence on Lori's family for both their house and Lori's job was more costly than they had realized. Such financial constraints inevitably exert a powerful influence over a couple's decisions, often placing limitations on independent choice-making abilities. They came to see how decisions ranging from which family to spend time with over the holidays to how they chose to spend their money were excessively influenced by a consideration of how Lori's parents would feel about such decisions. Like many couples, money was the number one source of conflict in their marriage. Therefore, these concerns regarding their financial connectedness to her parents served to motivate each of them to move in the direction of being more financially independent. Finally, they came to see how each of their families used different styles to deal with conflict. Tom's parents were more expressive with their anger, while Lori's kept much of their anger suppressed. This helped them to see not only some benefits in both styles but also the weaknesses as well. As a result, they established their own ground rules for arguing that reflected a balance of both.

In summary, from the insights gleaned through the construction of their family genograms, both Tom and Lori were able to become more objective and less reactive in their own relationship. The ability to observe the intergenerational family forces that were at work in their relationship inevitably helped each of them to depersonalize many of their disagreements and work toward a mutual goal of "leaving and cleaving."

4. Address the absence of mutual religious involvement—RFC Principle #2. Tom is not unusual in the sense that he had relegated religious involvement to a peripheral place in his life and their relationship. Unfortunately, their disjointed religious involvement also had been aggravated by the fact that each of them came from a fairly different religious background. In an effort to remedy this, they were each invited to share their history of religious involvement growing up and what if any desires they held for involvement in the future. This kind of gentle invitation into an area that often holds strong opinions by both partners is usually a good way to introduce a subject of vital importance to each partner, both corporately and individually. Negotiating discussions in this area of a couple's relationship requires a great deal of sensitivity on the part of the counselor and, as always, a conscious recognition of the need for the Lord's timing and guidance. Additionally, counselors must be aware of their own possible religious bias when dealing with couples from different Christian backgrounds and avoid allowing discussions of doctrinal differences to overshadow the potential common ground that a couple may share.

While Lori had already expressed her desires for Tom's involvement in church, these discussions led to her willingness to attend Tom's church on alternating Sundays so that they could worship together. Fortunately, Tom was attracted by her new flexibility on this issue. Further discussions prompted a new awareness for both of their mutual desire to work toward choosing ultimately one place where they could worship together (even if that meant attending a new church altogether). Despite Tom's under-involvement in the past, he felt a renewed commitment to work on this area of their relationship and was apologetic that he had neglected what they had both agreed before they married would occupy a central place in their future relationship. Needless to say, such discussions do not always proceed this smoothly but are nevertheless necessary and surprisingly fruitful when appropriately handled.

5. Explore ways to improve the sexual relationship—RFC Principle #12. Consistent with these changes, Tom and Lori's sexual relationship began to improve as the affection that they felt for one another increased. This was further assisted by the counselor recommending that they read a Christian book on sex, one chapter at a time, and discussing what they had learned. A couple's sexual relationship, like their relationship at large, needs to be consciously prioritized by each partner or else it will begin to suffer from neglect. Paul's admonition in 1 Corinthians 7:5 to "not deprive each other except by mutual consent and for a time" is a good reminder of the level of importance that both partners should place on this area of their relationship. Unfortunately, far too few couples enter marriage with an adequate understanding of this very complex area and often bring instead very distorted views of human sexuality. A good way to remedy this deficit is by periodically having couples read materials related to their sexual relationship and discuss with one another what they learned, agreed with, didn't agree with, and so forth. This will serve not only to increase their level of general knowledge and prevent monotony, but also to increase their level of emotional and spiritual intimacy.

Suggested Reading Resources

Client: Gary Chapman, *The Five Love Languages: How to Express Heartfelt Commitment to Your Mate*, 1992.

_____, *Hope for the Separated: Wounded Marriages Can Be Healed*, 1992.

Jim and Sally Conway, *When a Mate Wants Out: Secrets for Saving a Marriage*, 1992.

James C. Dobson, *Love for a Lifetime: Building a Marriage That Will Go the Distance*, 1987.

John Mordechai Gottman and Nan Silver, *The Seven Principles for Making Marriage Work*, 2000.

Willard R. Harley, Jr., *His Needs, Her Needs*, 1995.

Joseph Warren Kniskern, *When the Vow Breaks: A Survival and Recovery Guide for Christians Facing Divorce*, 1993.

Robert S. McGee, *The Search for Significance*, 1998.

Ronald W. Richardson, *Family Ties That Bind: A Self-Help Guide to Change Through Family of Origin Therapy*, 1999.

David Rosenau, *A Celebration of Sex*, 1996.

Ed Wheat, *Intended for Pleasure*, 1997.

_____, *Love Life for Every Married Couple*, 1983.

_____, *First Years of Forever*, 1988.

Norman Wright, *Before You Say 'I Do': A Marriage Preparation Manual for Couples*, 1997.

_____, *After You Say 'I Do'*, 1999.

_____, *Before You Remarry*, 1999.

Counselor: Larry Crabb, *The Marriage Builder: A Blueprint for Couples and Counselors: Now with Discussion Guide for Couples*, 1992.

John Mordechai Gottman, *The Marriage Clinic: A Scientifically-Based Marital Therapy*, 1999.

Ronald W. Richardson, *Family Ties That Bind: A Self-Help Guide to Change Through Family of Origin Therapy*, 1999.

Everett L. Worthington, Jr., *Marriage Counseling: A Christian Approach to Counseling Couples*, 1993.

_____, *Hope-Focused Marriage Counseling: A Guide to Brief Therapy*, 1999.

Norman H. Wright, *Marriage Counseling: A Practical Guide for Pastors and Counselors*, 1995.

_____, *Before You Say 'I Do': A Marriage Preparation Manual for Couples*, 1997.

Selected Scriptures That Address
Love and Marriage

Genesis 2:23, 24; **Ruth** 1:16b; **Song of Songs** 8:7; **Proverbs** 10:12; 18:22; 31:13-25; **Ecclesiastes** 4:10-11; **Matthew** 5:31-32; 19:6; **John** 3:16; 15:12; **1 Corinthians** 6:16; 7:1-40; 13; **Galatians** 6:2; **Ephesians** 4:32; 5:22-33; **Colossians** 3:18, 19; **1 Thessalonians** 3:12; **1 Timothy** 5:8; **1 Peter** 3:1-7; 5:14; **1 John** 4:7, 18; **Hebrews** 13:4

**Forgiveness: A Case Study–
Don and Sandy**

> *Be kind and compassionate to one another, forgiving each other, just as in Christ God forgave you. (Ephesians 4:32)*

> [21]*Then Peter came to Jesus and asked, "Lord, how many times shall I forgive my brother when he sins against me? Up to seven times?"* [22]*Jesus answered, "I tell you, not seven times, but seventy-seven times."* (Matthew 18:21-22)

Don had achieved more professional success in his relatively brief career than he had ever dreamed possible. A name partner after only four years in a law firm that employed more than one hundred attorneys, a $400,000 home where he lived with his wife Sandy and their two children in one of the city's most prestigious neighborhoods, and of course the obligatory BMW, were just a few signs of his varied accomplishments. Don was also actively involved with his family in a large local church, serving as a deacon and helping the church at times with various legal matters. All of this seemed to make their current predicament seem all the more confusing.

Ten years earlier Don and Sandy had met during their sophomore year in college, and nine months later decided to marry. Shortly thereafter, the financial strain of their joint college expenses coupled with Don's aspirations to go onto law school resulted in a decision for Sandy to drop out of school and go to work. Then, after struggling and sacrificing through the college and law school years, Don graduated at the top of his class and was hired by a prestigious law firm. Two years later they had their first child and a year later their second. Now it seemed as if they both had finally attained what they had desired for so long. Don was out of school and settled in his career. Sandy was now at home raising their children. From all outward appearances, the future never seemed brighter as the hardships imposed by Don's studies were now behind them.

However, the years of struggle had taken a toll on their marriage. An emotional distance had developed between Don and Sandy as career advancement and child-rearing activities had subtly taken center stage. Each felt lonely and hurt that the other was not more attentive. Sandy originally had been attracted to Don's ambitious nature and desire to make something of his life. This determination to achieve stood in stark contrast to the irresponsibility exhibited by her often-unemployed father. However, the satisfaction she had felt from his achievement was replaced by the same emotional distance that she experienced with her dad growing up. Similarly, Don, who had for so long been able to bury his dissatisfaction at home in his work, had become increasingly frustrated and unfulfilled with a career that had suddenly plateaued and which seemingly offered only more of the same in the future. His life cried out for a change to quiet the growing sense of emptiness and dissatisfaction. And the faith that had once provided his sense of moral direction was now, after years of neglect, little help in avoiding the choice that now rocked their marriage. Don had had an affair with a paralegal at work. Not so coincidentally, when Don was only seven years of age his mother also had an affair that ultimately ended in the termination of her marriage. He had resented her for years because of this fact but now found himself the object of his own resentment. How could he have ever done such a foolish thing?

Sandy was understandably full of resentment. All of the years of sacrifice left her feeling bitterly betrayed. By the time they showed up for counseling, it had been only five days since Sandy had discovered in

Don's jacket the receipt from a local hotel, leading to the confrontation and confession. While some of her anger had subsided, it had only given way to her profound hurt and growing ambivalence about their marriage. She was asking herself, "How could I ever forgive him for such a thing?" What's more, although Don was repentant and wanted to work on saving their marriage, Sandy was not sure she wanted to reconcile with him after the affair. She felt that scripturally she could divorce him under such circumstances and that "God would understand." Given this all-too-familiar problem in marriages today, the counselor needs to move decisively to promote the best chance at saving the marriage. In this case, the counselor took the following steps to assist in their reconciliation.

The Application of Structured Strategies to Forgiveness

1. Encourage a hopeful and redemptive course of action—RFC Principle #4. For the partner whose mate has engaged in infidelity, the feelings of betrayal are often so great as to make the concept of forgiveness, much less reconciliation, seem like a virtual impossibility. Fueling this idea are common misperceptions held by both parties that any hopes of ever having a happy and satisfying marriage have now been dashed and/or that ultimately most couples facing such circumstances go on to divorce. However, experience with couples dealing with infidelity reveals the fallacy of these beliefs. In fact, over 90% of couples who have experienced an affair and who are willing to pursue counseling remain married. Furthermore, when questioned a year later, a majority of these couples report a high level of satisfaction with their marriages. This is not meant to suggest that the forgiveness/reconciliation process is ever easy or that a lot of work is not required to get there. What is intended is that there are good reasons to hope that a redemptive outcome is not only possible but also likely if both parties are willing to stay and work on their marriage. Having this awareness, the counselor shared this information with Don and Sandy in an effort to secure Sandy's willingness to work on their relationship. Additionally, she was assured that if after working together for five sessions she still felt that there was no hope for their marriage, she could still choose to leave. The counselor then clarified that during this time neither Sandy nor Don must raise the question "Should I stay and work on the marriage or leave?" In other words, they must be willing to give 100% to restoring their relationship during this time without questioning the outcome.

This kind of invitation carries several advantages. First, progress is hindered and energy is wasted when couples allow themselves continually to raise the "stay or leave" question. The renewed bonding that needs to take place between marriage partners will only be frustrated by continuing to entertain this question. Even in the most strained marital situations, most partners are willing to commit to working together for five sessions. Second, by highlighting that they are only putting down the possibility of leaving for a time, not abandoning this idea altogether, they paradoxically become more willing to commit to working on the relationship given the freedom to leave they now know still exists. Ironically, the freedom to leave always exists with every couple, and a counselor is powerless to change this fact. However, if this freedom is acknowledged by the counselor, it can then become his or her ally. Third, outlining a five-session framework for working with highly distressed couples should not be seen as encouraging divorce. One partner choosing to leave does not mean they are choosing divorce, only that they desire a period of separation. Choosing separation does not mean the relationship is over and may at times, though not always, bring more productive change than merely talking about the issues involved. What this framework does ultimately is buy the counselor five weeks of time to keep a couple working together under the same roof. Given this time commitment outlined by the counselor, Sandy was willing to commit to work on the marriage.

2. Promote forgiveness and reconciliation—RFC Principle #1. Using the "Guidelines for Working Toward Forgiveness" outlined in appendix J, the counselor led Don and Sandy through the forgiveness and reconciliation process. After Sandy indicated her willingness to "try" to forgive Don, she was sent home following the first session with the assignment to make a list of all the hurts and losses she had experienced as a result of his infidelity. It is important that offended spouses be allowed time to reflect on all of their injuries so they will be able to look back and feel they were acknowledged by both themselves and their partner. Don't try to rush this process by simply having the spouse try to recall all of the hurts on the spur of the moment. They will inevitably miss important material and possibly regret or resent feeling hurried through the experience. During the next session, Sandy and Don were told to sit and face one another and look each other in the eye while she revealed all of these hurts and losses. (Don was told that he was not to try and talk or defend himself during this time except for taking periodic opportunities to reflect in the same or similar words what he heard Sandy saying. He was also told to try to imagine what it would be like to be in Sandy's place.) While some of her injuries had already been discussed during the past week, she now was able to tell Don how deeply betrayed she felt by his affair after the years of sacrifice and commitment she had shown in their relationship. She also described how vulnerable she had made herself to him by her willingness to quit school so that he could go to law school. She had even joked with Don when she agreed to quit school about how financially vulnerable she would be if he got his degrees and decided to get himself a "trophy wife." Now she described how she felt foolish for making this decision.

Don sat silently as Sandy talked, periodically tearing up as she described the nature of her losses. It is often difficult to predict how spouses will respond to all of the accusations of hurt and injury by their spouse. Some will become defensive and, even if they don't speak, give off the message that they are indifferent to these injuries or maybe even justified in their behavior. Fortunately, Don gave off no such messages. By the time Sandy had finished speaking, he gathered himself together and stated, "I don't know how you could ever forgive me, but I am very, very sorry for what I did. I hope you can forgive me because I would really like to make our marriage work." The sincerity of Don's contrition clearly resulted in a softening of Sandy's demeanor.

Before moving forward, the counselor asked Don if as a sign of "good faith and true commitment to work on the relationship" if he would be willing to deposit $10,000 in an account in Sandy's name for the purpose of allowing her to hire an investigator should she ever become doubtful of his fidelity again. (The statements were sent to her mother's address so Don would not know if she ever decided to exercise this option. Not only does such an agreement empower the offended spouse by reducing fears of a future affair and the fears of "not knowing," but it of course promotes accountability in their marriage. When trust in the relationship improves, they can acknowledge this by closing the account if they choose.) Don agreed. He also agreed to have the paralegal work in another department of their firm and if necessary switch places of employment if that is what it took to help save the marriage. Sandy was then asked if she was at a point where she was willing to release all of her anger and resentments related to her losses by choosing to forgive Don. In what appeared to be tears of relief, she agreed.

Following their forgiveness session, Don and Sandy worked on ways to enhance their relationship by becoming more sensitive to and working toward meeting the others needs. Both were able to recognize how they had allowed their relationship to suffer from neglect during recent years. Sandy willingly accepted responsibility for her contribution to their having slowly drifted apart. She realized that while she had not "caused" Don to have an affair, she had allowed her interest in the children to divert her from attending to their relationship.

3. Explore the need for "leaving and cleaving" and the impact of the "sins of the fathers"—RFC Principle #10. Both Don and Sandy needed to develop an appreciation of how their past and present experiences with their parents continued to impact their current relationship. By increasing their awareness of how the dysfunctional behavior patterns witnessed in each of their families growing up continued to exert an influence over their current behavior, they were better able to identify and change their own dysfunctional behaviors. In Sandy's case, it became apparent that her mother's relationship with her over the years had hindered her ability to "leave" home emotionally and "cleave" appropriately with Don. Due to the distant and often conflictual relationship that her mother and father experienced over the years, Sandy's mother often turned to her for support and consolation. This intense pattern of cross-generational over-involvement continued up until the time Sandy and Don presented for counseling. In fact, one of Don's complaints was that Sandy often told her mother too much about their private matters. He also felt that her mother did the same thing, often sharing personal details about her own marriage with Sandy that should more appropriately be discussed with her husband.

Sandy was at first reluctant to acknowledge this problem since this pattern of relating to her mother understandably seemed so normal and comfortable. Her mother had also been a source of consolation at various times in the past, so changing how she related to her might threaten this support. However, Sandy was beginning to see how this consolation came at a price. Her mother, upon hearing about Sandy's concerns about Don, would often go on to discuss the general failures of men and say that if her husband Jack "ever did something like that to me I would leave him." This placed Sandy in the undesirable position of actually having to displease her mother should she decide to stay in her marriage. In addition, she began to see how having such a "close" relationship with her mother inadvertently had undermined the potential intimacy she could have experienced with Don. Armed with these observations and a renewed commitment to work on the marriage, Sandy began to draw new boundaries with her mother that resulted in a more satisfying relationship with Don. Adultery, it seems, is almost "always a family affair" (Weil, *Adultery: The Forgivable Sin*, 30). Subtle permissions and predilections for infidelity can be witnessed in the family backgrounds of most individuals facing these problems. In fact, Bonnie Weil, a writer and family therapist widely known for her work with couples facing infidelity, states "in nine out of ten cases, either the straying partner, his/her mate, or both partners had adulterous parents" (30). More importantly, it is not so much that these families overtly encourage unfaithful behavior as they model disturbed patterns of intimacy. Such families usually reflect higher levels of divorce, conflict, arrests, enmeshment, disengagement, alcoholism, and or drug abuse than in families where divorces have not occurred. Each of these problems then, in turn, increases the possibility that an affair will take place. They also increase the chance that children who witness these behavior patterns will experience these same problems. Even if, like Don, individuals determine that they would rather not repeat some parental behaviors, research confirms that in the absence of corrective learning experiences they will still be inclined to duplicate these previously modeled behaviors.

This information made an impact on Don. Given his current situation and the profound impact of his mother's affair, he found it easier to be receptive to the idea of how relationships with his family growing up were relevant to his present dilemma. He did state that before his affair if anyone had asked him if he was vulnerable to such a problem he would have resolutely denied the possibility. However, he now saw how powerful such early learning experiences had been for him. He also recognized how he needed to be vigilant regarding this vulnerability and make a dedicated effort to learn new patterns of relating with Sandy. In order to make these changes, both Sandy and Don agreed to schedule structured times for sharing how they were each doing emotionally, relationally, and spiritually. Such discussions were to last only about 30 minutes, occur at least once a week, and be entirely focused on issues that pertained to these areas of their lives. During these times of sharing, each agreed to reflect periodically what they heard the other saying, help their partner stay on track with talking about "themselves," and resist the temptation to interrupt or challenge anything being said. Initially, couples are often surprised by how difficult it is to engage in such focused personal communication and may be tempted to change the content or discontinue the practice for this reason. However, persistence with these attempts will lead inevitably to an improved level of communication and need satisfaction in the relationship.

4. Encourage them to draw upon the resources of their spiritual heritage—RFC Principle #2. As reflected in each RFC principle, the Scriptures provide a rich resource for addressing the various concerns of counselees. In looking for a springboard for a more distinctly spiritual discussion, Don was asked what biblical character or story came to mind when he thought of the circumstances he was now facing. Not surprisingly, he identified the story of David's infidelity with Bathsheba. What was surprising for Don, however, was how informative this unfortunate account of a fallen hero could be for understanding and responding to his current situation. Specifically, this story introduced Don to the idea that parallel midlife forces may have served to precipitate in a crisis in each case.

A midlife crisis is often described differently between men and women. Descriptions differ even among members of the same sex. However, one thing is clear. For all individuals involved, there is *a real collision of expectations with reality*. A recurring theme here would be one of reevaluation. Frequently precipitated by stress coupled with a growing awareness of their age, the persons at midlife begins to reevaluate their lives. The time frame in question varies, but an average range would be between the ages of 35 and 45. In actuality, it is not so much about a person's chronological age as it is his state of mind, but this is the most common time of life. In the process, such individuals are often faced with the realization that not all of their life-long dreams will be fulfilled. Or as in the case with Don, individuals realize that they already have accomplished more than they had ever dreamed and experience a commonly noted type of post-achievement let down, a sense of "Is this all there is?" Despite which form it takes, these individuals feel a sense of disillusionment that their expectations are not being met with more satisfaction.

In this process an individual's relationships begin to receive more scrutiny. Marriage may be seen as dull and lifeless. Sex may no longer seem as satisfying. An emotional distance may have evolved in the marital relationship, leaving the person with a sense of being misunderstood, unappreciated, or just plain lonely. A sense of urgency develops that cries out for change! Unfortunately, this change often is seen as needing to be external, in terms of a person's environment or relationships, rather than as a clarion call to examine internal priorities and deepen spiritual roots. Couple these changes with the fact that this whole process is usually very subtle and one can see why midlife can be such a challenging time for individuals.

For Don, it was surprising to consider how both he and King David may have been influenced by such midlife forces and consequently how they may have increased their risk of having affairs. After all, here were two men who by most accounts had it all. Could it be that the expectations of David and Don came crashing into reality, leaving them both with a surprising sense of disillusionment, a sense of "What now?" Furthermore, David's demonstration of repentance when confronted was similar to Don's; and though they had each experienced difficult consequences,

David's story pointed to a hope that Don could also experience a new and revitalized relationship with God. Observing these parallels for Don prompted a renewed interest in rebuilding that personal relationship with God that previously had been so satisfying. Sandy also found comfort in making these connections. As a result, both she and Don renewed their commitment to prioritize their Christian walk as individuals, as a couple, and as a family.

5. Identify and modify counterproductive thought patterns—RFC Principle #6. Not surprisingly, both Don and Sandy struggled with rampant feelings of inadequacy or shame. For Don, his list of self-depricating thoughts included the idea that his choice to have the affair meant that he was a "bad person just like [his] mother." However, his own circumstances now propelled him to examine his previously negative appraisals of his mother. With the encouragement of his counselor, Don was able to see his mother in a more balanced and redemptive light, recognizing that she still possessed many positive qualities in spite of her choice to have an affair. Likewise, he was able to recognize that his worth as a husband and father could not realistically be evaluated simply by his recent failure. Indeed, rather than running from the marriage he was instead choosing the difficult process of taking personal responsibility to correct his mistake. The relationships he had with both himself and his mother were strengthened and improved as a result. Additionally, his marital relationship benefitted from Don's ability to move beyond despondency and toward contributing positively to his marriage.

Likewise Sandy was struggling with thought demons of her own, think-ing now how inadequate she was as a woman and a wife that her husband would need to seek the arms of another female. In a similar manner, the counselor was able to encourage Sandy to view her situation through a wider lens, helping her to see how affairs are not primarily about the inadequacy of a person's mate as much as they are about their mate's current and past life situation. Additionally, while recognizing her neglect of their relationship over the years had aggravated their current predica-ment, she came to see that Don alone would have to bear the ultimate responsibility for having the affair. And as time went on, Sandy was even able to empathize with Don's dissatisfaction with their relationship, denying that she would have gone so far as to have an affair but recognizing that she too had had fleeting thoughts of leaving over the years. Finally, reading and hearing about how other couples had successfully navigated similar circumstances was also useful in helping Sandy to think more redemptively about her current situation. These shifts in the ways that Sandy thought about her situation and her role in their current problem allowed for the same type of relational healing witnessed with Don previously. Ultimately, her more balanced thoughts provided the fertile ground necessary for a renewed and hope-filled view of their future together.

Suggested Reading Resources

Client: David W. Augsburger, *Caring Enough to Forgive—Caring Enough Not to Forgive*, 1981.

Paul Colman, *The Forgiving Marriage*, 1989.

Robert D. Enright, *Forgiveness Is a Choice*, 2001.

Gottman, John, *Why Marriages Succeed or Fail*, 1994.

McCullough, M. E., S. J. Sandage and E. L. Worthington, Jr., *To Forgive Is Human: How to Put Your Past in the Past*, 1997.

Robert S. McGee, *The Search for Significance*, 1998.

Debbie Morris (with Gregg Lewis), *Forgiving the Dead Man Walking*, 1998.

Lewis B. Smedes, *Art of Forgiving: When You Need to Forgive and Don't Know How*, 1996.

_____, *Forgive and Forget: Healing the Hurts We Don't Deserve*, 1996.

Counselor: David W. Augsburger, *Helping People Forgive*, 1996.

Robert D. Enright and J. North, *Exploring Forgiveness*, 1998.

Beverly Flanigan, *Forgiving the Unforgivable: Overcoming the Bitter Legacy of Intimate Wounds*, 1994.

John Gottman, *Why Marriages Succeed or Fail*, 1994.

Mark R. McMinn, *Psychology, Theology, and Spirituality in Christian Counseling*, 1996.

Bonnie Eaker Weil, *Adultery: The Forgivable Sin: Healing the Inherited Patterns of Betrayal in Your Family*, 1993.

Everett L. Worthington, *Dimensions of Forgiveness: Psychological Research & Theological Perspectives* (Laws of Life Symposia Series, vol. 1), 1999.

Selected Scriptures That Address
Forgiveness

Numbers 14:18, 20-24; **2 Samuel** 12:13-14; **Psalm** 103:12; **Isaiah** 1:18; 43:25; 55:6-7; **Jeremiah** 31:34; **Matthew** 1:21; 6:14-15; 11:25; **Mark** 11:24; **John** 3:16; **Acts** 2:38; **Hebrews** 10:17; **James** 5:20; **1 John** 1:7-10

Parenting Struggles: A Case Study– The Williams Family

> [18]*Fix these words of mine in your hearts and minds; tie them as symbols on your hands and bind them on your foreheads.* [19]*Teach them to your children, talking about them when you sit at home and when you walk along the road, when you lie down and when you get up. (Deuteronomy 11:18-20)*

Tom and Linda Williams first presented for counseling when their only son Brian (age 12) was given a three-day suspension for fighting on school grounds. Having never been an easy child to parent, Brian had a long history of misbehavior and poor school performance dating back to his early elementary school years. During this time, teachers had often complained of Brian's "poor impulse control" and problems with being disruptive in class. Frequently, it had been necessary to give him detentions for conflicts with both teachers and peers. Even Brian's current P.E. teacher, who stated he was used to "rough and tumble boys," had told Tom and Linda in a recent parent conference that their son might become a "future delinquent" if his behavior didn't change. However, unlike many delinquent youth, Brian generally seemed to be genuinely sorry for his behavior in retrospect and often had made commitments to change. But problem behaviors just seemed to continue. He struggled in school to make C's, even though his parents often spent time in the evening helping him with his homework. Complicating this picture was the fact that Brian often "forgot" to bring home assignments or to study for approaching tests. Even though Tom and Linda were careful to attend his report card conferences, the lack of consistent contact with his teachers often would result in weeks passing before these omissions were discovered. By this time, it was often too late to make a difference. Brian's active and often aggressive behaviors were witnessed not only at school but also at home and in church. His Sunday school teachers had to work hard to keep his behavior under control. In addition, Tom and Linda reported that getting

Brian to remember and/or complete chores at home was always a struggle. They reported that rearing their now 14-year-old daughter Celia had been a breeze compared to Brian.

The counselor wondered whether part of Brian's misbehavior and poor school performance might be a veiled cry for attention from his parents. Tom had for years been caught up in the demands of running his family's construction business and Linda had long been active on the city council. However, when investigating this possibility, Tom and Linda stated they had already considered this possibility and a year earlier had made several changes in their schedules to allow for more corporate and individual time with Brian. Unfortunately, his misbehavior had continued, although they reported that it seemed to have "helped a little." When asked about other things they had tried, they reported that they would sometimes ground Brian for a weekend or if his behavior got "really bad," Tom stated that he would "give him a spanking." Finally, the counselor strongly suspected that Brian's long-term struggle with both impulsive behaviors and poor academic performance might indicate the presence of Attention Deficit Disorder. Given this understanding of the family's situation, the following areas were addressed in the course of counseling with this family.

The Application of Structured Strategies
to Parenting

1. Investigate possible physical influences for problem behavior— RFC Principle #11. Pediatricians and parents have long recognized the impact that physical problems can exert on a child's behavior. For example, physical illnesses, hospitalizations, surgeries, and so forth, can all have a detrimental impact on the behavior of a child depending on the form and length of the illness, the reactions of the parents, and the coping abilities of the child. In addition, the presence of other physical limitations, often not described as an illness, such as mental retardation and attention-deficit disorder (ADD—with or without hyperactivity) may play a significant role in a child's problematic behavior. Suspecting ADD, the counselor referred Brian to a Christian psychiatrist who specialized in the identification and treatment of ADD. Using both computer-assisted assessment procedures and interviews obtained from schoolteachers and family members, Brian was indeed diagnosed with ADD and placed on a stimulant medication. Both his parents and school officials almost immediately noticed an improvement in Brian's ability to manage impulsive behavior and focus on assigned tasks.

2. Introduce and implement the "C-P-R Parenting Model"—RFC Principle #6. While a variety of medications may play a role in the management of child behavior problems, they should never be seen as a substitute for an effective behavior management program. The behavior management principles reflected in the C-P-R Parenting Model (appendix I) serve as a good starting point for parents seeking to improve their child management techniques. The consistency of Tom and Linda's parenting was enhanced by having both outline a few target behaviors that they especially desired to modify. Then they agreed on the appropriate rewards or consequences that would be applied to each behavior, depending on Brian's level of compliance with the task. They worked hard to ensure that consequences were always added or removed within 24-hours of the behavior in question to enhance the effectiveness of their efforts. Additional steps were taken to improve communication with the school by having Brian bring home a brief behavior report each day. This report involved little effort by the teachers (important in obtaining and maintaining their participation) as they would simply check and initial selected boxes on notes prepared by Linda to indicate Brian's success with behavior and schoolwork that day. Consequences for Brian's success or failure in these activities were administered the evening following the day in question. Failure to return the note automatically resulted in Brian receiving an undesired consequence. The "predictability" factor (appendix I) in their parenting was enhanced by working to improve communication in the family. Tom and Linda scheduled regular times to discuss their approaches to Brian's behavior and their commitment to "parent as a team" resulted in their willingness to com-promise when differences of opinions existed. Care was taken to ensure that Brian knew exactly what was expected of him. Vague goals, like requiring more respectful behavior, were reworded using language that specified the precise behaviors (i.e., tone of voice) that were expected.

3. Evaluate and enhance the couple's relationship—RFC Principle #8. Not infrequently, a child's problem behaviors can be traced to other distressed relationships in the family. This is particularly true when estrangement exists in a couple's relationship. Children are like relational barometers in the family, and their misbehaviors often signal an impending problem in the marriage relationship. While no overt conflict or discord seemed to be present between Tom and Linda, their busy schedules not only had limited the amount of attention required by Brian but also had started to impact negatively the satisfaction they felt from their relationship. Their marriage, like so many others in our hectic and often fast-paced society, was beginning to suffer from neglect. Recognizing how their lack of quality time together had affected their marriage, the counselor first commended them on their early insight and choice to modify their schedules so as to allow more time for Brian. He then highlighted how important this same kind of choice was going to be necessary to insure continued satisfaction in their marriage. Time management changes are never easy for busy couples like Tom and Linda, but the necessity to prioritize the marital relationship demands hard choices at times. When they began to identify how each missed the previously satisfying activities once present in their marriage, they jointly agreed to work on modifying their schedules in order to have more time together. While couples face a lot of time pressures these days trying to balance the multiple responsibilities of life, they need to be reminded that they are nevertheless not helpless victims of the demands of their schedules. Ultimately, we make time for those activities that we deed to be most important. If a marriage is going to survive long-term, it requires that we give it all the attention it deserves.

4. Discourage the use of counterproductive parental behaviors— RFC Principle #12. Not surprisingly, couples often embark on the road to parenting with little awareness of what actually will be required. Even if they were fortunate enough to have been raised in a home with appropriately caring and concerned parents, simply repeating the styles of parenting modeled in their homes will not insure the effectiveness of those same approaches if used today. While some ideas may continue to be effective, differences in time and circumstances will greatly affect the possibility that any given parenting approach will be successful. Tom had always been a fairly compliant child. On the few occasions when he did misbehave, he was quickly brought back into line with a few licks from a switch that his mother secured from the back yard. However, when he continued to use this approach to discipline Brian, not only did it not prove effective long-term, but it actually seemed to made his behavior worse. The counselor highlighted for Tom that using corporal punishment for certain children, especially as they get older or when they already are dealing with problems of aggression, often will have these kinds of detrimental consequences. By highlighting other options for consequenting misbehavior (i.e., time-outs, lost privileges, etc.), Tom learned to adopt more effective approaches for dealing with his son's behavior.

5. Re-initiate the use of family devotions—RFC Principle #1. While Tom and Linda had always been faithful in their attendance at church, they were encouraged to set aside time again each week for family devotions. This had been a regular practice several years earlier, but as the demands of their schedules increased they had discontinued this practice. These times were to be brief and structured to encourage open discussions surrounding previously selected Bible passages and stories. By continuing to model such faith involvements in the home, they again were helping to promote the critical spiritual development of both their children. They also were continuing a family tradition witnessed in their own homes growing up, opening the possibility that this practice might enrich future generations.

Suggested Reading Resources

Client: Henry Cloud and John Townsend, *Raising Great Kids: Parenting with Grace and Truth*, 1999.

James C. Dobson, *The New Dare to Discipline*, 1996.

_____, *Home with a Heart*, 1997.

Kevin Leman, Dave Jackson, and Neta Jackson, *Becoming the Parent God Wants You to Be*, 1998.

Myron C.Madden, *The Power to Bless*, 1999.

Bruce Narramore, *Help! I'm a Parent: How to Handle Temper Tantrums, Sibling Fights, Questions About Sex, and Other Parenting Challenges*, 1995.

Paul C. Reisser, *The Focus on the Family Complete Book of Baby and Child Care*, 1999.

Martha Sears and William Sears, M.D.,*The Complete Book of Christian Parenting & Child Care: A Medical & Moral Guide to Raising Happy, Healthy Children*, 1997.

Paul Warren, Jody Capehart, and Sandy Dengler, *You and Your A.D.D. Child: How to Understand and Help Kids With Attention Deficit Disorder*, 1995.

Joe White and Gary Smalley, *What Kids Wish Parents Knew About Parenting: What You Need to Know Before It's Too Late*, 1998.

Counselor: Matthew J. Fleischman, Arthur M. Horne, and Judy L. Arthur, *Troubled Families: A Treatment Program*, 1983.

Josh McDowell and Bob Hostetler, *Josh McDowell's Handbook on Counseling Youth: A Comprehensive Guide for Equipping Youth Workers, Pastors, Teachers, and Parents,* 1996.

Paul Warren, Jody Capehart, and Sandy Dengler, *You & Your A.D.D. Child: How to Understand and Help Kids with Attention Deficit Disorder,* 1995.

Everett L. Worthington and Kirby Worthington, *Helping Parents Make Disciples: Strategic Pastoral Counseling Resources,* 1996.

Selected Scriptures That Address
Parenting/Children

In answer to prayer:	To *Abraham,* **Genesis** 15:2-5, 21:1, 2; *Isaac,* 25:21; *Leah,* 30:17-22; *Rachel,* 30:22-24; *Hannah,* **1 Samuel** 1:9-20; *Zechariah,* **Luke** 1:13
Treatment of at birth:	**Ezekiel** 16:4-6; **Luke** 2:7, 12
The gift of God:	**Genesis** 4:1, 25; 17:16, 20; 28:3; 29:32-35; 30:2, 6, 17-20, 22-24; 33:5; **Ruth** 4:13; **Job** 1:21; **Psalm** 107:38, 41; 113:9; 127:3
God's care of:	**Exodus** 22:22-24; **Deuteronomy** 10:18; 14:29; **Job** 29: 12; **Psalm** 10:14, 17, 18; 27:10; 68:5; 146:9; **Jeremiah** 49:11; **Hosea** 14:3; **Malachi.** 3:5
A blessing:	**Genesis** 5:29; 30:1; **Psalm** 127:3-5; **Proverbs** 17:6; **Isaiah** 54:1; **Jeremiah** 20:15
Instruction of:	**Exodus** 13:8-10, 14-16; **Deuteronomy.** 4:9, 10; 6:6-9; 11:19, 20; 31:12, 13; **Joshua** 8:35; **Psalm** 34:11; 78:1-8; **Proverbs** 1:1, 4; 22:6; **Isaiah** 28:9, 10; **Joel** 1:3; **John** 21:15; **Acts** 22:3

Anger: A Case Study–
Bill W.

[26] "In your anger do not sin": Do not let the sun go down while you are still angry, [27] and do not give the devil a foothold. (Ephesians 4:26-27)

The voice that penetrated the levity shocked them all. Jerry's high-school classmates had gathered at his house to listen to music and basically hang out. It was a relaxed gathering. They were all sitting around talking and laughing, totally unprepared for what was about to happen. Suddenly, a rage-filled voice echoed across the room from a nearby doorway, Turn that d@#% stereo off!

Startled, they all turned to see Jerry's father Bill, glaring at their unsuspecting group. Having just returned from an evening out, his wild face, glazed eyes and slurred speech betrayed the fact that he had been drinking. Jerry quickly muted the stereo and everyone sat speechless, leaving a deafening silence in the room. Not dissuaded, he picked up his tirade of rebuke for roughly another minute before, just as suddenly, turning to leave. The group sat stunned, both offended and perplexed by the extent of Bill's anger. Several of Jerry's friends groped for words to lighten the moment. Few came. They basically excused themselves and went home.

As Bill's wife Gina and his son Jerry recounted this incident, they both reported how this was by no means their only experience with Bill's embarrassing and hurtful outbursts. They stated that for years he had experienced problems with his anger, an observation with which Bill painfully agreed. In spite of his decision several months earlier to recommit his life to Christ and his sincere desire to be a Christian father and husband, he continued to experience damaging eruptions of anger with his family, friends, and co-workers. These episodes often were followed by a temporary improvement in his behavior as he again determined to cage or stuff his negative feelings. However, as time passed and his pent-up emotions mounted, he again would succumb to his anger. Now, reinforced by his pastor's recent sermon on "Anger and Sin" and a sense of mounting guilt, he agreed with his family to seek counseling. (For a further discussion of anger and its relationship to this case, see appendix K.) As the sessions unfolded, the counselor worked to accomplish the following objectives.

The Application of Structured
Strategies to Anger

1. Identify and modify issues which diminish impulse control—RFC Principle #10. While Bill experienced problems with anger even when he was not drinking, the use of any mood-altering substances always increases the likelihood that individual will experience problems with impulse control. In reviewing his history of drinking and in conjunction with the observations offered by his family, Bill was challenged to recognize the role that drinking played in his angry outbursts. Convincing him of this fact was not difficult, and he readily agreed to discontinue drinking. However, before letting the issue drop entirely, the counselor asked whether he would be willing to attend AA recovery meetings should he fail to be able to keep this commitment. He also agreed to this. In addition, other situational variables that diminished control were identified. For example, the times that Bill most often exhibited anger were found to be just after coming home from work and/or days when work had been unusually stressful. Likewise, Gina would come home from work fatigued and frustrated, but her method of processing stress was immediately to begin talking through her day. Bill wanted to be left alone awhile. Therefore, they both agreed that Bill would benefit from having a 30-minute period of time to transition each day after coming home before assuming an active role in the family. In lieu of this, he agreed to give Gina a period of concentrated time to "process her day" and to deal with helping Jerry with his homework if that was necessary.

2. Outline the "RENEWAL" method for dealing with anger—RFC Principle #6. Utilizing the outline for dealing with anger found in appendix K, the counselor worked to educate Bill on how he could use the ideas represented in this acronym to deal with anger-provoking situations. A good deal of emphasis was placed on how a person's thoughts and behavior can either contribute to or diminish a person's tendency to get angry. Of particular help to Bill was his growing awareness of how a person's evaluation of an event, rather than the event itself, results in the presence or absence of anger. He came to recognize how situations such as difficulties at work don't *cause* his moods; it was his *interpretation of those events* that made the difference. Furthermore, his willingness to try to be empathetic with individuals involved in anger-provoking situations was demonstrated to be a powerful resource in the reduction of anger. For example, when presented with the scenario of a person cutting him off in traffic, a common point of vulnerability for Bill, he was asked whether he felt those situations caused his anger or his thoughts were primarily responsible for such reactions. He acknowledged that while he recognized that his thoughts "must control his reactions to some degree," he nevertheless felt that the average person would find such inconsiderate behavior offensive and be upset as well. Bill was then asked a qualifying question. What if he briefly caught a glimpse of a young girl's head on the passenger side of the car with blood coming down the side of her face? And what if the car was heading in the direction of a nearby hospital just down the road? Did he suppose that his reactions would be different and if so why? "Absolutely," he said, "since this would indicate to him that a father might be racing his injured child to the hospital." "Good," responded the counselor. "Now what has changed given the fact that the car still cut you off in both cases?" "The presence of the little girl," he stated, somewhat more cautiously. "That's true, but what has the presence of the little girl resulted in? Just a change in the situation or the way you think about the situation?" At this point, Bill began to sense how changes in the way persons think about or appraise a situation can result in significant alterations in their mood. At this point, special emphasis was given to how this situation involved a particular form of thinking that we often refer to as being "empathic." Being empathic involves learning how to view a situation from the other person's perspective and circumstances. For anger-prone people, the ability to consider another person's circumstances is critical in learning how to take control of their anger. As we have seen, learning to be empathic significantly aids a person's ability to forgive. For example, an offended person's willingness to consider variables such as the offender's family background, level of fatigue, recent exposure to stress, physical well-being, history of trauma, social skills, and so forth, often will serve to provide a more redemptive and less anger-provoking perspective than just focusing on the offender's current situation. In fact, few situations exist where such thinking cannot be utilized. As a result, Bill was given the assignment to journal each evening for 10-15 minutes and write about that day's anger-provoking situations. With each incident, he was challenged to develop 2-3 alternative ways that he could have viewed or reacted to the situation, utilizing the principle of empathy as a guide. Not only did this writing serve as a way of releasing built-up tensions, but Bill began to see how the careful deliberation of his thoughts and actions allowed him to be less reactive in future situations. This also allowed him to identify additional common anger provoking situations, giving him a further edge on anger with this predictive element in hand.

In addition to changing his thinking, Bill found that literally giving himself a "time-out" when the early signs of anger emerged often would help him to be more deliberative and constructive in his responses. For example, by carefully beginning to recognize early signs of anger, he would first mentally acknowledge this rising feeling and then, if possible, leave the immediate situation until he could respond in a more thoughtful and less reactive way. If leaving the situation was not possible, he would take a mental time-out by counting to 10. If this was not possible, he would literally look at his watch and while fifteen seconds were passing, force himself to consider alternative ways to think about and respond to the situation.

3. Utilize the Scriptures to develop a balanced view of anger—RFC Principle #2. As an extension of his journaling, Bill was encouraged to dialog with God about his anger while considering the selected Scriptures offered below. As is true with most individuals who struggle with anger, there is a tendency either to justify its misuse or to see anger as a bad or sinful emotion. Therefore, in order to develop a more balanced perspective, Bill was encouraged to recognize both the potential beneficial and harmful aspects of anger. He also was encouraged to bring his journal to the session each week to dialogue with the counselor about what he discovered. An example of how the Scriptures influenced his progress in counseling could be seen in several ways. First, he began to memorize those passages that had been helpful during his journaling activities. Second, Bill found that selected Scriptures such as "do not provoke your children to wrath" provided an expanded awareness of the damaging role his anger had played in his family. In particular, rather than parenting by example, he now recognized how his misuse of anger had modeled the very behavior he wished to discourage in his son. Therefore, he no longer saw his son's increasing problem with anger as rebellious but instead an extension of his own behavior. This new way of *thinking* about the interrelated nature of relationships in his family and specifically his role in those relationships provided the additional encouragement and motivation needed to sustain his commitment to change. Finally, Bill found that his study of the Scriptures helped to revitalize his faith and encourage a greater reliance on God through prayer.

4. Screen for contributing emotional or physical sources of anger—RFC Principle #11. There are many potential emotional or physical issues that may encourage a tendency toward anger in individuals. For example, persons who are diabetic often experience changes in their mood or find they have problems with irritability when their blood sugar levels are out of balance. Alternatively, persons with undiagnosed depression may find that an increase in anger is one of the prominent symptoms indicating the presence of this problem. While the counselor generally is not equipped to identify the presence or absence of all potentially complicating anger triggers, an awareness that they exist is essential. Every attempt should be made to become as knowledgeable as possible regarding the varied sources of anger and make appropriate referrals when necessary. As is often true of working with other emotional problems, a multidisciplinary approach frequently is key to effective anger management. Unfortunately, rare is the counselor who has not spent weeks or even months seeking a spiritual solution to problem feelings, in this instance excessive anger, only to discover that their resolution came by addressing the person's physiology.

Suggested Reading Resources

Client: Gary Chapman, *The Other Side of Love: Handling Anger in a Godly Way*, 1999.

James C. Dobson, *Emotions: Can You Trust Them*, 1997.

Tim F. LaHaye and Bob Phillips, *Anger Is a Choice*, 1982.

David Mace, *Love and Anger in Marriage*, 1982. (Out of print but a useful resource for couples if a copy can be secured through a library or used book service.)

Robert S. McGee, *The Search for Significance*, 1998.

Norman Wright, Gary J. Oliver, and Sharon Dahl, *Fears, Doubts, Blues, and Pouts: Stories About Handling Fear, Worry, Sadness, and Anger*, 1999.

Counselor: Robert E. Alberti and Michael L Emmons, *Your Perfect Right: A Guide to Assertive Living*, 1995.

Mark P. Cosgrove, *Counseling for Anger* (Resources for Christian Counseling, vol. 16), 1988.

Larry Crabb, *How to Deal with Anger*, 1991.

Aaron Beck, *Prisoners of Hate: The Cognitive Basis of Anger, Hostility, and Violence*, 1999.

Glenn Taylor and Rod Wilson (contributor), *Exploring Your Anger: Friend or Foe?* (Strategic Christian Living Series), 1997.

Selected Scriptures That Address
Anger

Destructive expressions of anger: Of *Cain* slaying Abel, **Genesis** 4:5-8; *Simeon and Levi,* on account of the humbling of their sister, Dinah, **Genesis** 49:5-7; *Pharaoh,* toward Moses, **Exodus** 10:11,28; *Saul,* toward Jonathan, **1 Samuel** 20:30-34; *Ahab,* because Naboth would not sell his vineyard, **1 Kings** 21:4; *Naaman,* because Elisha directed him to wash in the Jordan, **2 Kings** 5:11; *Uzziah,* toward Azariah, the priest, because of his reproof, **2 Chronicles** 26:19; *Elihu,* because Job had beaten his friends in an argument, **Job** 32:3; *Nebuchadnezzar,* on account of the insubordination of the three Hebrews who refused to worship his idol, **Daniel** 3:13, 19; *Jonah,* because the gourd withered, **Jonah** 4:1,2, 4, 9; *Herod,* toward the wise men who deceived him, **Matthew** 2:16; *people of Nazareth,* toward Jesus, **Luke** 4:28; *Paul,* toward Ananias, **Acts** 23:3; *Jews,* against Stephen, **Acts** 7:54-58

Selected Expressions of God's Anger: **Exodus** 22:24; 33:5; **Numbers** 11:1, 10, 33; **Deuteronomy** 6:14, 15; **Joshua** 7:1,26; **Judges** 2:12; **1 Samuel** 28:18; **2 Samuel** 6:7; **1 Kings** 11:9; **2 Kings** 13:3; **Psalm** 7:11; 69:24; 74:1; 76:7; 78:21, 38, 49, 50; **Isaiah** 5:25; **Jeremiah** 3:12; **Lamentations** 2:1, 3, 6; **Ezekiel** 5:13, 15; **Daniel** 9:16; **Hosea** 11:9; **Nahum** 1:2, 3, 6; **Matthew** 21:12 (Jesus and the money changers) 22:7, 13; **Romans** 1:18; 2:5; **Ephesians** 5:6; **Colossians** 3:6; **Hebrews** 3:11; 4:3; **Revelation** 6:16, 17; 14:10, 11; 15:1, 7; 16:19; 19:15

Alcohol and Substance Abuse:
A Case Study–Ted

> [29]*Who has woe? Who has sorrow? Who has strife? Who has complaints? Who has needless bruises? Who has bloodshot eyes?* [30]*Those who linger over wine, who go to sample bowls of mixed wine.* [31]*Do not gaze at wine when it is red, when it sparkles in the cup, when it goes down smoothly!* [32]*In the end it bites like a snake and poisons like a viper. (Proverbs 23:29-33)*

For the past 18 years, Ted (age 37) has specialized in installing marine electronics in yachts, cabin cruisers, and other high-end watercraft. His second wife, Cindy, and their two children live in a houseboat near the marina where he works. Having dropped out of college when he was nineteen to help his father run the family business, Ted had managed to revive a company that had suffered from years of neglect due to his father's problem drinking behavior. And as a result of his years of dedication and willingness to often work 14 to 16 hour days, Ted enjoyed professional relationships with some of the most wealthy individuals in his community. His reputation allowed him to command an impressive fee for his services; and when he worked, he was able to make significant amounts of money.

However, in spite of this success, business was not always steady. The winter season often resulted in a slowdown that meant he might be without work for days at a time. In addition, his exposure to the affluence of his clients had resulted in Ted's adopting a lifestyle of attempting to live far beyond his means. In spite of his wife's desire for them to purchase a home and the private school tuition expenses of their two children, Ted had recently purchased a brand new BMW, citing that it was necessary for "appearances" given the type of clients that he serviced.

Complicating Ted's management of their money was the fact that he often was invited to lavish parties being hosted by his clients. These gatherings usually involved a lot of drinking where again, for the sake of "fitting in," Ted had started to drink with his clients. However, over the years this drinking behavior became more widespread and problematic. In recent months, Ted frequently had come home drunk after one of these weekend parties and was drinking now after work during the week to "relieve stress." Additionally, he had started to gamble at these parties, which often involved high-stakes poker games, resulting in a gambling debt that had soured some of the relationships with his clients.

For several years, Cindy had excused Ted's behavior, often buying into Ted's excuses that he was in control of his drinking and that "he would never allow himself to be like his father." She would even make excuses to Ted's client's at times when he would miss appointments, saying "he was sick." However, recently Ted and Cindy had experienced a point of crisis when he was witnessed making a pass at another woman after becoming intoxicated at a party. Initially, Cindy had threatened to leave. However, after sleeping on this possibility and heeding the advice of a Christian friend, she decided to give counseling a chance and called to make an appointment. In working with this couple, the counselor utilized the following series of interventions.

The Application of Structured Strategies
to Alcohol and Substance Abuse

1. Get clients to acknowledge their drinking/drug-using problem—RFC Principle #7. In situations involving the abuse of alcohol and/or drugs or in cases that exhibit high levels of other addictive behaviors, such problems should be the initial target of any intervention efforts. The reason for such an emphasis is that addictive behaviors tend to affect adversely most other aspects of a person's life and relationships. At their most basic level, they threaten the survival of the system, whether that system is represented by an individual, couple, or family, due to the harmful and insidious ways that addictions work to undermine the physical, emotional, and relational welfare of persons so compromised. Therefore, any attempt to address other problem areas without first addressing prevalent addictive behaviors will in most cases result in a less than favorable outcome due to the continued negative effects exerted by such addictions. The importance of acknowledging the problem in the journey toward recovery can be seen in the fact that the first of the twelve steps in A.A. emphasizes this point. Step 1 requires that addicts recognize they are "powerless" over their particular addiction and that their life has become "unmanageable."

In the present situation, the counselor worked with Cindy, her children, Ted's brother, and one of Ted's concerned clients to carry out what is often referred to in treatment circles as an "intervention." An intervention involves having persons who are close to the individual in question, persons who have emotional or financial leverage of some type, such as wives, husbands, children, employers, siblings, friends, and so forth, come together in an effort to convey their concern over that person's addictive behavior. They are each encouraged to develop a message or a script stating their specific concerns relating to specific observations they have made of that person's behavior. They are also encouraged to set some kind of limit should that person choose to continue their behavior. For example, Cindy shared specific instances of how Ted's drinking was jeopardizing their financial well-being and their marriage. She followed these concerns by a statement that she wanted him to agree to address his drinking problem, and if he didn't she had decided to at least pursue a separation until their situation "improved." Likewise, the children shared their specific observations and their fear that their relationship with their father would be more difficult should he continue with his drinking. Ted's brother, who had successfully dealt with his drinking problem, shared observations and concerns and his belief that Ted's future involved only one of three options, "A.A., insanity, or death." Finally, his client, after sharing his specific observations regarding Ted's problem drinking, stated that he would no longer be willing to do business with Ted unless he sought help.

It needs to be emphasized that in order for an intervention to be successful, an initial meeting with these concerned persons should be held to rehearse what will be said. It is critical that everyone involved be of the same mind and resolved not to accept the excuses of the individual in question. Addicts can be very convincing and often enlist emotionally susceptible persons to change their stance through any number of strategies. Participants must be alerted to this fact and be resolved to remain committed to the agreed on course of action for the intervention to be effective. They also must avoid harsh or blaming attitudes, assaults on a person's character, or messages that come across more as angry ulti-matums than voices of concern. The focus of everyone's comments needs to remain on the specific *behaviors* of the individual in an effort to challenge the addict to recognize his or her problem.

As is common in such cases, Ted initially denied his problem and tried at first to minimize his drinking and then to blame his drinking on others, including his family. However, when this previously successful approach failed to weaken the resolve of his family, he defiantly stated that he would show everyone that he did not have a problem by stopping his drinking on his own. However, the group had been advised by the counselor to anticipate this eventuality. Therefore, they were encouraged to agree with this arrangement only if Ted would offer voluntarily to seek help should he fail to keep this agreement. Ted agreed. In one week, Ted and the family returned after he had again been found drinking in his office.

2. Provide medical support—RFC Principle #11. Ted reported that his "nerves had gotten much worse" during his period of abstinence and as a result he had started drinking just two days after the intervention. The counselor immediately realized that Ted's drinking was even more severe than he had suspected and that what Ted was describing as nerves were in reality tremors associated with his body's attempt to adjust or withdraw from the use of alcohol. Withdrawal symptoms stemming from the long-term use of alcohol are some of the most severe and potentially harmful symptoms seen in the substance abusing community. For this reason, anyone attempting to discontinue long-standing abuse of alcohol should consult with a physician for assistance with the medical management of withdrawal. Ted was referred to the family's physician, who then closely monitored Ted during this time.

3. Address the behaviors and core beliefs (thoughts) enabling addiction—RFC Principle #6. There are a variety of ways that alcoholics and addicts can undermine their recovery by engaging in faulty forms of acting and thinking. Counselors should help the recovering person to identify these behaviors early in the recovery process in an effort to help such persons avoid or reduce future relapses. For example, not uncommonly, alcoholics who previously frequented certain bars, streets, parts of town, and so on, when they were drinking will return to these high risk areas to prove to themselves that they no longer have a problem. At other times, they will allow stress in a certain area of their life to go unaddressed, leaving them again vulnerable to relapsing in an effort to cope. Therefore, previous patterns of high-risk behavior should be identified in order to avoid such eventualities. (It should be noted that learning better ways to handle stress is vitally important to the recovering addict.) Additionally, the thoughts of addicts surrounding the use of their "drug of choice" contain vital information that will help the counselor in redirecting undesirable forms of thinking. Often addicts harbor forms of thinking such as "I need this drug" or "I can't function without using" as justifications for continued used. They also often rationalize or minimize the damaging effects of their drug using behaviors with such thoughts as "If my boss would just lay off" or "I never drink before noon." By investigating the thoughts related to the addicts' behavior, the counselor can help the clients begin to identify and correct distortions in their thinking which leave them vulnerable to future relapses. For Ted, his belief that he "needed to drive a BMW for his business" only served to add to the stress of their already difficult financial situation and increase the conflict that he experienced with Cindy. In reality, such self-imposed standards threatened his recovery much more than his business.

Finally, as is true with all emotional and relational problems to a greater or lesser degree, damaging thoughts related to shame also operate in the addict's life. However, in regard to addictions, a host of writers and practitioners in the field isolate shame as a central component in all addictive processes. In fact, recognizing and addressing the dominant role that this emotion plays in such repetitive behaviors is widely recognized as key to any long-term counseling success. Therefore, helpers working with these populations would do well to address the addict's core beliefs stemming from feelings of inadequacy or shame. More information on shame, its role in addictive behavior, and ways to remedy problem forms of related thinking, can be found under the "Suggested Reading Resources" section for counselors found at the end of this case study.

4. Reduce the isolation and increase support for addicts and their families—RFC Principle #1. Addictions of all types tend to promote isolation among those who are so afflicted. As a result of this breakdown in social and spiritual connectivity, both addicts and their families often are left without the support systems necessary for the recovery process to begin or continue. It should be emphasized that addicts are being asked to give up a lifestyle that has become firmly established and a substance that they have long valued. Experience reveals that it is very unlikely that such changes can be undertaken and maintained with only one or two counseling sessions each week. Therefore, it becomes critically important for both addicts and their family members to connect with these helping resources. One of the most widely available and effective resources in this regard is the twelve-step support group known as Alcoholics Anonymous (A.A.) and its related family-focused groups known as Al-Anon and Alateen. Nobody knows the world of the addict better than other addicts. Not only can these mutual sharing and support systems provide vital direction for struggling addicts and their families, but also they encourage members to secure what they call "sponsors" in their quest for recovery. Sponsors are people who have a long-standing history of solid recovery and can therefore provide invaluable feedback and individual support to those early in the recovery process. In addition, they make themselves available 24-hours a day to those they agree to support.

5. Work to encourage a healthy religious faith—RFC Principle #2. In spite of the generic nature of the spirituality advocated by most twelve-step programs, their emphasis on addressing this vital subject provides a helpful springboard for the counselor to initiate discussions in this area. For recovering alcoholics to experience true wholeness and lasting meaning in their lives, they must come to see the essential nature of a relationship with Christ. As always, initiating such discussions should be a matter of much prayer. In addition, many addicts are used to shallow forms of religious involvement witnessed in much of the mainstream media these days. They are acutely aware of how to manipulate people and are quick to spot insincerity. Therefore, counselors need to be a living witness of the vital faith that they hold so that they may communicate in their lifestyle and actions, not just in words, a genuine relationship with Christ. On the other hand, helpers should guard against becoming too moralistic in their attempts to help addicts or allowing recovery to be "spiritualized" to the point where those strugglers discount the necessity of other corrective types of actions or personal effort on their part.

6. Provide family counseling—RFC Principle #10. Addictions have long been recognized as family problems. Not only does an addict's behavior negatively impact others, but often other family members inadvertently enable the addict to continue drug-using behaviors. This situation is readily witnessed in the present case in which Cindy engages in the frequently observed pattern of making excuses for her chemically dependent spouse. While such actions are motivated by an attempt to shelter the addict from short-term consequences, they ultimately result in exaggerating the long-term consequences of the using behavior. For all of these reasons, the addict's family members deserve attention and support. During the process of work-ing with the family, Cindy and her children were able to begin to share the pain of dealing with Ted's alcoholism and ways that they could offer support to one another. They also were able to share valuable insights into signs in Ted's behaviors that in the past had helped to signal future drinking behavior. The increased vulnerability of both Ted and his family to problems with alcohol were highlighted by examining the continuing influence that genetics and poor parental modeling (both Ted's and his father's) would have on any future decisions to drink. Finally, efforts were made to work on improving both the marital and parent/child relationships which had suffered from neglect over the years from Ted's alcoholism and excessive work habits.

Suggested Reading Resources

Client: Stephen Arterburn and D. Stoop, *The Life Recovery Bible,* 1992.

Robert Hemfelt and Richard Fowler, *Serenity: A Companion for Twelve-Step Recovery Complete with New Testament Psalms and Proverbs,* 1990.

Robert S. McGee, *The Search for Significance,* 1998.

Keith Miller, *A Hunger for Healing Workbook,* 1992.

_____, *A Hunger for Healing: The Twelve Steps as a Classic Model for Christian Spiritual Growth,* 1992.

Zondervan Publishing Company, *Recovery Devotional Bible: New International Version,* 1993.

Counselor: Aaron Beck, et al., *Cognitive Therapy of Substance Abuse,* 1993.

Gerald May, *Addiction and Grace,* 1991.

Keith Miller, *A Hunger for Healing Workbook,* 1992.

Lewis B. Smedes, *Shame and Grace: Healing the Shame We Don't Deserve*, 1994.

Daniel R. Green and Mel Lawrenz, *Encountering Shame and Guilt: Resources for Strategic Pastoral Counseling* (Resources for Strategic Pastoral Counseling), 1994.

Merle A. Fossum and Marilyn J. Mason, *Facing Shame: Families in Recovery*, 1989.

Patrick Carnes, *Out of the Shadows: Understanding Sexual Addiction*, 1992.

Selected Scriptures That Address
Alcohol and Substance Abuse

Deuteronomy 21:20, 21; 29:19-21; **1 Samuel** 1:14; **Psalm** 69:12; **Proverbs** 20:1; 21:17; 23:20, 21, 29-35; 31:4-7; **Isaiah** 5:11, 12, 22; 19:14; 24:9, 11; 28:1, 3, 7, 8; 56:12; **Jeremiah** 25:27; **Hosea** 4:11; 7:5, 14; **Joel** 1:5; **Joel** 3:3; **Amos** 2:8, 12; 6:1, 6; **Micah** 2:11; **Nahum** 1:10; **Habakkuk** 2:15, 16, 17; **Matthew** 24:49; **Luke** 12:45; 21:34; **Romans** 13:13; **Galatians** 5:19-21; **Ephesians** 5:18; **1 Thessalonians** 5:7, 8

Chapter 6

Applying RFC in Pastoral
Preaching

Before We Begin

A pastor who reflects on RFC in association with his work in the pulpit can easily come to the conclusion that the ministries of counseling and preaching share a great deal of common ground. Both ministries affirm a high view of Scripture, hold to a firm conviction that the Bible reveals a way for people to experience reconciliation in a variety of relationships, and focuses on Jesus as the centerpiece of the message of God's reconciling love.

Preachers and counselors also share a common awareness that troubled people need someone to guide them toward reconciliation and that the process of tearing down walls can take time. They also know that ministers don't have magic wands to make pain simply go away at the utterance of a few select verses of Scripture. Even though the walls may come down in a dynamic act of God's grace, learning to live without the walls may still take a while.

Because of so much common ground, developing sermons along the lines of RFC has not been a particularly difficult assignment. In fact, preparing the following sermon briefs has been a joyful experience. Hopefully they reflect the insights of RFC and serve as worthy examples of how a pastor can focus on reconciliation in his preaching ministry.

Before you get into them, though, consider some influences that shaped the way they were designed. A variety of contextual, pastoral, and homiletical propositions surfaced along the way, and some of them made their way into the preparation process. Please consider six of them as you read the sermons and as you prepare your own messages so they can focus on reconciliation.

First, every sermon begins with a text of Scripture that serves as both the foundation as well as the means of developing the message. Even if the sermon idea originates in the mind of the preacher apart from a text, perhaps as he deals with the pain of his people, it must be surrendered to a Scripture portion that he selects in keeping with the idea. Once selected, the text should always be examined by using the procedures of sound, reliable exegesis and interpreted in accordance with the principles of solid exposition.

Second, each sermon text either implies or explicates a redemptive message. The Bible is God's message of redemption. God's Word is the account of what went wrong with people and what He has done to redeem us, centered ultimately in the death, burial and resurrection of Jesus Christ, His Son and our Savior. Each text, therefore, has a part in that redemptive message and can somehow point to the redemptive centerpiece, Jesus Christ. Accordingly, every sermon text has the potential to show implicitly or explicitly the need and the means of our redemption (see Chappell, 1994).

Third, biographical-narrative Scripture passages provide ample opportunities to develop reconciliation-focused sermons. Narrative texts relate stories about people or episodes in the Bible. Since approximately 70% of the Bible consists of narrative literature, a preacher does well to master the art of preparing and delivering sermons based on passages from this rich and fascinating genre. No matter how sophisticated people may become, they are still captivated by well-told stories. When people in pain identify with people in the Bible who bore the same kind of pain, the stage has been set for a reconciliation-focused message.

Fourth, tension can be built into a sermon as a way of engaging the people in the pew from start to finish. Biographical-narrative sermons have built-in tension by virtue of the fact that they are stories that have characters who interact along the lines of plot and conflict. Other kinds of texts can be developed by a two-point approach that sets in tension the human problem underlying the passage and the divine solution that ultimately centers in Jesus.

Fifth, every congregation includes people who listen and learn in uniquely different ways. Some of the people learn by way of reading and writing. They will likely favor a sermon that follows a logical progression of thought or line of reasoning. Since that is the way reading and writing influences their cognitive process. Other people listen orally, using their eyes and ears to study people and to hear discourse, not to read or write books. Generally speaking, oral people come in two shapes. Either they are illiterate or at least beneficially illiterate, or they are literate but prefer to listen and learn out of their preliterate orality. Oral people must be taken into account by a preacher who is intent on preparing and delivering reconciliation-focused sermons. They are a large and growing segment of the population in this country, and their way of learning produces a culture all its own that becomes an interpretive filter for the sermons they hear.

Sixth, a pastor knows that guiding people toward reconciliation takes more than preaching one sermon on a topic that deals with emotional and relational pain. It takes time to help hurting people through preaching. And it takes effort on the part of a pastor who loves his people so much that he continues to fine-tune his homiletical skills so they can be used to help people tear down walls. Most of all, it takes a pastor who is willing to live as a person of integrity, someone who the troubled people in his congregation can trust.

As you study the following sermons, keep these propositions in mind. In them you can see the common ground between preaching and counseling. As you read them, think about a pastor in his pulpit and in his counseling room trying to do only one thing: help hurting people tear down the walls.

A Sermon about Depression:
Getting Back on Track
(1 Kings 19:1-18)

Imagine Elijah as he awaited Queen Jezebel's response. He was sure she would sit up and take notice that God had done something amazing at Mt. Carmel, according to 1 Kings 18. God had won the day on that mountain top and everybody saw it. Jezebel's gods never showed up for the divine showdown. But God Almighty did, igniting a water-soaked alter with fire from heaven.

Ahab, Jezebel's husband, saw it. And he rushed back to the palace to give her the news. Elijah outran the royal chariot, perhaps breathless with anticipation over Jezebel's reaction. Maybe she would repent. Or she might begin to inquire of him about the Almighty God.

But the story didn't turn out that way. Not at all. Jezebel didn't repent; she only got angry. In her rage, she promised Elijah that she would kill him within the next twenty-four hours.

The news must have crushed Elijah, the otherwise bigger-than-life prophet who had developed a reputation as a fearless man of God. But the concrete of Jezebel's heart shattered his confidence, and he felt he had no other choice but to run. He ran as fast and as far as he could.

He got as far as his tired legs would take him. Then exhaustion got the best of him, and he found a resting place under the shade of a juniper tree. There he uttered a grim wish to die. After all, he must have thought to himself, death would be his friend who would take him away from his sorrow and despair. With the death wish on his lips, he slipped into a troubled sleep.

Can you identify with Elijah? James tells us that Elijah was an ordinary person made of flesh and blood just like you and me (James 5:16). I might not be able to identify with Elijah when he called down fire from heaven, but his story resonates with mine when he fights the battle with depression. It's good to know that even some of God's choice servants get depressed. It means that people like you and me are in good company.

The story of Elijah under the juniper tree shows how God works with us to get us back on track. Anybody can experience depression, but not everyone finds a way out of the dark shadows and back into the light. Getting back on track, as the story of God working with Elijah teaches us, means taking some important steps under the Lord's direction.

Granted, some people need the help of a physician or a therapist in their quest to work through their depression. Anybody, however, can benefit from this moving story of a loving God helping a depressed prophet. It suggests how the Lord can guide us toward the light when the shadows of depression lengthen over us.

The first step toward getting back on track may come as a surprise to people who look for some sort of complex, spiritually charged principle. In fact it actually sounds more like common sense. The first step has to do with getting some rest and something to eat (vv. 5-7).

After Elijah slept a while under the juniper tree, an angel awakened him. Now you might have expected the angel to be a divine drill sergeant, yelling in Elijah's ear and commanding the tired prophet to ignore the despair in his soul and to finish what he had started. That's the way we tend to think about God when we get tired but we still have work to do. We expect His angel to rebuke us with "Hey, you deadbeat, get up and get back to work. What do you think this is, a picnic in the park?"

But the angel didn't say anything like that to Elijah. On the contrary, the gentle messenger from God awakened the weary man of God and placed some water and bread right in front of him. Elijah couldn't miss it, neither the food nor the water nor the kind hand of God who had given both to him. What did Elijah do? No, he didn't get up immediately, muster his courage and walk all the way back to Jezebel's door with renewed eagerness. No, he didn't repent of his gross sin of negligence, and neither did he confess that he had failed God. According to the story, Elijah simply went back to sleep. He must have been tired, weary to the bone.

The angel knew Elijah needed food, so he awakened the prophet a second time. Like before, the angel didn't treat the prophet like he was about to miss the school bus because he overslept. He simply awakened Elijah to feed him. Twice now the angel of God did something to help the prophet get back on track. He helped the weary preacher to get some rest and something to eat.

These days when we find ourselves under the juniper tree of depression, we don't need to wait for an angel to send us food and water or for divine guidance to get some rest. We can substitute an angel carrying bread with a grocery store, and we can replace a juniper tree with a bed. God knows what we need. Rest assured He is not going to be disappointed with us because we get tired and hungry.

I know what you're thinking; this step is not very profound. You're right. But that does not mean it's not important. How many times have you made poor decisions when you were hungry or tired? Do you remember the last time you went grocery shopping when you were famished? Your pantry probably still contains some of the stuff you bought that day!

The second step toward getting back on track can be a little disconcerting (vv. 8-14). For Elijah, it took him to the mountain of God. For us, it takes us to a place where we can hear from God in a fresh way.

After Elijah got some nourishment and rest, God led him to a distant place, a place where a depressed person could listen to Him without being distracted. The place God had in mind for Elijah was Mount Horeb, the mountain where Moses encountered God through a burning bush (Exodus 3:1). After a forty-day walk, Elijah would soon encounter the Lord there too.

Elijah climbed the mountain and situated himself in a cave. Then God showed up and asked him a soul-searching question: Why are you here? As it turns out, that's a good question to ask when depression sweeps over you like a plague, shrouding all your hope with an ominous cloud of confusion. Why are you here? What's your purpose? What do you need to hear God say so you can step out from beneath the cloud?

How would you answer such a question? Elijah answered by pouring out his heart. First he whimpered about the job God had given him to do. Then he moaned about the way he felt so alone. All by himself. Nobody cared. All alone. The words probably echoed down through the mountain side. All alone. Nobody cared.

It's funny how we convince ourselves of ideas that are light years from the truth. What's even more curious is that God doesn't lose His temper when we utter such foolishness as "nobody cares" and "we are all alone." Instead He gets us ready to hear him in a new way that will neutralize the poison from the bowl of bad information we've been feeding ourselves.

God told Elijah to brace himself for what would happen next. Then Elijah experienced the wind, but God wasn't there. After that, the prophet encountered an earthquake, but God didn't make Himself present then either. Fire followed the earthquake, but God didn't come along. God had spoken to Elijah in all of these ways before, but now they didn't work any more.

Have you ever wished you could talk with God like you did right after you became a Christian, when everything was simple and exciting? Perhaps you have longed for the day back when knowing God was as simple as waking up in the morning and brushing your teeth.

Those days have come and gone, never to return. Frankly, I am not sure God wants us to wish our lives away, longing for simpler days when we could hear His voice in ways we could understand without any trouble. He seems to be more interested in speaking to us where we are right now.

The wind, earthquake, and the fire represented the ways God had spoken to Elijah before. Now God spoke to him in a new and different way, through the sound of a gently blowing breeze. God had never spoken to him that way before. It might have been a little confusing or bewildering to Elijah at first. But it was the way God wanted to speak, so Elijah had no choice but to listen.

We don't always know what we like, but we like what we know. Getting back on track may mean accepting the fact that God wants to speak to us in a different way. Perhaps in the middle of the darkness of depression, God is closer than He has ever been before and He wants to speak to you, but not like before. While it may not be what you've grown accustomed to, it's probably the best way for God to show you some things about the relationship He wants to have with you right now.

The mountain where you encounter God does not have to be located in Palestine. In fact, it doesn't have to be an actual mountain. It can be any place where you can meet God, a place where you won't be distracted by the things around you. In that place, you can spend time with God's probing question: Why are you here? And you can spend time with Him listening for His answer spoken in His way in His time.

The story shows us the third step toward getting back on track (vv. 14-18). Study Elijah's reaction to the gentle blowing breeze of God's presence and you will see that the encounter didn't have an immediate effect on the tired prophet. He still misunderstood and told himself things that were not true. That's the way it is when we meet Him. Sometimes results don't come immediately. It takes time for the reality to sink in and for a lasting difference to be made in how we see ourselves in our relationship with God. We can't expect God to wave a magic wand over us and make all of our troubles vanish into thin air.

What's the third step God wants us to make in order to get back on track? After He refreshes us with nourishment, rest, and a new sense of His presence, He wants us to get on with the work He intended us to do all along. No, we might not be completely restored. That process may take some time, and it may be a while before we can really see the big picture. But in due time He orders us to get on with the task at hand.

When God sent Elijah to resume his prophetic work, He had not taken Jezebel out of the picture either. She was still there when he came down from the mountain. So will the problems that put you under the dark cloud. They will probably still be right there when you return, waiting for you.

What changes is our perspective on them. Instead of looking at the overwhelming challenges before us, we do well to ask God to show us what we can do right at the moment. We can't do everything, but we can do something. We may not be able to solve the big problems, but we can do what God wants us to do today, in the next hour, for the next few minutes by taking action in baby steps.

Along the way we can trust God to give us information on a need-to-know basis. God didn't tell Elijah about how Jezebel's story would end . That information would come much later. Instead, God gave the prophet his immediate marching orders and nothing more. He wanted Elijah to anoint three people whose lives would fit into the national puzzle that only God could solve. Like Elijah, sometimes we do our best work for the Master when we are satisfied with His short-term orders for us.

The third step in the process of getting back on track can be very tough. It's a little easier, though, if we know we have somebody on our side. When we struggle to fight our way out of depression, the notion of being alone troubles us because we know we lack the strength that comes in numbers. God can clear our thinking if we listen to Him. He can remind us of the countless people who share our commitment to Christ and our desire to walk in the light of His presence. With that awareness, we can grow more courageous for the hard work ahead of us.

That's how God propped up Elijah's courage. He left the prophet with a critical reminder: Elijah was not alone! In fact, God told him about a small army of people who stood shoulder to shoulder with the prophet in his devotion to the Lord.

The devil's lie couldn't work any longer. And it has a short shelf life today if we remember that in serving Christ we work in the company of many good people who share our love for Him and His kingdom.

Getting back to the Lord's work can be difficult. It's easier, though, if we remember that others share our love for Him and His Kingdom.

The steps Elijah took to get back on track seem simple enough, but they are almost impossible for us to take them if we try by ourselves. Our Savior enables us to use our common sense, get a fresh word from the Lord, and get on with the work before us with a new assurance that we labor in the company of fellow followers of the Master. The story of Elijah and the juniper tree challenges us to trust Him to guide us along the way from the darkness of depression to the light of His presence.

A Sermon about Confusion and Worry:
Diminishing the Distance
(Luke 11:5-13)

What if you had the chance to ask Jesus to do just one thing for you, what would it be? If you had Him to stand right in front of you, what would you ask Him to do?

When they got the opportunity, Jesus' first disciples asked Him to teach them to pray (v. 1). You can understand why they would make such a request. After all, on more than a few occasions they had seen Him slip away to a quiet place early in the morning to talk with his Father. He always returned more than ready to face the challenges of the day.

Or they had watched Him handle the weariness that accompanied His ministry. He would stop right in the middle of the pressure of it all, spend some time praying, and get back to work with the fire of God in His eyes.

Apparently they got to hear Him sometimes when He prayed. Just imagine what they must have overheard. Not only did they get to hear the words spoken in the prayer, but they also picked up on the intimacy between the Father and the Son.

Like the disciples then, we need Jesus to teach us to pray. We know what it's like to be disappointed with what happens—or doesn't happen

—when we pray. We long to know how to talk to God so that it makes a difference.

Do you get frustrated when you pray and nothing seems to come of it? Over time does the frustration fosters a kind of unhealthy distance between you and God? The more we pray without hearing from God, the wider the gap. After a while the silence of God confuses us, and then it begins to worry us. It make us want to throw up our hands and quit trying.

Like a wise old Christian said, we can take it when God says "Yes" to our prayers. And, even though we don't like it, we can handle it when God says "No." But what drives most of us up the wall is when God doesn't say anything. When He is silent, we draw the conclusion that He must be absent. Few things in our lives trouble us like the feeling that God has left us.

Like I said, the disciples asked Jesus to teach them to pray. So He did. In His instructions about prayer He answers many of the confusing questions about talking to God that worry us. With some of our troublesome questions answered, the distance between us and the Father can be diminished when we pray.

Jesus gives us a model for praying (vv. 2-4). Sometimes we refer to it as the Lord's Prayer, and we might even recite it in worship services. But Jesus didn't intend for us only to recite it. He wants us to use it as a model when we pray. You might think of it as a blueprint for guiding us through our prayer time with the Father.

Once Jesus gave us his model for praying, He went on to talk about one of the primary concerns we deal with when we try to pray. It's the concern about talking to God but not hearing anything from Him in return. When we ask Him for something, and He doesn't respond, we feel the distance. And it grows wider as the silence of God continues to be His only response to our efforts in prayer. After a while, we wonder if God is even listening to us any more.

To give us a clear picture of what's actually going on when we pray, Jesus tells us a story about three friends (vv. 2-4). The story along with Jesus' remarks after it gives us assurance that God hears us when we pray. Although God may respond to our prayer by being silent, we don't need to confuse the silence of God with the absence of God.

Sometimes God can be almost impossible to figure out. As God said himself, his ways aren't our ways and our thoughts are not his thoughts (Isaiah 55:8). Because of the difficulty we get lost in the confusion and start to draw our own conclusions about what God is or is not doing in response to our prayer.

The story of the three friends helps us to understand that God listens to us. To help us follow the story line, let's contemporize it some and give names to each of the three friends: Fred, Harry, and Bill.

At the beginning of the story, we find Fred in his house at about midnight sipping tea and watching television in the den. He was dozing a little because it's past time to go to bed. That's why he jumped like a rabbit when he heard the doorbell ring. Trying to wipe the sleep out of his eyes, he stumbled to the front door and fumbled with the lock until he could get it open.

There he saw Harry, standing with his traveling bag in his hand and a hungry look on his face. Fred blurts out with characteristic bravado, "Fred, I'm glad I found you at home! I was passing through on my way to a sales meeting tomorrow and thought about you. I figured that if anybody would have something to eat or a spare bed for a good night's rest, it would be you. "I'm starved." With that, Harry pushed himself past Bill and walked into the den.

In the day of Jesus, travelers didn't have the luxury of hotels and all-night cafes. They had to depend on the hospitality of the local folks for a good meal or a place to sleep for the night. As you might imagine, a town got a reputation for being kind or cruel to travelers and other strangers. A respectable town had a reputation for being hospitable, and every town wanted to be known as respectable.

Think about it. If the rule of hospitality applied to strangers, it certainly applied to unexpected friends like Harry. Fred must have been of that opinion because he got busy trying to rustle up something for his old friend to eat. That's when he made a startling discovery: his cupboard was bare. He didn't have any food in his house.

What would you do if you had an empty refrigerator and a hungry friend? You would probably do exactly what Fred did. He welcomed Harry into his den, ushered him to his personal recliner, gave him some tea, and offered him the television remote control. Then he excused himself by saying, "Harry, make yourself comfortable. I'll be right back."

Out the back door Fred went as fast as he could. He worked his way through the gate in the fence between his property and Bill's place. Fred always considered Bill a good friend. They went to college together. Fred had landed Bill a good job with a growing company in town. Their wives were like sisters, and their children played together all the time.

Rushing to Bill's back door, Fred began to tap gently but firmly on the glass window. Persistently he kept tapping until Bill finally came to the door, wiping the sleep from his eyes as he turned on the patio light.

You've heard the expression: a friend in need is a friend indeed. Fred depended on his friendship with Bill to solicit some food for his other friend Harry.

Bill cracked open the door only slightly. With a note of slight surprise and subtle indignation in his voice, Bill asked Fred, "What in the world are you doing here at this hour? It's after midnight."

Fred tried to explain, "Sorry to wake you, Bill, but I have a big problem. You see, Harry just showed up at my door and he is as hungry as a horse. I don't have anything to eat, but I know you've got some bread. I came to see if you could give me some of it for Harry."

Bill whispered through the crack in the door, "Fred, you know I'd love to help you but I can't, at least right now. The kids have just gone to sleep."

In those days, the term "family room" would have meant something entirely different than it does today. The house had a family room alright. In fact, that's the only room in the whole house. The family lived together in one room. More to the point they slept together in the same room. Bill's children had settled in on their mats sound asleep. And Bill intended them to stay that way until morning.

"Sorry, I can't help you," Bill said to Fred before he gently but firmly shut the door in his face.

Fred probably stood there, puzzled and confused. Perhaps he began to ponder what it meant for Bill to call him a friend. What kind of friend would leave you high and dry at the very time when you need him? After all, Fred probably thought to himself, it wasn't like he was selfish in asking Bill for bread. No, the bread was for Harry. But it didn't matter; Bill turned Fred down. Fred must have thought Bill had abandoned him.

Jesus reflected a sense of humor in the way he ended the story. He speculated that Bill might not have given Fred a loaf of bread because of their friendship. However, if Fred kept on rapping on Bill's back door, he eventually would have given Fred all the bread he wanted just to get him to go away!

Do you sometimes think that God acts a lot like Bill? You know He's supposed to be your friend and you also know He's the only one who's got what you need. But he shuts the door in your face when you ask Him for help. Does it frustrate you when He seems to act that way, especially when you are asking for something not for yourself, but for someone you care about?

Some people reason that the best way to get what we need from God is to badger Him. If we pester Him enough, we argue, He will cave in and give us what we need. We even use Bible passages like Luke 18:1-8 to build our case. According to that passage, a widow kept on nagging a judge until he eventually wore down and granted her request. We reason that the only way we can get God to answer us is to wear Him down.

When God doesn't answer our prayer, we get confused and frustrated. In turn, the gap between us and God grows wider. Factor in the troublesome, haunting notion that God might be absent and the situation can get completely overwhelming. It can get to the point that may decide to give up on prayer all together.

Jesus diminishes the distance created by God's silence by assuring us that, indeed, God hears us. He encourages us to keep on asking, seeking, and knocking. At the right time, God will answer. In the silence, we can rest in that assurance (vv. 9-10).

No, God's not like Bill. Jesus assures us that we can trust the Father to hear us when we pray. In His time and in His way, He will answer us. We can count on it. Just because He's silent, it doesn't mean He's absent.

I know what you're thinking. You've tried that approach to prayer and so far it hasn't worked. I understand your confusion. Frankly, I don't always understand why God has not responded to my prayer as I think he should. But you and I can trust Him to be listening. Jesus encourages us to put or faith in God to work by continuing to talk to Him about what we need.

God hears us. In addition, He gives us what is best for us (vv. 11-13). Jesus made that point by asking a most curious question: What self-respecting parent would give his or her children something that would hurt them when they asked for something that would help them?

Think about it. Suppose your son or grandson asked for a piece of bread. Would you give him a hand grenade? What if your daughter asked you for a Bible? Would you give her a bag of cocaine? Absolutely not!

Neither will God give something that will hurt us when we need something that will help us. That's why He promises to give us his very best gift: the Holy Spirit.

Perhaps, though, you had another gift in mind. You may have already decided on the best gift that God could give you. And what you had in mind was something a little more tangible.

Why is the Holy Spirit the best gift God offers to us? God showed me the answer to that question through my children. My wife and I have three sons. When our oldest son was born and we brought him home from the hospital, we assumed that he would be just fine since he was such a healthy baby. We noticed that something was wrong with him, however, not long after we put him down for a nap. He slept only a couple of hours. Then he woke up screaming for food. After we fed him, he went back to sleep—but only for a couple of hours, and the process would repeat itself. The day turned into a week and into two weeks before we finally decided to take him to the doctor. Certainly, we reasoned, something must be dreadfully wrong with our son.

There we were at the doctor's office, confused and worried. We assumed that we would get some medicine to help our baby—and us—to sleep all night. What the doctor gave us, however, was good advice. At the time, though, it didn't sound so good. In fact, we began to wonder if the doctor was nothing more than a quack.

Our doctor advised us to feed our baby well and make sure he had on a clean, dry diaper each night before we put him to bed. Then he advised us to put him to bed and leave him alone until the next morning. In time the baby would adjust to the new schedule and sleep all night.

I went to the doctor looking for medicine because I thought that's what I needed for my son. What the doctor gave me was better than medicine, even though at the time I didn't think so. Medicine would have been good, but what the doctor gave turned out to be best.

My sons have taught me something else. When they got sick in the night or they were paralyzed with fear because of a nightmare, a teddy bear or an action figure couldn't comfort them. They felt better only when somebody who loved them got into their bed with them and held them close. Having teddy bears might be good. But being there yourself is best.

The best gift God could ever give us is not necessarily when he gives us the things we think we need. No, the best gift is when he comes himself. He's a God who listens and gives. Jesus told us so. You can count on Him.

A Sermon about Marriage Problems:
How Marriage Works
(Ephesians 5:21-33)

Marriages go through tough times. Some people say the toughest times take place during the first two years. Others say it's the seventh year of marriage. Still others say it's much later.

It's probably a little bit of all of the above. Every stage in marriage presents its own challenges to a couple. Adjusting can be difficult no matter how long a man and woman have lived together "in the holy estate of matrimony."

Adjustment usually involves changes in the way couples relate to their families, handle their money, and communicate with each other. Husbands and wives have to learn to adjust in theses areas from the beginning, and they keep on making adjustments until death separates them.

A newly wed couple has to work together to carve out a lasting relationship with each other. At the same time, they may have to help other folks in their families to accept the fact that they have cut the apron strings. Stressful and troublesome, it's only one of many more family adjustments to come.

Money gets its meddlesome paws in the middle of matrimonial bliss early on in a marriage too. Organizing the household budget and putting it into practice takes loads of time and energy. New couples have to be patient with each other as they come to terms with how the bills will be paid and how the extra money—if any exists—will be spent. Again, that's just the beginning of the many hurdles they will have to encounter when it comes to their money.

Communication challenges have to be addressed early on in a marriage, too. When either the husband or the wife begins to think that the dating days have come to an end, problems can begin. Instead of planning a nice, quiet dinner with his sweetheart, a husband can easily slip into a pattern of thinking that Friday nights can be spent better in front of the television. Likewise, instead of thinking about ways to impress the man of her dreams, a wife can settle into a routine that leaves little doubt that she has lost interest in making good impressions on him.

Bad habits picked up at the beginning of a marriage can torment a couple for a long time. Over the years the problems in a marriage can fester. Hope can give way to resignation as the couple lives like they have decided to tolerate each other through the misery they created for themselves.

Paul offers us a way of doing marriage that can put a couple back on solid ground. His admonitions about husbands and wives can help a couple retrieve a sense of fulfillment in their relationship. If they ask God to help them put Ephesians 5 into practice, they can begin to build a strong and lasting marriage. Even a marriage in serious trouble can get back on solid ground if the couple would be willing to put the passage seriously into practice.

Ephesians 5:22-33 follows Paul's instruction about believers practicing mutual submission in their relationships with one another (v. 21). For couples, his instruction has some definite implication for their marriage.

In a marriage relationship, a wife has a definite responsibility (vv. 22-24). According to Paul, she submits to her husband. That makes perfectly good sense in a relationship in which mutual submission is the standard. When left to stand alone without such a standard, the notion of a submissive wife doesn't fare too well in the marketplace of ideas.

For years now, feminism in America has devoted significant attention to the ways women are treated in society. In fact, the scholarly and popular discussion on the subject has flourished in every conceivable direction since the 1960s. Much of it seems to have one common theme: women must be treated equally with men. For feminists, Paul's notion of a woman submitting herself to a man is at least unthinkable and at worst repugnant.

Feminists aren't the only people who protest. Many battered women oppose a female submitting to a male. After all, they insist, that idea kept too many women in abusive and dangerous relationships for too long. Women who have the impression that their husbands see them as property wouldn't advocate Paul's precept either. How fulfilling would it be for a woman to live out her days as some man's doormat?

The precept gets beaten up as well because of the husbands who abuse the idea of submission. Such a husband sees his easy chair as his throne, his television remote control as his scepter, and his house as his personal castle. His wife serves him in his little kingdom like a slave serves a master. When she gets out of hand by having an idea of her own or a dream that he didn't approve, he lifts the submission standard right out of the Bible and forces her to yield to his authority. Every time that happens, she erases a little more of who she is in Christ in order to become a little more what her selfish husband expects her to be.

No wonder some people detest the idea of a wife submitting to her husband! Its misuse has led to a misunderstanding of the precept that, in turn, has prompted an awful backlash. And so it should. Any Christian should oppose the misuse of this or any other standard of Scripture for the purpose of manipulating people. Rest assured that Paul's principle can be put into practice in a wholesome way so that both husband and wife can benefit and God can be glorified in the marriage.

Jesus didn't exhibit a male chauvinist attitude. Quite the contrary, with what He said and what He did, He emancipated women. The culture of His day viewed women as little more than a man's property, but He saw women as human beings worthy of being redeemed. That's why some of his best friends were women. That's why he spent time talking to a woman at Jacob's well and to another who had been caught in the act of adultery. That's why he healed a woman with a twelve-year-old disease and used a widow as an example of giving that pleases the Lord.

His attitude must have rubbed off on Simon Peter, the disciple that teaches us that God can use anybody. A coarse fisherman-turned-preacher, Peter wrote to Christians who were suffering at the hands of oppressors about the value of submitting to authority. In his letter, he talked about wives and how they shared equally with their husbands in the grace of life. He also urged husbands to understand that their relationships with their wives had a definite impact on their personal prayer lives (1Peter 3:7).

The idea of a wife submitting to her husband, then, can't be all that bad. Perhaps it makes more sense when you consider it in light of the husband's responsibility in the marriage. Again, under the broad category of mutual submission, Paul gives some clear instruction on how a man submits himself to his wife (vv. 25-32). Read his instructions and you will probably notice that Paul goes into considerable detail on the matter. Obviously, Paul knows that a husband needs to shoulder his responsibility for the marriage if he intends for his relationship with his wife to grow toward maturity.

Helping people grasp difficult concepts sometimes requires the use of analogies, little stories that help us understand big truths. That definition doesn't quite fit Paul's instruction to husbands because the analogy turns out to be a bigger story than the big story. Paul tries to tell husbands how to submit to their wives by using Jesus and the church as the analogy. Jesus gave up everything for the church, even to the point of laying down His life on the cross. You couldn't ask for a better, more perfect analogy of a husband's relationship with his wife. Just like Jesus gave up everything for His church, a husband gives up everything for his wife.

Think about it for a minute. Jesus gave up *everything* for the church. He gave up Heaven with the Father to be born in a manger in Bethlehem. He gave up His freedom of movement and accepted the limitations of being every bit a human. He gave up His right to an easy life by taking twelve rag-tag men on as disciples and marching up and down Palestine preaching the gospel of the Kingdom of God. He gave up self-glorification by submitting to the kiss of a traitor who would hand him over to a mock court who would carry out a farce of a trial so they could kill him. He gave up His safety by submitting to the cross, dying there, and being buried in a borrowed grave from which He arose on that first Easter Sunday.

Was it in His best interest to give up so much? No, but it was in the best interest of His bride. That's why He did it. He died, because He loved the church to the point that she mattered more to Him than His own life. Like Jesus gave Himself up for His church, a husband gives himself up for his wife.

As an act of loving submission, a husband thinks about his wife's well being before he considers his own. He looks out for her best interests, not his. To extend the image of 1 Peter 3:4, a husband devotes himself to finding ways to help his wife nurture the inner person of her heart.

What effect would such unselfishness have on a man's wife? She would appreciate him. Moreover, she would trust him. Furthermore, she would entrust herself to him, knowing that he would always try to do what's in her best interest. In other words, she would submit to him because she has faith in him to lead the family in a direction that would be most beneficial for her as well as their children.

Besides the example of Jesus, Paul goes on to say, a husband has to consider another compelling argument. When a man and a woman become husband and wife, the two become one flesh (Genesis 2:24). Therefore, Paul argues, when a man takes care of his wife, he is actually taking care of himself. Conversely, if he ignores his wife, it's as if he has ignored himself. What self-respecting man would do something so foolish? If he is convinced that his wife and he are one unit, then it must certainly make a difference in the way he treats her.

With the powerful examples of Jesus and the church, Paul nails down the obligation of a husband to his wife. By bringing up the reality that marriage merges two people into one, he leaves little room for a man to back out of his commitment to submit himself to his wife.

There you have it, the precept of mutual submission as Paul applies it to marriage. Perhaps you're thinking: It looks good on paper, but does it really make a difference in a real-life marriage? How can a husband and wife put the precept to work in their relationship?

Meet Tom and Brenda, a couple trying to work through a troubled marriage. It's been on the rocks for a while now, and neither of them knows what to do to get it back on solid ground. But they both want the marriage to work. How can the principle of mutual submission help them to recover their marriage?

For starters, Tom will do well to take responsibility for leading the couple toward health. Why Tom? Because he is the head of his house. That's not a crown he wears, but a duty he fulfills. He must accept his responsibility for letting his marriage get out of hand, and he must also take the initiative to set it back on track. That's an act of submission to his wife's best interests.

Then Tom has the obligation to seek help if necessary so he and Brenda can restore the lines of communication. Through the conduit of communication will flow the energizing current that can revitalize their relationship.

Also, Tom may have to do other things to demonstrate to Brenda he has given up himself for her. It may take time, a long time. It may require him to be patient with Brenda. Depending on the circumstances, she may need plenty of time to be persuaded that his intentions are authentic. In time, she will begin to see that he means business.

As you can tell, Tom can't do it by himself. The Lord must help him. Brenda needs the Lord's help too. Through the struggle of trusting each other and restoring the relationship, they will have to rely on Him to give them what they can't give themselves.

Of course, Brenda will have to make up her mind that Tom's intentions are pure. If she does, she can begin to take the risk of trusting him. Over time, trust will turn into respect. Eventually, respect will turn into a willingness to put her life in his hands with full assurance that Tom has her best interest in his heart. At the same time she will have to take the initiative for her role in both the problems and the solutions in their marriage.

Across the years Tom and Brenda can develop a positive and rewarding cycle of growth in their relationship. The more she sees him lead with her best interest in his heart, the more she will respect him and submit to his leadership. The more Tom sees that Brenda respects him, the more he will want to give himself up for her. And the cycle continues.

Try it for yourself. You'll agree that the Lord's way of doing marriage is indeed the best way. But don't try it by yourself. The most important step you can take is toward Jesus, surrendering your life and your marriage to Him.

A Sermon about Forgiveness:
The Power of Forgiveness
(Genesis 50:19-21)

Let me introduce you to Joseph, Jacob's son, Isaac's grandson, Abraham's great-grandson. And through his story, let me introduce you to the miracle of forgiving.

Joseph's father loved him deeply, and he even made him a multicolored coat to show it. Joseph knew how special his coat was and he wore it proudly, much to the resentment of his eleven brothers.

What the coat didn't do to make Joseph's brothers hate him, the dreams he kept having certainly did. Joseph dreamed about a day when he would rule over his brothers, and he told them about his dreams so much that they thought they couldn't stomach him any more.

One day, their anger and resentment got the best of them. They tied Joseph up like an animal and sold him as a slave. He was only seventeen when it happened.

Joseph didn't see his brothers again for about twenty years. His last recollection of his brothers must have been awful. First they threw him into a pit and plotted his murder while they snacked on the food he probably brought them from home. He heard every word of their conversation. He knew what they wanted to do to him, and he couldn't do one thing about it.

They saw some Ishmaelite traders passing through and changed their mind about killing him. Instead they sold him. Joseph heard them cut the deal with the nomads before they handed him over. How he must have begged his brothers not to do what they had already done, but his pleading went unheard.

Through tear-filled eyes he gazed at his brothers for the last time. There they were, laughing and celebrating and plotting a lie to tell Jacob about what happened to his favorite son. That cruel image got smaller and smaller as Joseph's slave owners took him farther away. In time, the image faded and disappeared. It would be the last image Joseph could remember about his brothers, and it would last him for about two decades.

Joseph wound up in Egypt, and because of some God-given administrative abilities, Potiphar soon put the young man in charge of his household affairs. Speaking of affairs, Potiphar's wife wanted to have one with Joseph, but he resisted because of the values that came from his walk with God. A woman scorned, she got even and hatched a lie that would top the one his brothers told to Jacob, and Joseph got thrown into prison. There his administrative abilities were put to work again, which may have made his situation a little more tolerable. But he was still in prison, and for something he didn't do.

To make matters worse, Joseph helped a fellow prisoner by interpreting a dream for him. In turn, he promised Joseph that he would seek the release of his dream-interpreting friend once he himself got out of jail. He got out of jail alright, but he forgot about Joseph, who had to languish in prison for two more years before getting released.

Good things started to happen for Joseph, though, on the day Pharaoh called for him out of the prison to interpret a couple of his royal dreams. The dreams had to do with what God was about to do. Seven years of abundance for the land of Egypt, Joseph told Pharaoh, would be followed by seven years of famine. Being an administrator at heart, he recommended that Pharaoh put someone in charge of collecting the food during the good days so the people would have something to eat during the bad days. Impressed with how God lived in Joseph's life, Pharaoh put him in charge of the entire operation. A fairly formidable assignment for a thirty-year-old man, don't you think?

Seven good years passed, just like Joseph said, and the seven years of famine followed. Everyone ran out of food and ran to Egypt because they heard they could get food there.

One day Joseph's brothers showed up on his doorstep, oblivious to the fact that the brother they had sold into slavery stood at the door. But Joseph recognized them. He went off to a place by himself and wept like a baby after he laid his eyes on them. After all, he hadn't seen them for twenty years or so, and the photograph he carried in his head wasn't exactly what you would call a Kodak moment.

He didn't hurt them, and he had no intention of getting revenge. Granted, he took them down a road of confusion, fear, and misery before he revealed himself to them. He did not want to hurt them, but wanted to make sure he could see his father again. To make a long story short, not only did he get to see Jacob again, but he got to relocate his entire family to the land of Goshen, some of the best farm land in Egypt. He took good care of his brothers and their families. Moreover, he took care of his father until the old man died.

They say that revenge is a dish best served up cold. That thought probably crossed Joseph's brothers' minds after their father's funeral. Now they were at the mercy of Joseph, whose wrath, they thought, would not be delayed any longer. Payback was coming; they were certain of it. To keep Joseph from revenge, they hatched another lie this time a whopper, about Jacob telling them to tell Joseph not to hurt them. Once they crafted the lie, they served it up to Joseph and waited to see what he would do with it.

They were scared, and they should have been. At least forty years had passed since that miserable day in the desert with the Ishmaelite traders. They had denied Joseph of many good years with their father. They forced him to learn how to survive in a far-away place, they contributed to his imprisonment, they were responsible for his loneliness, and they deserved to pay for what they did to him.

Joseph didn't have revenge on his mind, though, and he tried to console them by telling them something that has echoed across the centuries. What he said could be considered profound because it reflected his heart, a heart that carried no bitterness at all for his brothers. Can you imagine such a feat, to be able to forgive people who had led to memories of cruelty and years of pain?

With what Joseph said to his brothers, he reminds us that we can get bitter because of injustices that have been committed against us. Or we can get better. To get bitter, all we have to do is hold on to the hurt and let it grow and take deep roots in our soul. To get better, however, we have to forgive. That's what Joseph did, and you can see the evidence of it in what he said to his brothers.

First he told them, "You meant it for evil" (v. 20). He didn't sugar-coat what his brothers had done, neither did he sweep it under the rug. What his brothers had done to him could only be described as something evil. What made their actions even more repulsive was the fact that they acted with intense malice. They wanted to hurt him. In fact, they initially wanted to kill him, but they eventually settled for sending him into permanent exile. There's no way around it; they meant evil against Joseph.

We never cease to be amazed at how cruel one person can be toward another. After a while you think you've heard it all. Then you hear another report of something awful that happened to a person at the hands of another. What makes such reports even more difficult to bear is the fact that it's obvious that the perpetrator acted with evil, cruel intent. You can overlook a guy who hurts you accidentally. How do you respond when he hurts you on purpose?

Probably the most difficult reports involve injustices done to innocent victims by people who were supposed to protect them. It's tough to hear about adults hurting children, parents being cruel to their sons and daughters, aunts and uncles causing pain to their nieces and nephews, and brothers and sisters acting with intentional injustice toward their siblings. These kinds of things should never happen; but they do. Hard as it is to conceive, they are acts of evil performed by people who intend to inflict pain.

The victims of such meanness constantly bear in their hearts the deep scars of mistreatment and injustice. Perhaps you have been victimized at the hands of someone who treated you cruelly. You bear the scars too, and they won't just go away. You know first hand what it's like for Joseph to tell his brothers, "You meant evil against me."

Like Joseph, you have only two choices when it comes to responding to the evil done to you. You can get bitter, or you can get better. Getting bitter is easy. Just do nothing. Your heart will take it from there.

The journey from pain to bitterness takes less time than people think. Before you know it, bitterness has consumed you like a cancer, sapping all the life out of you. Once that happens, you will be the ultimate victim. You've already been crippled by a mean act of cruel injustice. Because of the bitterness you harbor in your aching heart, over what happened, you will waste away to nothing as the life God intended you to enjoy smolders into ashes.

When I talk about your bitterness, you might get the impression that I'm being flippant about your misery. I'm not. I'm only trying to be realistic. Sometimes people who harbor bitterness give themselves permission to nurture it, like a favorite houseplant. Over time it becomes such a vital part of them that they are lost without it.

You can't hold on to bitterness without it consuming you. You've got to find a better way.

You have to forgive. There's no other way to get better. No other way.

Encouraging you to forgive puts a knot in my stomach because I can only begin to imagine how hard it must be for you to take that option. But dying a bitter person is harder and more miserable than going down the long road of forgiveness.

Joseph forgave his brothers. That's the only reason he could ever come to the place in which he could tell them, "God meant it for good" (v. 20). He could see God's hand at work throughout the ordeals that he faced.

You might be confused by Joseph's statement about God. Did he mean that God planned for his life to be so miserable for so long? Had God approved of the evil plot to have Joseph forcibly removed from his home and family? Can God do something that cruel to someone as innocent as a seventeen-year-old boy?

God didn't plan the ordeals Joseph faced, but He didn't waste them either. He made sure they wouldn't be lost on Joseph. In fact, every step of the way, God walked with his young follower. From the time his brothers sold him until the day he saw his brothers face to face after decades had passed, God has been there with him. He healed Joseph's broken heart, gave him opportunities in Egypt, and gave him a family of his own. Joseph's two sons, Manasseh and Ephraim, got their names from their father who knew God's presence. Manasseh reminded Joseph that God helped him forget the past. Ephraim reminded him that God made him fruitful in the new world in which he had been placed. God had made his life good. He hadn't wasted anything, even Joseph's mistreatment.

God did something else for Joseph. The Lord turned his affliction into fulfillment. Joseph told his brothers that he bore no resentment toward them because of what God had done in his life as a result of their evil. God had placed him in charge of feeding thousands of people every day. What a fulfillment it must have been for him to wake up every day of his life and know that his work made it possible for people everywhere to stay alive.

Perhaps now you understand why Joseph harbored no bitterness. And you can praise the Lord for His great work of turning Joseph's lemons into lemonade.

Through the centuries God has done the same thing in the lives of lots of people who have given their pain to Him. No, God didn't have a hand in the injustices performed at the hands of people who acted with evil intent. But, yes, He can do something with what happened so the ordeals won't be wasted. He can make it possible for something good to come out of the torment.

Would you be willing to let Him do in you what He did in Joseph? Of course, it means forgiving and starting over. While that may be a hard step to take, remember that you won't be taking it alone. And if you are a Christian, remember how He forgave you. Now it's your turn.

So you see, forgiving begins with knowing Jesus personally. Without Him we can't expect to do much more than grow bitter. But with Him working in us, we can get better because He can help us to forgive.

Who knows, perhaps the day will come when you can say to the person who hurt you so deeply, "You meant it for evil, but God meant it for good." You could actually be able to bury the bitterness and experience the releasing joy of forgiveness.

Who knows, you might find yourself in work more fulfilling than you could have ever imagined. God could place you in a position to turn the pain into productive service for Him.

Who knows.

A Sermon about Parenting Struggles:
Blessing the Children
(Mark 10:13-16)

You might say Jesus was a dead man walking when he traveled along the road from Capernaum to Jerusalem with His disciples. He had the cross in view, and nothing would stop him from the divine appointment with death on our behalf.

Needless to say, the air was tense as He and his disciples made their way down the road together. The disciples had not been playing off the same sheet of music as Jesus. As He walked, He thought about what He needed to say to the disciples so they would be ready when the time came for Him to leave them. As they walked, however, they thought about which one of them would be Jesus' right hand man when He came into his Kingdom.

Because they thought in different directions, you could understand why they responded so differently to the children who gathered on the side of the road, waiting for Jesus to pass. To the disciples, the children got in the way of the Master, who didn't need the racket that kids could make. To Jesus, the children meant something completely different. They were people who mattered to Him a great deal, as the disciples would discover soon enough.

When Jesus saw the disciples tried to shoo away the children, He became indignant. The word "indignant" isn't normally associated with Jesus. It's usually associated with the religious leaders Jesus confronted. After He would put them in their place, so to speak, they would become indignant. Sometimes His disciples would even be indignant toward Him, especially after He corrected their thinking or behavior.

But we hardly ever think about Jesus becoming indignant. Indignation and Jesus usually don't wind up in the same sentence. Later on the disciples would see Jesus get hot under the collar about the money changers in the Temple. He showed his righteous indignation with a few well-chosen words about God's house being a place of prayer, a whip, and an overturned table or two.

Jesus got mad, really mad, when He saw the disciples dismiss the children with a coarse rebuke. In His indignation, He told the disciples to bring the children to Him. On the face of it, His command doesn't sound that stirring. After all, the words of His instructions lie there on the page of your Bible, just looking at you. They sting only when you lift them from the page and put them in the mouth of a Master who had just gotten mad.

One way to hear how Jesus might have uttered those words is to remember the day you took your mother's good spoons to the back yard. As you recall, you got the good spoons from the cabinet because somehow you could dig deeper into the dirt. At your age, you didn't have a clue as to why your mom called them good spoons. As far as you were concerned, they were good only to the extent that they helped you dig deeper and faster. That made them valuable to the successful completion of your excavation project near the oak tree. Using the good spoons would get you to China much quicker, which was, by the way, the goal of your quest.

You can almost see it now, can't you. Your mother's shadow lengthens over your hunched form as she gets closer and closer to you. The shadow gets your attention first. Then you turn and you see her face. Her angry stare and pursed lips give you a clue that good spoons mean something more than you had previously considered. Then she says the words you have never forgotten, "Bring those spoons here to me right now." And just for good measure, she calls you by the full name listed on your birth certificate, which, as you had already learned, means big trouble.

When Jesus instructed the disciples to bring the children to Him, He had a bite in His voice too. They knew they were in big trouble. Reacting to the sting of his words, they quickly obeyed Him and brought the children to Him. Probably a little perplexed, they listened closely to what He would say next and they watched intently to see what He would do next.

If you are a parent you should listen and watch too. What Jesus said and did in the presence of the children can change your life and the lives of your children. If you wear the wounds of bad parenting, pay close attention as well. Jesus does something that will make a lasting impression on you.

In the presence of the children, Jesus taught the disciples about the Kingdom. In particular, He said that if you wanted to enter the Kingdom, you would have to come like a little child. Imagine that, Jesus used a child as a model for Kingdom citizenry.

What does that statement mean to you? For me, it means that Kingdom citizens can look to children to identify some important character traits that please the Lord. For instance, children are helpless. When they are babies, they can't do a thing for themselves. As they grow older, they become a little more capable of doing some things for themselves, but they still need a lot of help. For years, they need the help of parents to provide them food, a home, and transportation.

If you watch children for long, you notice that they grow comfortable with their helplessness. It's a fact of their lives, so they accept it, respecting the people who care for them. As they blow out more and more candles on their birthday cakes, though, they yearn to be more and more independent. All too quickly they become adolescents and then adults who think they can do things for themselves. They don't need anybody. In growing older, they swap childlike innocence with adult-like cynicism.

Kingdom citizens do well to be childlike when it comes to helplessness. In our adult Christianity, we tend to think we don't need anything from anybody, even the Lord. For instance, one particularly cynical believer admitted her discomfort with the Lord's Prayer. In particular, she confessed, she didn't like the part that started with, "Give us . . . ." As far as she was concerned, she didn't need God to give her anything. She could get it herself.

It's sad when we as Christians lose our childlike helplessness. When we do, we miss the adventure that comes in trusting the Lord. Children learn to trust people to fill in the helpless places in their little lives. They don't worry or fret much about what they need. They simply trust someone to tend to them. They don't even have to think very much about what's best for them. Someone else will carry that burden for them. All they do in their simple world of trust is ask for what they want. They trust others to take it from there.

Perhaps the loss of a sense of helplessness has contributed to more than a few believers losing their passion for the Lord. You've probably noticed that children are motivated by what they get to do. Serving the people they love is something they get to do. They can hardly wait to take out the trash for Papa, wash dishes for Aunt Marie, or help their teacher by cleaning the erasers.

Adult Christians grow cynical as we lose that childlike eagerness to serve Jesus. We serve him not because we *get* to do it, but because we've *got* to do it. We go to church because we've got to. We give because we've got to. When was the last time you served Jesus with the eagerness of a child?

After Jesus said that Kingdom citizens could take a lesson about living from children, He did something that you don't want to overlook. He blessed the children.

How do you think Jesus blessed the children? Do you think he gestured in a priestly sort of way? Do you think he said some ritual words to convey a blessing on them?

I picture Jesus doing something far more personal and a great deal more meaningful. But in order to understand it, we need some orientation to the value of a blessing in the family. For that information we look to God's Word.

Genesis 49 recorded the value of a blessing in Jacob's family. Jacob, old and tired and close to dying, called for his sons so he could bless them. If you read the story, you notice that he gave a unique blessing to each of his sons. He didn't have a blessing for Reuben, the oldest son, because of something shameful the boy had done years earlier. But the other sons got a blessing, and each blessing was appropriate to the person.

In my opinion, Jacob isn't much of a role model for parenting, but the way he blessed his sons is worth our consideration. Today, children still seek a blessing from their parents. In other words, they still need their parents to tell them that they matter in the world, that they are special. With a blessing a child has the approval needed to make a difference in the world. Without a blessing a child lives with something important missing, a piece of the puzzle that's still not in place.

Suppose you got a blessing from your parents. It might not mean you are perfectly suited to take on life. However, it certainly means that down deep inside you know that someone special to you approves of you, thinks you matter, and considers you to be a valuable human being.

What if you didn't get a blessing from your parents? Many people didn't. And many children get passed over for a blessing today. Too often, such people get up in the morning, put their feet on the floor, and walk out the door every day in search of it. They excel in order to feel approved by someone, or they act out in destructive ways in order to send a message that they still haven't found the blessing they've been looking for all their lives.

Now go back with me to Jesus on the road to Jerusalem blessing the children. One at a time, he put the children in his lap. He looked at them right in their eyes, and he told them how much they mattered to the Father. Perhaps He even told them that the Father had worked overtime on them, making them so impressive and promising. Then He hugged them and sent them on their way.

As each child left His lap, don't you think they skipped away happy? Someone important told them they mattered to the Father. Who knows what kind of impact it made on those little fellows. More than a few of them may have been named among some of the leaders of the church in the generation that would follow. Rest assured that Jesus' blessing made a significant impression on them.

His blessing can make the same kind of impression on you. If you don't think you ever received a blessing from your parents, then you can look to Jesus to bless you. If you have received Him as you Savior and Lord, you already know the peace in your heart that comes from being one of His children. Now think of yourself crawling up into the lap of the Savior and hearing Him say to you the words that will fill your heart with His blessing. He thinks you are important enough to die for you so you could receive the blessing that comes with the smile of God.

Perhaps you consider yourself to have received a blessing from your parents. Even so, don't overlook the blessing of Jesus in your life. As important as it is to have the blessing of your parents, it's even more vital for you to allow the blessing of Jesus to penetrate your soul.

If you are a parent, think about the blessing you need to give your children. They desperately need your approval; they await your blessing. Bless them by telling them in word and deed that they matter to you. Talk with them about the way that God wants to make a difference through their lives. Let them know they are special because they are your children.

Don't make them jump through hoops in order to get your blessing. When parents do that, they have a tendency to move the hoop once the children start trying to jump through it. Real blessings don't require hoops.

One more thing. Act like a child yourself. Not childish, mind you, but childlike. Jesus will be pleased.

A Sermon about Anger: The Destructive Force of Anger (Genesis 37)

The story told in Genesis about Abraham only gets better by the time we turn the page to Isaac, his son. Then along came Jacob, his grandson. The beginning of his story includes deceit that victimized Esau, his brother. By the time we are introduced to Jacob's sons, twelve of them in all, the story includes something else: anger. In fact the story shows what anger can do to individuals as well as to entire families.

Jacob has taken two wives and has named all of his sons by the time we pick up the story in Genesis 37. Like so many of the people in his day living in that part of the world, Jacob owned sheep and assigned his sons the chores of taking care of them. Sheep always need fresh grass, so the boys had to lead the flock to new pasture ground, and they had to work together whether they liked it or not.

The brothers didn't seem to like Joseph at all, and with a modicum of good reason. Jacob had made it painfully obvious that Joseph was his favorite son. It didn't take a rocket scientist to figure out that Joseph was the apple of his daddy's eye. All Joseph had to do was put on the multicolored coat Jacob had made for him. The coat symbolized Jacob's favoritism and the brothers' resentment of Joseph.

Joseph added his own fuel to the fire of sibling jealousy. He wore the coat proudly in front of his brothers and talked about the dreams he had. One dream had Joseph's sheaf of wheat towering above the sheaves of his brothers. In turn, their sheaves bowed down in humble servitude. When he told them that dream, they turned green with envy. As you know, envy fuels the fire of anger quite well.

Then Joseph told about another dream. This dream placed Joseph in authority over the sun, the moon, and—you guessed it—eleven stars. His brothers knew what the dream meant. Joseph would exercise sovereign rule over his father, his mother, and his brothers. What do you think the brothers said under their breath as they heard Jacob's favorite son talk about being a potentate over them? Although his father didn't appreciate the dream either, he tended to take it all in stride. Not so with the brothers, whose heated jealousy continued to bring their anger to a boil.

As the plot thickens in the story of the brothers' anger, the scene shifts to a placed called Dothan. It's a place that you and I might forget about, but Joseph would never forget it. What happened to him there changed his life. Near Dothan he went from being the favorite son of Jacob, his father, to being a nameless slave who belonged to an Ishmaelite trader.

His father had sent him to Dothan to check on his brothers and the flock of sheep. As the brothers saw him coming closer, they said to one another, "Here comes the dreamer" with a definite sound of disgust and resentment in their voices. As he got ever closer, they could see the many colors on the coat that branded him as favored. The closer those colors got to them, the more the brothers turned red with rage.

What made the situation worse was that the boys, all of them, were a long way from home. Daddy could not see them, fuss at them, and protect Joseph from them. In far-away Dothan, they could act out their anger without fear of recourse because of the one ingredient that had been missing before: opportunity.

A lion caged in a zoo cannot act on the rage that results from the poking taunts of mean bullies. Let the zookeeper forget to lock the cage door, though, and the situation changes, and the bullies become the prey. It happens because of one key ingredient: opportunity. Unknowingly, Joseph walked into a lion's den where restraint had been removed on the brothers' anger. Joseph wouldn't last long.

Immediately one of the brothers suggested that they kill the dreamer. Then, after thinking about it, he proposed that the brothers could tell Jacob that a wild animal got hold of his favorite son and had him for lunch— literally. Can you imagine their anger boiling over to the point it would make them want to see Joseph dead?

Reuben, the oldest brother, stepped in and snatched Joseph out of their hands. He didn't care for Joseph either, but he had not let his anger get the best of him. With a cool head, he told his brothers to throw Joseph into the nearby pit and leave him there. Secretly, he intended to sneak back to the pit later and rescue Joseph.

On the face of it, you might be compelled to say that Reuben was a hero. But think about it. Telling your brothers to get lost, that nothing should make them mad enough to hurt someone would have been a noble gesture. So would telling the other brothers that Joseph didn't deserve such torment, no matter what they thought about his dreams. How noble was it for Reuben to deliver Joseph from the hands of death only to throw him into a pit?

Either way, Joseph was left humiliated and alone, vulnerable to the meanness that anger fostered, and no one stood up for him when he needed an ally. Can people get so mad with a person that they would really do something so despicable?

Judah, another brother, acted as "nobly" as Reuben. After they threw Joseph into the pit, they let him wither in the hole without water while they enjoyed their lunch. They looked up from their food long enough to see a band of Ishmaelites coming their way. That's when Judah rose to the occasion telling his brothers that Joseph didn't need to die. After all, Judah suggested perhaps with a touch of piety, Joseph was still their brother.

Don't kill him, Judah insisted. Sell him instead. With brothers like Judah and Reuben, Joseph didn't have a chance. Ice water must have been flowing through their veins as they flagged down the Ishmaelite traders, pulled Joseph out of the pit, and bargained over the price of his hide. Eventually they settled on a price, selling him to the slave traders for twenty shekels of silver. As Joseph pleaded with them, they counted their money with smirks on their faces.

The only thing left to do now was to figure out how to break the news to Jacob. They knew he would take the news hard, so they created a whopper of a lie that would exonerate them completely. The lie would include a wild animal and their young brother. They rigged a prop that would help the old man's imagination finish the lie that they could only start to tell. Again, their blood must have run cold as they rehearsed what they would do and what they would say.

Can you believe that anger would turn brothers into cold-hearted animals who would be willing to kill a member of their family? How can anger could go so deep that it would prevent the brothers from feeling just a little bit guilty about breaking their father's heart?

Although the story may hard to believe, it really happened. And the sad truth is that it continues to happen every day in families across the country. Anger enslaves some people while victimizing others, sometimes in the same family.

The brothers of Joseph serve as examples of how anger can enslave people, turning them into persons who would act in ways that don't make sense at all. Their anger toward him apparently grew more intense as the days turned into weeks, months, and years that they lived together. Notice in the Bible story how many times the brothers got angry at Joseph. They hated Joseph because of the coat his father made for him (v. 4). Their hatred made it impossible for them to carry on a friendly conversation with him. When he told them about his dream of domination over them, they hated him for it (v. 8). Their anger over what he said fueled the fire of resentment already burning in their hearts. When he shared with them the next dream, again his sovereignty over them, it stirred them to jealousy, and they would spend time worshiping the green-eyed monster who stoked the fire in the oven of their angry hearts (v. 11).

No wonder when they finally got the opportunity, they acted. They must have been so full of rage by the time they saw him in the field at Dothan, they could not control themselves. At that very moment, their anger took complete control of them.

Anger can be a good emotion that can help us make a positive impact for Christ. Let's face it, sometimes we ought to get angry. When we see injustice, mistreatment, neglect, or manipulation of human beings, we ought to get mad about it. Jesus certainly got hot under the collar when he saw the holy people had turned the Temple into a strip mall. He had a right to be angry, to grab the whip and drive out the money changers, turning over tables in His way (John 2:13-16). Even though He showed anger, it never controlled Him. He just put it to good use.

Anger out of control, actually, takes control. That's why Paul admonished Christians not to let the sun go down on their wrath. When they let it simmer, it intensifies. The more they allow it to grow hotter, the more they give the devil an opportunity to take over their lives through their rage (Ephesians 4:26-27).

Christians should take the necessary steps to check their anger at the door of their hearts (Matthew 5:21-26). Talking to His disciples, Jesus pointed out that what's way down deep eventually comes to the surface. If anger has been planted in the soil of our hearts, we are obliged to pull it out like a bad weed. We can't afford to let it stay. Otherwise it'll take over the whole garden.

Suppose you have been victimized by anger. You probably can identify with Joseph, who suffered as an innocent seventeen-year-old boy the insurmountable torment that anger fosters. And you might have asked the question that begs to be asked from the story of Joseph and his brothers: Where was God when the brothers hurled their torment at poor Joseph? Why didn't God protect him or retaliate on his behalf?

If you look closely at the story, you see that God had showed up. No, He didn't make the mean brothers go away. That's not always His way of solving problems. He moved in the situation, however, to guide Joseph through the ordeal his brothers created for him.

For instance, God nurtured a special love in Jacob's heart for Joseph. He also gave Joseph a couple of impressive dreams. Coupled with the awareness that his father loved him, Joseph had a healthy self-concept that would enable him to endure the rigorous transition to the Egyptian culture. Because the Lord was with him, he flourished as a leader in the land of his captivity. And yes, God opened Reuben's eyes to the brothers' plan to kill Joseph. And God prompted him to do something that would keep Joseph alive.

One more thing needs to be mentioned about where God was during Joseph's torment. God went with Joseph all the way to Egypt. He held the frightened boy in His mighty arms as Joseph cried for his brothers to have mercy on him. Every day of his journey, God stayed with him. He never left Joseph. Not once.

We can trust God to be with us when anger has victimized us. We do well not to tell God how he should act on our behalf. He can be trusted to be with us, to take care of us, and to get us where He wants us to go on His terms. Like Joseph, we have a purpose for living that comes straight from the heart of God. One way or another, we can count on God to move us through the rough waters that have been stirred by the storms of anger coming our way.

Jesus reminded Kingdom citizens to expect people to respond out of anger when we try to introduce Him to them. Out of their anger, they may say awful things to and about us. If they have the chance, they might even try to do terrible things to us too. When it happens, and it will, He told us to keep in mind that we are in good company. People got angry at the prophets, too. When folks get mad at us in the same way they got steamed at Isaiah or Jeremiah, we should take it as a complement (Matthew 5:11-12).

If you are a Christian, yet anger controls you more than Jesus, why not surrender the anger to Him? Agree with Him about how wrong it is to harbor anger, and ask Him to help you live under His control alone. He will if you ask Him. He wants to liberate you from the prison your anger has built for you.

If you are a Christian who has been victimized by anger, look around you. God is at work in your life right now. Trust Him, and watch Him do His redeeming work.

A Sermon about Alcohol and Drug Abuse: A Condemning Heart (1 John 3:18-22)

Ben had been drinking for a long time when he called Joe. They had been friends for years, and now Ben needed to lean on that friendship if he intended to survive. They had grown up in the same church and had sung in the same choir. They had become Christians at about the same time. Joe went on to college and got busy with his career. Ben stayed behind and drank. They hadn't talked to each other in a long while. You could understand Joe's surprise when he heard Ben's voice on the other end of the telephone line.

After exchanging a few brief pleasantries, Ben got right to the point. After his last DUI, he had checked himself in to a treatment center. He knew he couldn't keep on going in the same direction. Eventually, it would kill him. You might say he bottomed out. Like the Prodigal Son in the hog pen, he had finally come to himself.

He wanted to put his addiction behind him, but he really didn't know how to do it. In his therapy sessions, he had heard about depending on God. When he called Joe, he wanted to ask one simple question: How can I get past all the pretense of religion and get into a relationship with the Lord that would make a difference to me now?

Ben had been a Christian for years, but he never had been taught how to walk with God. He had learned how to be a good church-goer, but not how to be a mature disciple. Being a good church attender never went deep into his soul to help him with the inner turmoil that came with the life-sapping sense of shame he lived with for as far back he could remember.

In fact, Ben drank to numb the pain of his shame and guilt. Privately he tried to drink his torment away, and publicly he tried to pretend it didn't exist. Now he wanted, or needed, someone to show him how to scrape off the veneer and get to the heart of the problem. That's where his need for God came into the picture.

Ben's problem is not a rare occurrence. People everywhere live with overwhelming doses of shame and guilt. Sometimes they try to deal with it using everything from drugs or alcohol to work or pleasure. In time they get addicted.

John had something liberating to say to people caught in the web of addiction. He said that a Christian's love for the Lord showed through truth and deed, not through meaningless words that rolled off their tongues (v. 18). According to John, you can't find pretense in truth and deed. What we think and what we do, not the empty words we utter, show how much we love Jesus.

Therein lies the problem. For some of us, getting closer to Jesus can be difficult. Sometimes it hurts so much that we can't tolerate it. We resort to a religion of words because a relationship based on truth and deed causes too much pain. For a number of Christians, the more we try to get close to the Lord, the more we feel ashamed of ourselves. Intense guilt overwhelms us. The more we try to make it go away, the longer it remains and the more frustrating and painful it gets. Self-condemnation has set in.

John must have known that some Christians would have this problem. That's why, he addressed guilt and shame in his letter to Christians who apparently struggled with some menacing half-truths they must have heard about Jesus. These half-truths had come their way by self-styled experts who believed they had the inside track on what God's Word meant. The self-perception of these experts and their spiritual superiority apparently had almost trampled the spiritual life out of honest-to-goodness Christians in the church. As a result, some believers carry around a biting sense of self-condemnation, their wagons loaded with unnecessary guilt and shame.

John knew they needed assurance in the face of their self-condemnation (vv. 19-20). To reassure them, he went right to their hearts. He wanted to assure them in the face of their struggle that God was greater than their hearts. Three times in the same simple sentence he referred to their hearts. It was a good place to start in order to get to the root of their problem.

If it's good enough for John, it's good enough for us. Let's take a look at your heart, especially if you tend to be overrun by a foreboding sense of guilt and shame. Starting there can help you get to the root of your problem.

And it's quite a big problem for some of us. It affects our view of ourselves, always reminding us that we are not good enough. It affects our relationships with other people, forcing us to keep everybody at arm's length. After all, our hearts tell us, if people really knew us like we know ourselves, they wouldn't like us either.

Worst of all, a condemning heart affects our relationship with God. Every time we try to get closer to Him, our hearts remind us of the times we failed Him in the past, the mistakes we made, and the promises to Him we didn't keep. Because of the pain inflicted by a condemning heart, we distance ourselves from God. With no other place to go, we lapse into a religion of words. It's a dull place to live all right, but it's safe.

Perhaps that's the root of your problem of guilt and shame, otherwise known as condemnation. Your problem could lie in your heart. It's been described as the seat of our emotions, the throne room of our feelings, command central of our passions. The heart manifests feelings of hate and love, fear and courage, anger and calm. Romance novels and old wives tales encourage us to follow our hearts, trust out hearts, go where our hearts tell us. Because of the heart people have gotten married, chosen careers, and relocated themselves and their families in different parts of the country. Indeed a person's heart drives a great deal of what he or she does.

The tricky thing about your heart, though, is that you really can't trust it. The prophet Jeremiah said so, and he used the words like *deceitful* and *wicked* to describe how the heart really works (Jeremiah 32:6). Your heart can fool you, guiding you to have certain feelings that have no basis whatsoever in truth. That's why the old community proverb still makes sense: you should think with your head, not your heart.

What's your heart been telling you about your relationship with God? Is what you hear based on the truth of God's Word, or is it based on raw emotion? On guilt and shame? On self-condemnation?

One spring afternoon Lydia talked to her pastor about an overwhelming sense of conviction she kept on feeling about a mistake she had made years ago. She took the feeling to be the convicting work of the Holy Spirit. It was so intense, she confessed, that she couldn't even enjoy the flowers in her garden, which were some of the most beautiful in her neighborhood. She had been beaten down by something inside, and her heart told her it was God's conviction.

She and her pastor began to talk about the mistake she had made when she was a young girl in a new town with a new job where new temptations got a hold of her. She had stolen some money from her boss, which was easy to do since he didn't mind the store, so to speak. In time she felt horrible about what she had done. She replaced the money without anyone knowing she had taken it. And she asked God to forgive her for stealing the money. Ever since, she never stole another thing in her life.

But she was still troubled about what she had done, even after all those years had passed. Every time she felt guilty, she would ask God to forgive her again. For a little while, the guilt and shame would diminish, only to return to torment her again. She cranked up her level of activity at the church to in an effort to do some kind of private restitution for her sin. After years of church involvement, she still felt guilty.

What did her pastor do in response? He began to teach Lydia the difference between God's conviction and the devil's condemnation. In essence, he told her that when God convicts us, we confess. After we confess, the joy of the Lord returns, because He has removed our sin and the guilt that accompanies it.

By contrast, when the devil condemns, even when we confess, the pain won't go away. What's the difference? When God convicts, He tells us we have done something bad. Once we confess it, He forgets it. When the devil condemns us, we don't just hear that we've done something bad. No, the devil makes sure we hear that we are bad, really bad and that nothing we do will ever fix us.

Lydia's pastor explained to her that the devil enjoyed whispering in her ear the lie that she was a bad person. And the devil would make sure to whisper that message in her ear at every possible opportunity. The evil one worked especially hard to bring up the lie to Lydia every time she go a little closer to the Lord.

The time had come, the pastor encouraged Lydia, to tell the devil to get off her back. Confidently, he showed her from the Bible how to ignore the lies of the devil and how to ask God for discernment and courage to listen to His Word about her situation. As she walked out of her pastor's office, Lydia had a new appreciation for Romans 8:1. In fact, she quoted it as she shut the door behind her: "There is now, therefore, no condemnation to those who are in Christ Jesus."

Like Lydia, you could be troubled by the lies the devil whispers in your ear, lies that make you feel guilty and ashamed. Granted, guilt and shame go along with the Holy Spirit's conviction, but go away with God's forgiveness. Not so with the condemning whisper of the devil.

How can you hush the whispered lie of the evil one? Listen to the truth that speaks loud and clear. John knew the truth, and he wrote to our benefit that the Word of God carried more weight than the messages emanating from a heart bent on condemnation. Just think about it; God knows everything. For Lydia, God knew about her sin, and He also knew about her confession and His forgiveness. Furthermore, He knew she wanted nothing more than to love and serve Him. She didn't have to convince Him of any of those realities. He already knew.

He knows about the day we received His free gift of salvation through Jesus Christ. And He knows we want to serve Jesus as a loyal disciple. Also, He knows about the time we spend with Him each day, and He knows about the struggle we face with the great liar called the devil. Moreover, He knows what He wants us to become in Christ, and He is paving the way for His will for us to be a reality in our lives.

What would happen if we could get past the lie that we can't measure up? What if we could embrace the truth that God knows us and that He has qualified us to be a Kingdom citizen through Jesus Christ? What if we could hush the whispered lie and listen to the truth?

For one thing, we could be confident before God (v. 21). Based on the truth we receive, we can come confidently into the presence of God as a friend and not a stranger. Just think of the changes that confidence in the Lord could make in your life.

John points out that confidence before God carries with it the potential to empower a Christian's prayer life (v. 22). We can experience a dramatic change in the way we come into the presence of God. A self-condemning Christian fights off feelings of guilt and shame that crop up while he or she tries to pray. On the other hand, a confident Christian approaches God with a sense of gratitude that comes from having been forgiven through Christ. Gratitude opens the door for clarity when it comes to what we need to get His job done in our world. We ask and receive because we see clearly what we need. That's only one of the many ways in which confidence can be put to work in prayer.

Confidence puts feet to your prayers in a fulfilling way (v. 23). Self-condemning Christians serve God in order to get His approval. Remember that such a person constantly lives with the lie that acceptance has to be earned, or that it's always out of reach. Every day such a person does Kingdom work with the slim hope that God may smile on his or her efforts. But before the day is started, he or she is convinced that measuring up would be impossible.

By contrast, confident Christians work hard in the Kingdom because we know we have God's approval. It came in Christ the day we received Him as our Savior. When we wake up every morning, we sense the smile of God on our lives, not because we earned it, but because of the grace of Jesus. We work hard to serve the Lord out of sheer gratitude to Him for naming us among His children.

Now let's go back to where we started, to Ben and his addiction. The help he needs comes from what John said about a condemning heart. Perhaps it's the help you need too.

It's the only way to hush the whispers.

Conclusion

Dear Martha and Matt,

When we wrote this book we had you in mind. In fact, we talked about you and people like you in the first few pages.

For a long time we have seen your pain, and we have tried to do something about it. We want the walls to come down between you and God, other people, and even yourself. In other words, we want you to experience the joy and hope of reconciliation. We believe that if you do, you can be on your way to wholeness and health.

Of course, what we have written about doesn't work like a magic wand. It takes time for the walls to come down. After all, it took time for them to be built in the first place. The counseling process that leads to reconciliation can be slow and painstaking. In our instant-is-not-fast-enough culture, it may get frustrating.

You could say the same thing about the sermons. Although they have been designed to help you be reconciled in your relationships, the sermons may only crack open the window of possibility. By listening to them you might feel the gentle breeze of God's reconciling grace. But what you think you really need is a roaring typhoon to destroy the wall!

It may take time. Lots of time.

Ministers who care enough to focus on reconciliation with you in mind are not miracle workers. They have been called by God to proclaim the good news of reconciliation in Jesus Christ and to help believers in Christ to grow toward maturity. That's a tough assignment, and they may not have all the skills necessary to do everything well. But if they love you enough to try to help you, they are special people indeed.

Lord willing, you will run across just such a minister, one who cares enough to try to help you tear down the walls that alienate you. Through preaching or through counseling, or both, you will be led to the place in which you can come to Christ. There, in His presence, the walls can come down.

When that happens, thank God for his reconciliation in Christ. And thank God for the minister who loved you enough to point you in the right direction.

In His Service,

Asa and Argile

Appendixes

Appendix A
RFC Thought Journal

Precipitating Event	Unbalanced/ Distressed Mood (Dominant Feeling)	Related Unbalanced/ Distressed Thoughts (I.D. Primary Concern) Strength of Belief 0-100%	Evidence That Supports Primary Concern	Evidence That Does Not Support Primary Concern	Scriptural Resources	Alternative/ Balanced Thoughts	Signs of Reconciliation Balanced Mood/ Relationship New Strength of Belief 0-100%
	Feelings of Inadequacy, Low Self-Worth	"I'm so stupid!" (80%)	"There were 3 mistakes in the last letter I typed."	"The four previous letters that I typed were error free."	For in the day of trouble he will keep me safe in his dwelling; he will hide me in the shelter of his tabernacle and set me high upon a rock. (Psalm 27:5)	"Typing mistakes are inevitable. Overall, I am a very accurate typist."	"I'm so stupid!" (35%)
Repeated Criticisms from Boss	Frustration/Anger	"My boss is a real jerk!"	"I forgot to remind him of his business lunch."	"This is the first time I have ever failed to remind him of a lunch engagement."		"His schedule is one of the busiest of all the lawyers in our firm. However, I will allow more time to review his calendar each morning."	"Overall, I have been a very capable worker." (90%)
	Hurt/Sadness	"I can't believe how he speaks to me."	"I was late to work on Monday."	"I have been late to work only twice in the last six months and then only because my children were sick."	Cast your cares on the LORD and he will sustain you; he will never let the righteous fall. (Psalm 55:22)		More Confident
							Feel Restored

A bruised reed he will not break and a smoldering wick he will not snuff out. In faithfulness, he will bring forth justice. (Isaiah 42:3) When I called, you answered me; you made me bold and stouthearted. (Psalm 138:3) So God created man in his own image. . . . God saw all that he had made and it was very good. (Genesis 1:27, 31)	"The care of my children will always have to come first. He will just have to understand." "It is good to know that God values me."

Appendix B

RFC Activity Log

Use the following chart to log your Activities for one week. Record the amount of Pleasure derived from each activity using a 1-5 scale with 1 = very little and 5 = a great deal.

Time/Day	Monday	Tuesday	Wednesday	Thursday	Friday	Saturday	Sunday
6:00–6:59 A.M.	A: P:	A: P:	A: P:	A: P:	A: P:	A: P:	A: P:
7:00–7:59 A.M.	A: P:	A: P:	A: P:	A: P:	A: P:	A: P:	A: P:
8:00–8:59 A.M.	A: P:	A: P:	A: P:	A: P:	A: P:	A: P:	A: P:
9:00–9:59 A.M.	A: P:	A: P:	A: P:	A: P:	A: P:	A: P:	A: P:
10:00–10:59 A.M.	A: P:	A: P:	A: P:	A: P:	A: P:	A: P:	A: P:
11:00–11:59 A.M.	A: P:	A: P:	A: P:	A: P:	A: P:	A: P:	A: P:
12:00–12:59 P.M.	A: P:	A: P:	A: P:	A: P:	A: P:	A: P:	A: P:

Time											
1:00–1:59 P.M.	A:		A:		A:		A:		A:		A:
	P:		P:		P:		P:		P:		P:
2:00–2:59 P.M.	A:		A:		A:		A:		A:		A:
	P:		P:		P:		P:		P:		P:
3:00–3:59 P.M.	A:		A:		A:		A:		A:		A:
	P:		P:		P:		P:		P:		P:
4:00–4:59 P.M.	A:		A:		A:		A:		A:		A:
	P:		P:		P:		P:		P:		P:
5:00–5:59 P.M.	A:		A:		A:		A:		A:		A:
	P:		P:		P:		P:		P:		P:
6:00–6:59 P.M.	A:		A:		A:		A:		A:		A:
	P:		P:		P:		P:		P:		P:
7:00–7:59 P.M.	A:		A:		A:		A:		A:		A:
	P:		P:		P:		P:		P:		P:
8:00–8:59 P.M.	A:		A:		A:		A:		A:		A:
	P:		P:		P:		P:		P:		P:
9:00–9:59 P.M.	A:		A:		A:		A:		A:		A:
	P:		P:		P:		P:		P:		P:
10:00–10:59 P.M.	A:		A:		A:		A:		A:		A:
	P:		P:		P:		P:		P:		P:

Appendix C—Relationship Inventory

Age	History of Presenting Problem	Self-Described Nature of Relationship with God/Self/Others	Events Related to Changes in Presenting Problem	Critical Patterns/ 1st Step Changes
16	Experienced first depressive episode	God—saved at 12 y/o; "felt that He let me down" Self—"thought something must be wrong with me" Others—Just had a few friends	Dropped by girlfriend	
18	Mood improved when I started attending college		Met new friends Change of environment	* Views God as untrustworthy, impersonal, not longsuffering
27	First diagnosed Major Depressive Episode Given 1st antidepressant Temporary improvement in mood No therapy	God—"God must have long ago scratched me off. Been away from Him for years." Self—"Felt like a loser; I had no sense of who I was without my job." Others—Had no real friends during this time, working 60 hours a week.	Laid off from work Conflict in marriage	* Isolated from supportive relationships; God, wife, friends, children

32	Wife threatens to leave unless he goes to see a therapist for his depression, tired of his dark mood.	God—"Indifferent to my needs" Self—Something must really be wrong with me. Now my wife wants to leave me" Others—Feel disconnected from my wife and kids	Started therapy, lasted two months	* Interpersonal deficits hindering healthy attachments?
45	Depressed all the time. Considering suicide	Self—felt like a failure as a father and husband, felt guilty about co-worker Others—Met a female friend at work. Discussed mutual relationship problems. Only time I felt happy.	Youngest daughter went off to college Wife went back to work	* Overly self-critical, persistent thoughts of inadequacy
46 (Present)		God—Started going back to church at a friend's request Others—Separated from wife	Separated one month from wife Seeking help from Christian therapist	* High risk relationship with female co-worker

The chart above illustrates how a relationship inventory could be used to help identify relationship deficits with a depressed client. This is similar to the "life chart" described by Weissman, et al. but with several modifications. In the example below, this depressed client was first asked to select critical years during which significant changes occurred in his mood and these were listed down the left hand side of the page. In the second column he was asked to offer a brief description of those mood changes. The third column was used to record brief descriptions of his perceived relationships with God, self, and significant others during those times. Any noteworthy events related to changes in his mood during these important periods were recorded in the fourth column. Finally, the fifth column was used to record critical patterns observed in the relationship column (#3) over the years in response to significant changes in the client's mood. These patterns, revealing relational deficits and critical self-talk, were then highlighted and used to by this therapist to help the client determine the "First Step" he could take to make an improvement in each relational domain. Successive sessions involved making additional relationship changes identified through collaborative interchanges.

Appendix D

RFC Common Problem/Symptom Checklist

Fill in: 0 = none, 1 = mild, 2 = moderate, 3 = severe

___ aging/dependency
___ alcohol/drugs
___ anger control
___ child custody
___ children
___ church/ministry
___ codependency
___ communication
___ depression
___ disabled
___ divorce/separation

___ family
___ fear/anxiety
___ God/faith
___ grief/loss
___ in-laws
___ intimacy
___ loneliness
___ marriage
___ money/budgeting
___ mood swings
___ other addictions

___ parents
___ past hurts
___ premarital
___ school/learning
___ self-esteem
___ sexual issues
___ singleness
___ stress management
___ weight control
___ work/career

Appendix E
RFC Sadness Scale

Over the past _2 weeks_, to what degree were the following true for you:

0 = not at all   **1** = a little   **2** = moderately   **3** = quite a bit   **4** = extremely

(Circle correct response)

1. Not looking forward to things as much as you used to	0 1 2 3 4
2. Feeling sad, down, or heavy	0 1 2 3 4
3. Experiencing difficulty making decisions or concentrating	0 1 2 3 4
4. Feeling guilty about thoughts or behaviors, past or present	0 1 2 3 4
5. Gained or lost more than five pounds	0 1 2 3 4
6. Feeling irritated more than you used to	0 1 2 3 4
7. Finding that you cry more or that it is more difficult to cry	0 1 2 3 4
8. Diminished interest in sexual activities or the opposite sex	0 1 2 3 4
9. Decline in your appetite	0 1 2 3 4
10. Feeling disappointed in yourself	0 1 2 3 4
11. Feeling fatigued, tired, or worn out	0 1 2 3 4
12. Having thoughts of killing yourself or wishing you were no longer around	0 1 2 3 4
13. Worrying about your appearance	0 1 2 3 4
14. Worrying about your health	0 1 2 3 4
15. Difficulty getting out of bed in the morning, even after spending sufficient time in bed	0 1 2 3 4
16. Waking up early and having difficulty going back to sleep	0 1 2 3 4
17. When bad things happen, in my life, I tend to see them as being my fault.	0 1 2 3 4
18. The future seems rather hopeless	0 1 2 3 4

Total Score _____

A study assessing the validity of the **RFC** Sadness Scale revealed a concurrent validity of $r = .74$ when compared to the BDI. The internal consistency estimate of reliability using an equal-length Spearman-Brown revealed a corrected correlation of $r = .96$. The two-week delay test/retest reliability estimate was $r = .88$ (all results significant at $p \le .01$). In addition, an expert panel of raters judged this instrument to be high in both content and face validity. A more complete study of criterion validity is ongoing. However, based upon a preliminary pilot study for assessing criterion validity, this instrument demonstrated a high level of proficiency in distinguishing between depressed and non-depressed individuals. This initial information lends support to the conclusion that this instrument should be helpful in measuring a client's general sense of emotional distress resulting from a depressed mood. Gratitude is extended to Philip Coyle, Ph.D. and his research design and testing class for their invaluable assistance in evaluating this instrument.

Scoring

0 - 10 Within Normal Limits
11 - 21 Mild
22 - 33 Moderate
34 - 72 Severe

High scores on questions #12 and/or #18 may indicate a significant risk of suicide.

(See "RFC Suicide Risk Assessment Guidelines")

Appendix F
RFC Anxiety Scale

Over the past _week_, to what degree were the following true for you:

0 = not at all   **1** = a little   **2** = moderately   **3** = quite a bit   **4** = extremely

(Circle correct response)

1. Feeling anxious or tense — 0 1 2 3 4
2. Sweating when you have not been exercising or exposed to high temperatures (sometimes known as a "cold sweat") — 0 1 2 3 4
3. Struggling with persistent thoughts, images, and/or impulses that are disgusting, unwanted, or simply don't make sense — 0 1 2 3 4
4. Numbness or tingling in different parts of your body — 0 1 2 3 4
5. Repeating a behavior over and over again, contrary to what seems normal (i.e., checking, washing, counting, cleaning, etc.) — 0 1 2 3 4
6. Experiencing your face as being flushed — 0 1 2 3 4
7. Frequent changes in your emotions, often due to changes in what is going on around you — 0 1 2 3 4
8. Feeling of having wobbly legs — 0 1 2 3 4
9. Difficulty falling asleep or staying asleep at night — 0 1 2 3 4
10. Problems with diarrhea, indigestion, or upset stomach — 0 1 2 3 4
11. Feeling exhausted, weak, or fatigued — 0 1 2 3 4
12. Difficulty relaxing or taking it easy — 0 1 2 3 4
13. Heightened sensitivity to sounds or touch — 0 1 2 3 4
14. Worrying about your health or about dying — 0 1 2 3 4
15. Tension in your back, neck, head, or shoulders — 0 1 2 3 4
16. Feeling dizzy or lightheaded — 0 1 2 3 4
17. Feeling shaky or jittery — 0 1 2 3 4
18. Having difficulty catching your breath, even when you have not been active — 0 1 2 3 4
19. Feeling a choking sensation or lump in your throat — 0 1 2 3 4
20. For no apparent reason, feeling like something terrible is about to happen — 0 1 2 3 4
21. Feeling foggy, strange, or detached from your environment or body — 0 1 2 3 4
22. Having your heart race or pound for no apparent reason — 0 1 2 3 4
23. Coolness in your hands and feet or sweaty palms — 0 1 2 3 4
24. Carrying tension, pain, or pressure in your chest — 0 1 2 3 4
25. Feeling terrified or scared — 0 1 2 3 4
26. Difficulty concentrating due to racing thoughts — 0 1 2 3 4
27. Feeling unsteady or faint like you might fall — 0 1 2 3 4

28. Worry about situations that may occur in the future or that
   in the past have caused a lot of excessive tension or anxiety   0   1   2   3   4
29. Avoiding going places due to the tension and anxiety they
   cause   0   1   2   3   4

Total Score _____

A study assessing the validity of the **RFC** Anxiety Scale revealed a concurrent validity of $r = .95$ when compared to the BAI. The internal consistency estimate of reliability using an equal-length Spearman-Brown revealed a corrected correlation of $r = .95$. The two-week delay test/retest reliability estimate was $r = .76$ (all results significant at $p \leq .01$). In addition, an expert panel of raters judged this instrument to be high in both content and face validity. A more complete study of criterion validity is ongoing. However, based upon a preliminary pilot study for assessing criterion validity, this instrument demonstrated a high level of proficiency in distinguishing between anxious and non-anxious individuals. This initial information lends support to the conclusion that this instrument should be helpful in measuring a client's general sense of emotional distress resulting from anxiety. Gratitude is extended to Philip Coyle, Ph.D. and his research design and testing class for their invaluable assistance in evaluating this instrument.

Copyright © 1999 by Asa R. Sphar III, Ph.D.

Scoring

    0 - 25   Within Normal Limits
26 - 43   Mild
44 - 59   Moderate
60 - 116   Severe

High scores on questions #3 and/or #5 may indicate the presence of obsessive and/or compulsive tendencies.

Appendix G
RFC Suicide Risk Assessment Guidelines

The following suicide assessment guidelines are intended to provide a systematic and structured means of assessing an individual's potential for suicide. Even though each content area is subject to broad interpretation, following this approach will assist users in reaching a better approximation of a person's lethality than unstructured interviews alone. However, any client who is considered a significant risk for suicide should be immediately referred for evaluation by a licensed mental health specialist.

It is very common for persons experiencing a significant amount of emotional distress to consider the possibility of suicide. Generally, many such considerations are only suggestive of the person's level of emotional discomfort (often referred to as passive suicidal ideation) and not necessarily an indication of any serious intent to attempt self-destruction (active suicidal ideation). However, helpers should always exercise an "abundance of caution" by asking all potentially suicidal clients questions such as, "Have you ever considered committing suicide? If so, how recently? Have you ever made an attempt before or ever come close?" Positive responses to any of these questions indicate a need for further inquiry into the following content areas, outlined according to the acronym "**SAD TRIP**." (*For persons with previous suicide attempts, the following questions can also be asked in the past tense.*)

Specificity—Following an admission of suicidal thinking, the counselor should follow up by asking the client something like, *"Tell me about your plans. Specifically, how would you go about killing yourself?"* The more specific the plan, the higher the degree of risk. Some client's may respond to this question with statements like, *"Oh I don't know, I guess I might try 'so and so."* Responses of this type usually indicate less risk than those reflecting definite plans. Distinct plans are indicated by statements like, "I have a loaded 38-caliber revolver in my bedside table that I plan on using tonight." In such cases, immediate preventive measures should be taken to assure the client's safety.

Availability—How *available* is the proposed method? In the previous example, the person with the gun in his bedside table would definitely be a higher risk than someone who wants to throw himself off a skyscraper when he is coming to see you in a isolated rural community. However, even when a person's plan poses no immediate risk of injury, care should be taken not to dismiss even the most outrageous scenarios.

Dangerousness—How *dangerous* is the proposed method? Suicide attempts utilizing guns or hanging allow virtually no time for a potential rescue. Granted there have been cases in which persons who have used these methods have been saved, but proportionally very few when compared with other less lethal methods. On the other hand, cases involving an overdose of medicine or even cutting one's wrist, while potentially lethal, allow more time for such clients to change their mind and seek help or for others to intervene. Therefore, the more lethal the method, the higher the risk that someone will successfully complete a suicide attempt.

Time—How long ago did the client make an attempt or was the client considering suicide? As a general rule, the more *time* that has elapsed since they last struggled with suicidal thinking or behavior, the lower the degree of risk. However, even when a previous attempt occurred months or even years earlier, the helper may still wish to review the specifics of past suicidal episodes to determine the potential lethality of any future suicidal behaviors. Since most initial inquiries into this area reflect the counselor's uneasiness with a client's safety, it would seem only appropriate to evaluate thoroughly the helper's suspicions.

Reasons—What *emotional, relational, physical/developmental,* and *spiritual reasons* exist that would serve to deter or prevent the client from harming himself? For example, helpers should ask the client questions such as, "What reasons can you identify for not killing yourself?" Or, if they seem pressed to identify any, follow this question with "What has kept you from choosing suicide up to this point?" Reasons given vary considerably, but include such answers as: "I am just too chicken or scared to ever make a real attempt" (*emotional*); "I could never do that to my parents or to my children" (*relational*); "Right now, I at least have my health. I look around and a lot of people who don't even have that seem to have a pretty good life" (*physical/developmental*); or, "I am afraid that God would not forgive me" (*spiritual*). All of these responses, along with the client's related strength in that belief, can be used by the helper to measure a client's current risk for injury. These thoughts may also serve to increase a client's resolve to resist future suicidal thinking and behavior.

Conversely, what *situational factors* exist that may expose the client to a higher risk for self-harm? This is where additional reading on the subject and personal experience will greatly assist the helper in evaluating client risk. For example, studies indicate that well over 50% of suicide attempts occur within 24 hours of persons ingesting a mood-altering substance. Therefore, the presence of addictive behavior such as alcohol or drug dependency may add considerably to a client's suicidal risk. While many additional risk factors have been identified, some common ones include recent losses, particularly in the areas of personal relationships or vocation; clients who are under the age of 20 and over the age of 55; clients with chronic or terminal illnesses; and/or clients without a meaningful or positive relationship with God.

Intention—Just how serious is the client in actually killing himself or herself? Even though a plan to commit suicide may not involve methods sufficient to bring about death, the client may not realize this. For example, if a client who plans on taking six aspirin really thinks that this amount of medicine is sufficient to kill her, then her **intention** indicates a higher *actual* risk than does another person who may use this choice as a plea for help. Once they discover that their method is not reliable, they may simply just change their procedure and attempt again. Also, helpers should ask questions like, "Given that you have been feeling suicidal, how hard would you work to conceal it? Would you give any signs to those around you?" While this may seem like a ridiculous question since it would seem unlikely that a person bent on concealment would answer this honestly, many times even highly evasive clients will reveal their intention to conceal their attempt when confronted in such a direct manner. For those who don't, the cryptic nature of their reply will indicate that their report for no self-harm cannot be trusted.

Proximity—What is the proximity of help? Would it be reasonable to assume that someone would be around who could prevent the client from self-harm or assist in her rescue? Often clients plan to make attempts when, for example, they know that their spouses will be coming home from work or that someone will be around. As a general rule, unless the identified method is extremely lethal, the less a suicidal plan reflects intentional isolation, the less serious the client is about actually committing suicide.

Appendix H
Managing High Suicide Risk

Helpers should remember that *most* persons who consider suicide are considerably ambivalent about pursuing such action. There is a part of them that wants to die, and another part that wants to live. Helpers can capitalize on this tension by highlighting this dividedness within the client and highlighting and encouraging the part that wants to live. Making statements such as *"I suspect that while part of you wants to die, another part of you wants to live. Tell me some of the reasons that you would not choose to kill yourself"* can help in this regard.

Additionally, redemptive responses to individuals considered a high risk for suicide will necessarily reflect an appreciation for the following guidelines.

1) **Work to establish rapport.** Once again, people don't care how much you know until they know how much you care. Helpers must communicate their sincere interest in and care for the individual in order to be maximally effective.

2) **Identify central concerns.** Just allowing persons an opportunity to voice their pain can help to relieve their suicidal urges. Listening carefully to their complaints can also provide important information that may be helpful in formulating an effective response. However, counselors should attempt to transition clients' discussions about their problems to a greater focus on solutions to those problems. Just allowing clients to obsess endlessly about their difficulties will only result in greater despair.

3) **Seek to remove or discard the means of suicide.** Covenant with the individual and any family members to discard or remove dangerous items identified in the suicide plan. While not all potentially dangerous items can be removed from a client's environment short of hospitalization, removing those items that are highlighted in their *primary* plan is usually sufficient to reduce substantially the immediate risk of injury. For example, if certain medications are named, they should either be thrown where they cannot be retrieved or flushed down the toilet. Firearms should be removed from the household and given to other family members or friends for safekeeping (not a place which is

frequented by the suicidal person). Never leave firearms in the house with a suicidal person, even if other family members say they will lock them up or separate the shells from the gun. Persons intent on self-injury can be very industrious when it comes to locating hidden firearms. Remember methods such as shooting or hanging oneself allow very little if any time for rescue.

4) **Strive to involve significant others.** Professionals in the field often refer to the fact that a person's choice to attempt suicide is dyadic by nature. What this implies is that suicide is generally not an isolated act but really involves two people. One person is the suicidal individual. The other is someone whose opinion or influence is considered paramount in the suicidal person's life. While this person may not be someone actually close to the individual (i.e., a movie star or public figure), often such an individual is known personally by the client. Asking questions like "If you were to leave a suicide note, to whom would it be addressed" or "Who would you be most concerned about finding out about your death" can be used to help identify this person. Responses to these questions vary but often reflect people such as ex-boyfriends, girlfriends, family members, teachers, wives, husbands, therapists, and so forth. Once identified, the client's involvement with such people is often characterized by dependency. Usually their emotional well-being is wrapped up in the actions and opinions of the other individual. Commonly, there has been some kind of rupture in the relationship that has precipitated the client's choice to consider suicide. Therefore, attempts should be made to get these individuals together and to restore the lines of communications. Often the other person will be shocked to find out what the client is considering and encourage if not plead with the client to reconsider. If however the other person does not want to be of assistance directly, he or she may provide helpful information regarding what is important or valuable to the suicidal individual. Finally, other significant others may need to be identified and brought into the picture.

5) **Never leave the person alone.** Engage caretakers to stay with the client until it has been determined that the risk for suicide has diminished. Remember that an actual attempt to harm oneself may only take a few seconds so high-risk individuals should be subject to visual contact at all times. This means that persons who agree to provide such "watch care" stay in the same room or accompany these individuals wherever they go.

6) **Identify client resources.** What has helped them to resist the urge to kill themselves up to this point? What kinds of coping skills have been utilized in the past? These responses often involve certain identifiable actions and thoughts that can be utilized again in the future.

7) **Mobilize as many sources of support as possible.** Persons who are suicidal are often also suffering from other medical, addictive, or mental health problems as well. Consideration should be give to referring the individual to an appropriate twelve-step group, physician, or other appropriate adjunctive support person to complement other helping efforts.

8) **Refer to a trained mental health professional.** Any seriously suicidal person should be referred for ongoing care to an individual trained to handle such situations. While ministers and lay persons can provide invaluable assistance to at-risk individuals, they are not usually trained to handle such cases nor do they have the time needed to address adequately the needs present in these individuals.

Appendix I
Parenting C-P-R: Straightforward Principles to Enhance Effectiveness

Have you ever felt like your parenting needed to be resuscitated? Probably so. Parenting is a challenging task. Rare is the parent who has not drunk from the well of humility in the face of a crying infant, tantruming child, or defiant adolescent. And what concerned parent, having experienced these challenges, has not attempted to remedy this dilemma by consulting a local book store, attending a workshop, or simply talking with other parents, only to feel overwhelmed by the abundant and often contradictory parenting advice available today?

These experiences reveal a consistent need among parents for a straightforward yet effective *method* for "reviving" their parenting efforts that will serve to highlight key behavior management fundamentals. By focusing on the three principles of **Consistency**, **Predictability**, and **Reasonableness** (C-P-R), parents have ready access to practical reference points that will help to guide and modify their parenting approaches. These three qualities, operating in an atmosphere of love and forgiveness, represent the basis of effective parenting.

Consistency

And let us not grow weary in well doing, for in due season we shall reap, if we do not lose heart. (Galatians 6:9)

How often have you found yourself complaining to your children or another person about the fact that your children "don't listen" or are "hardheaded" or "stubborn"? Do you find yourself having to raise your voice or get upset before your children will obey? Or maybe they have stopped doing what you ask all together. A primary reason for such problems is inconsistency in a parent's approach to changing the child's behavior.

Few parents are surprised to hear that consistency plays a vital role in effective parenting. In fact, most parents readily identify consistency as one of their parenting weaknesses. However, consistency involves several parental behaviors that often fail to be appreciated. A failure to identify and apply the actions that contribute to parental consistency will, of course, lead to unintentional participation in the problem that most parents seek to avoid.

Consistency in child management is cultivated when parents are able to **identify** specifically the

(a) Behaviors they would like to see increased/decreased along with a system for monitoring them. Monitoring selected behaviors may involve a daily charting of the behaviors or simply careful observation.

(b) Consequences/rewards that will accompany the previously specified behaviors. Remember, rewards and consequences tend to be unique to each child. Finding the ones that are right for your child may take some time. Social rewards such as praise or positive attention are powerful incentives and are free!

(c) Time limits required for their children to either begin or end the specified behaviors. Frequently, children fail to initiate desired behaviors because they lack a sense of urgency.

Additionally, consistency is culminated when parents are able to **apply** diligently the

(a) System for monitoring those behaviors.

(b) Consequences/rewards and time limits to the monitored behaviors *without significant interruption.* A good rule to remember is that consequences should be administered and/or terminated within 24 hours of the behavior in question. The greater the length of time between the behaviors to be modified and the consequences for those behaviors, the less influence the consequences will hold for modifying those behaviors. For example, if a child fails to clean her room when told, the consequence of less T.V. time, for example, should be administered the same day. (She should still, of course, be required to clean her room.) Immediate consequences are necessary for several reasons. As time passes the consequences in the child's mind begin to lose their connections with the problem behaviors, reducing the behavior-modifying impact of the consequence. Also, as these associations decrease, children are more likely to become resentful of the consequences due to their seeming unfair. Finally, by starting fresh with a clean slate each day through restoring privileges that were removed the day before, parents are less likely to run out of rewards to manipulate should problem behaviors continue.

One way for parents to improve their consistency rating is to identify what is inconsistent about their approach to parenting, or obstacles to consistency. These frequently involve a failure to follow through on warnings, random punishments and/or rewards; giving in to pleadings or tantrums; failure to check for task completion; and poorly defined behaviors/routines, consequences/rewards, or time limits. It should be highlighted here that the rewards for consistency can be seen in what I call the "7-10 Day Rule." Whenever parents attempt to discourage unwanted or encourage desired behaviors in their children, it may take seven to ten days before the behavior begins to change.

Predictability

The secret things belong to the Lord our God, but the things that are revealed belong to us and to our children for ever, that we may do all the words of this law. (Deuteronomy 29:29)

Imagine for just a moment the following scenario. Tommy has just come home from school and decides that he would like to get a snack. He goes to the cabinet and begins his search for something to eat. Upon finding a new variety pack of chips, Tommy begins to open the box and make his selection. Suddenly, his mother appears from the other room clearly perturbed. She informs Tommy that he has lost the privilege of having a snack that afternoon since he was not supposed to eat that particular box of chips. What's missing? Predictability. Tommy didn't know that Mom had previously decided that they were for school lunches.

Or let's assume the same scenario as above except that Tommy knowingly attempted to eat chips from the forbidden box and was caught. This time Mom informs him, for the first time, that he was going to lose snack privileges for a week. What is missing? Again, predictability. While it was inappropriate for Tommy to disobey his mother, what responsibility should Mom carry for informing Tommy of the consequences ahead of time so he might have this information to react to?

Predictability in child management is cultivated when parents are able to **resolve** any

(a) **Differences** that may exist between their child-rearing practices or others involved in providing care for the children.

(b) **Conflicts** that may exist in relationships between individuals within the parenting group that may impede the parenting process. Parents need to parent as a team.

(c) **Skill deficits** that may hinder their ability to communicate information effectively to their children. Such skills involve knowing effective ways to get a child's attention; telling a child what you want and how you want it done; and using clear, specific, and respectful words.

Additionally, predictability is culminated when parents are able to **communicate** clearly with their children the

(a) **Behaviors** that they would like to see increased or decreased as well as the **rewards/consequences** and **time limits** that apply to the previously specified behaviors. Whenever possible, this needs to take place before the administration of the rewards or consequences for the previously specified behaviors.

(b) **Parenting as a team** concept that outlines the unity with which the parents will be parenting. Children need to be discouraged from attempting to divide and conquer. This does not mean that parents are always expected to agree with one another. Disagreement is frequently healthy in parenting, but a commitment should be made to seek compromises together *in private.*

A good way for parents to check their predictability rating would be to ask themselves the question, "Can my children reasonably predict what I expect from them and/or the consequences/rewards that will follow certain identified behaviors?" (Just assuming that your children ought to have known something may unnecessarily instill resentment.) Difficulty in responding to this question with a "Yes" may result from some of the following obstacles to predictability: poor communication between the parents or between the parents and children, a conflicted or estranged couple relationship, or a lack of or a poorly defined routine for the children. These problems frequently lead each parent to address different behaviors, to fail in their support of one another, or to overlook the help provided by routines.

Reasonableness

Fathers, provoke not your children to wrath: but bring them up in the nurture and admonition of the Lord. (Ephesians 6:4)

Timmy is an adopted six-year-old boy who has just entered the first grade. Within the first week, the teacher had to send a note home to his parents reporting that Timmy had to be corrected frequently during the week for being too aggressive with his playmates. Evidently, when Timmy did not get his way at playtime, he would walk up and push down the child whom he felt was responsible for his frustration.

When Timmy's dad received the note, he was understandably upset and decided that he needed to punish Timmy for his behavior. The news was especially upsetting to him as he began to worry that the violence Timmy had witnessed in his natural family growing up, which had led to his being taken out of the home, was now beginning to be imitated in his behavior at school. He decided therefore to handle the situation firmly by administering a spanking in order to "nip the problem in the bud." However, the next week he again received the same note only this time it said that the problem was getting worse. Again he used spanking, only this time there was much more anger in his countenance as he administered the discipline. By the third week the teacher was asking for a conference with Timmy's family. The frustration and humiliation that resulted from not being successful in curbing his son's behavior began to panic Timmy's dad. He began to worry that his son might grow up to be like his natural father. The following week, Timmy's father guiltily admitted to his son's teacher that he was so exasperated with Timmy's continuing misbehavior that the week before he was screaming in his son's face.

What is missing in this illustration? You guessed it. Reasonableness. While spanking is an appropriate form of punishment for some types of misbehavior in six-year-olds, for a youngster who is already having problems with aggression, another approach is advisable. Additionally, the lack of self-control, while a common problem for most parents at some time or another, is modeling the very behavior that Timmy's dad desperately wants to curtail.

Reasonableness in child management is cultivated when parents are able to **evaluate** accurately the

(a) Expectations they hold for the previously specified behaviors recognizing Judeo-Christian standards, developmental issues, social norms, a child's age/health, and just good common sense as legitimate fields of reference in making such determinations.

(b) Rewards/consequences and time limits to see if they are appropriate for the previously specified behaviors.

(c) Environment to learn how a child's physical surroundings may contribute to the possibility that a desired behavior will occur (i.e., providing a quiet place to do homework helps to encourage the completion of studies; arranging shelving at the proper heights and providing hangers in ample supply can promote clean rooms).

Additionally, reasonableness is culminated when parents are able to **exercise** properly

(a) Self-control when conducting parenting tasks

(b) Environmental alterations that encourage the desired behaviors

(c) Attitudes that reflect the spirit of love and forgiveness

One way to check on your "reasonability rating" might be to ask the question, "Is what you are currently doing achieving the desired results in your children?" This question may sound ridiculously self-evident, but it is not. One primary roadblock to effective parenting is the faulty belief that "more of the same will somehow produce different results." Frequently, as in the previous case involving spankings for Timmy's aggressive behavior,

Helping Hurting People

the solution becomes the problem. In this instance, corporal punishment only made the problem worse. New alternatives to handling the problem needed to be considered. Other *obstacles to reasonableness* occur when a parent exercises poor self-control, reflects harsh attitudes, or fails to give attention to environmental variables. Notice at this point that the first step toward exercising each parenting principle involves **preparation** for the parenting task. It is only the second step in each principle that involves **application** of the various principles through direct interactions with the children. Adequate preparation at each stage is extremely important to exercise these principles in parenting.

What becomes evident as parents begin to exercise this approach to parenting are the similarities between these three fundamental principles and God's actions toward his people down through the ages. The *consistency* of His love toward us is reflected throughout the Bible but especially in that "... while we were yet sinners, Christ died for us." The *predictability* of His actions is highlighted by virtue of His being a God of revelation and his open communication through the Word of God regarding expectations for our behavior. The *reasonableness* of His actions is shown by the redemptive results that come from His disciplines as well as affirmations. Guided by such examples, we too can use these principles with confidence with our children.

Appendix J
RFC Forgiveness Guidelines
for Couples

"Forgiveness is letting go of the need for vengeance and relinquishing negative thoughts of bitterness and resentment." (DiBlasio, 1997)

Implications

- Forgiveness is an act of the will, a choice, and therefore not contingent on feelings (Mt. 18:21-35, Lk. 6:37, Eph. 4:3).
- Forgiveness is not forgetting. Only God can forget (Jer. 31:34). Also, forgiveness is not condoning, ignoring, suppressing, repressing, allowing future abuse, placating, or excusing and is not always the end of pain and consequences.
- Letting go of anger and resentment helps to release an individual from the offending party and allow for a new beginning or start in a couple's relationship.
- Forgiveness is life enhancing and freeing (Jn. 10:10). It has been said that "the only thing that costs more than forgiving is *not* forgiving."
- This definition emphasizes the distinction between hurt and anger. The *choice* is to release feelings of bitterness and any desire to retaliate (anger). Feelings of hurt often remain, even when forgiveness has taken place, since the offense represents a loss for the individual. Feelings of hurt, though they usually decline over time, may require additional work and usually don't subside entirely.
- Forgiveness does *not* necessarily imply or demand *reconciliation*. It is possible to forgive someone for something but not seek reconciliation. However, the ability to remain free from negative thoughts toward another requires cultivating an *attitude* of care toward that person. The mind hates a void and will return to previously undesirable attitudes unless more well-intentioned thoughts are in place.

The following is offered as a definition of reconciliation:

> *Reconciliation involves the re-establishment of a **caring relationship** in which mutually trustworthy behaviors and thoughts replace previously untrustworthy behaviors and attitudes.*

Notice the differences between *forgiveness* and *reconciliation*. Forgiveness is a **gift** that persons give to their offenders and themselves; reconciliation is **earned** by re-establishing trust through mutually trustworthy behavior. Forgiveness occurs **within an individual**; reconciliation occurs **within a relationship**. Forgiveness can happen **instantaneously** (although it may take time) while reconciliation always occurs **over time** (trust can only appropriately be granted over time).

Steps to Forgiveness

Initially, you must identify the couple's readiness for forgiveness work. While the Bible does not present the choice to forgive as optional, couples cannot and should not be forced or coerced into forgiving their mate. Such an approach will make the counselor seem insensitive and often increase resistance to the process. Also, some individuals or couples may recognize the need to forgive but choose to postpone any action until later in the reconciliation process. However, by following the preliminary steps given below, a couple's reluctance to initiate this process often subsides as the personal and relational advantages of timely forgiveness (Ephesians 4:26) are outlined.

Preliminary Steps

First, set the stage for forgiveness. Inform the couple that frequently before moving toward reconciliation, others couples have found that they needed to let go of the bitterness that has come from past hurts. Therefore, many couples find that before they can move toward reconciliation in their relationship, they need to learn a way to let go of the bitterness that has come from past hurts. Ask, "Would you like to talk about how you can let go of your anger toward you partner at this point?" (Most frequently, the couple will respond affirmatively. However, if the response is "no" or they are unsure, proceed to allow for more ventilation of feelings around past hurts and move on with counseling until another opportunity arises to revisit the issue.)

Second, present the idea of forgiveness. Offer "The Choice to Forgive" as a reasonable alternative that many couples find they can utilize early in the reconciliation process. *First*, carefully define forgiveness and reconciliation. Often an individual's misunderstanding of forgiveness stands in the way of a willingness to choose this option (i.e., they equate forgiveness with forgetting and therefore something they have understandably never been able to do). *Second*, highlight how choosing to forgive early in the counseling process often speeds up reconciliation by allowing the couple to experience a new start in their relationship. By choosing to forgive you are saying to your partner that while you know that the pain and hurt of past offenses may not be resolved by this choice, you are forever giving up the right to use the anger and resentments related to these hurts against your partner in the future. This means that both partners take responsibility for monitoring their anger as it relates to past hurts and not allow it to infect their relationship or future discussions of hurts. Then ask, "Given this understanding of forgiveness, are you willing to consider offering this gift to your partner and the relationship at this time?" (Again, most couples recognize the benefits of this process and readily agree. However, if reluctance is demonstrated, then seek the opportunity to revisit this idea at a latter time.)

Formal Forgiveness Session

1. Maintain rapport. Again, people don't care how much you know until they know how much you care. We need to guard against allowing the idea of building and maintaining rapport to become just a technique (i.e., reflective listening). Empathy is not just a technique; it is an attitude of caring. In forgiveness work, it is critical that individuals feel they can be fully transparent without fear of being judged and sense that we care enough to hear their story.

2. Recall mutual hurts. Work in the abstract doesn't produce much change. The couple needs to be specific. Generally, *both* individuals have contributed in some way to the conflicts they have experienced and can therefore own a share of the hurts they have each experienced. Having partners first identify how their own behaviors have hurt the other person rather than initially pointing to the other person's offensive behaviors helps to limit defensiveness.

Techniques:

   (a) Have one partner recall experiences of being hurt while the other practices being empathic and caring. When the expression of hurt is met with an attitude that expresses care, concern, and/or regret, the extinction of negative feelings is promoted.

   (b) Acknowledge the presence of the feeling of ambivalence in the offended party that is often rekindled by this process. It is common for clients to feel divided on the issue of forgiveness, with part of them wanting to forgive and another part resisting this notion. In a sense, their mind is struggling to decide where to spend its energy. They can either continue to be angry and bitter or work to invest that energy in the work of forgiveness. Remind them that by attending to their positive inclinations and choosing to forgive, they will not only save themselves energy in the end but also provide a better platform for their relationship to survive.

3. Assess the risk of future victimization and aid in setting appropriate boundaries. Explore the appropriate role that anger may initially play by providing the energy and motivation to set relationship and safety-enhancing boundaries. For example, spouses may need new rules to foster improved communication. Such rules may include requiring that no derogatory terms or foul language will be used when discussing their differences or that they each will respect the other's requests for time-outs during times of anticipated or renewed conflict. In cases where there has been infidelity, anger may assist the injured spouse in setting new requirements for reconciliation. Examples of such boundaries would include requiring the offending spouse to discontinue all contact with the third party; establishing a "Trust Fund" (a private sum of money [$1,000.00+] voluntarily given by the offender to the mate which can be used to hire an investigator if another affair is suspected); obtaining approval for victims to call their mates at any time to check on their locations or activities, and so forth. Once clients have been empowered by appropriate boundaries, they can let go of anger more easily. Forgiveness does not mean that new boundaries do not need to be in place. Also, the rebuilding of trust and the lowering of boundaries are the work of reconciliation and not forgiveness. When trust has improved, boundaries can be relaxed.

Techniques:

   (a) Relapse prevention plan in the case of infidelity. A plan to stop the affair needs to be in place as do steps that are to be taken to prevent its recurrence.
   (b) For cases involving abuse, contingency plans must be formed and validated by the therapist.

4. Encourage empathy between partners. Research has demonstrated that empathy is strongly related to helping people forgive. In fact, couples who are encouraged to utilize empathy (trying to see things from their partners perspective) to approach forgiveness as opposed to seeing forgiveness as just self-enhancing (i.e., forgiveness is good for you) are able to arrive at forgiveness at a much faster rate. Therefore, many identify the encouragement of empathy as the *core technique* or *central key* of forgiveness work. Furthermore, remaining free from negative thoughts about another is encouraged by empathy and the attitude of concern it fosters for the offender's emotional, physical, and/or spiritual well-being. In the final analysis, it is difficult to harbor resentment and share concern for someone at the same time.

Techniques:

   (a) Write a letter to yourself supposedly from the other person explaining the opposing point of view.
   (b) Present the idea that research has shown that persons who have been offended by others tend to omit the pressures that were operating on the other person and minimize their own contribution to the problem. Also, they tend to see the effects as permanent and the offender as more evil or malicious than is actually the case. On the other hand, studies also demonstrate how offenders tend to omit the long-lasting effects of their behavior, minimize their own negative intentions, give justifications, and/or stress that they were trying to accomplish positive things.
   (c) Have partners role-play their mate's position based on how they think their partner might have thought, felt, or seen the situation.

5. Identify forgiveness as an altruistic gift. Encourage each partner to recall when they have received unmerited forgiveness in their past. (For Christians, this is a readily available idea.) In all successful relationships, forgiveness is the price you pay for choosing to care for someone.

Techniques:

   (a) Say, "Tell me about a time that you received forgiveness that was undeserved."

(b) For those who say this has not happened or who have trouble remembering, ask for a time when they witnessed someone else receiving undeserved forgiveness.

6. Formalize the choice to forgive through a ritual or ceremony. Rituals or ceremonies like those presented below help to punctuate or emphasize a person's choice to forgive. These help to serve as signposts for forgiveness.

Techniques:

(a) Burn the list or letter outlining the hurts and throwing ashes away.

(b) Burn the letter and keep the ashes in an urn as a reminder.

(c) Say out loud that you forgive the person.

(d) Write a letter expressing forgiveness and read it in the presence of the therapist and partner.

(e) Write a Certificate of Forgiveness for the offense or person.

7. Maintain forgiveness. Couples are going to have to live with this forgiveness, and not uncommonly they begin to doubt it. Therefore, the following ideas can help individuals hold onto their positions.

Techniques:

(a) Predict the *extinction burst phenomenon.* In the case of forgiveness, this phenomenon involves experiencing resurgent feelings of anger from memories of past offenses during new times of conflict or stress. Individuals need to be reminded that such reactions (habituated thoughts triggered by similar past circumstances) are common and do not necessarily signal that forgiveness has not occurred. The success or failure of forgiveness is really measured by how they choose to handle those resurgent memories (forgiving is not forgetting) by assuming personal responsibility for not allowing renewed anger from the past to re-infect their current relationship.

(b) Remind them of the distinction between hurt and anger. Lingering hurt is a natural and often lasting result of experiencing a loss.

(c) Challenge them to review their letter, certificate, etc.

References

Coleman, Paul. *The Forgiving Marriage*. Chicago: Contemporary Books, 1989.

DiBlasio, Frederick A., and J. H. Proctor. "Therapists and the Clinical Use of Forgiveness." *American Journal of Family Therapy* 21 (1993): 175-84.

Enright, Robert D., and J. North. *Exploring Forgiveness*. Madison: University of Wisconsin Press, 1998.

Flanigan, Beverly. *Forgiving the Unforgivable*. New York: Macmillan, 1992.

Gottman, John. *Why Marriages Succeed or Fail*. New York: Simon & Schuster, 1994.

Markman, H., S. Stanley, and S. Blumberg. *Fighting for Your Marriage*. San Francisco: Jossey-Bass, 1994.

McCullough, M. E. "Marriage and Forgiveness." *Marriage and Family: A Christian Journal* 1 (1997): 81-96.

McCullough, M. E., and E. L. Worthington, Jr. "Encouraging Clients to Forgive People Who Have Hurt Them: Review, Critique, and Research Prospectus." *Journal of Psychology and Theology* 22 (1994): 3-20.

_____. "Models of Interpersonal Forgiveness and Their Applications to Counseling: Review and Critique." *Counseling and Values* 39 (1994): 2-14.

_____. "Promoting Forgiveness: A Comparison of Two Brief Psycho-educational Group Interventions with a Waiting-List Control." *Counseling and Values* 40 (1995): 55-68.

McCullough, M. E., E. L. Worthington, Jr., and K. C. Rachal. "Interpersonal Forgiving in Close Relationships." *Journal of Personality and Social Psychology* 73 (1997): 321-36.

McCullough, M. E., S. J. Sandage, and E. L. Worthington, Jr. *To Forgive Is Human: How to Put Your Past in the Past*. Downers Grove, IL: InterVarsity Press, 1997.

Veenstra, Glenn. "Forgiveness: A Critique of Adult Child Approaches." *Journal of Psychology and Christianity* 12, no. 1 (1993): 58-68.

_____. "Psychological Concepts of Forgiveness." *Journal of Psychology and Christianity* 11, no. 2 (1992): 160-69.

Worthington, E. L., Jr. "An Empathy-Humility-Commitment Model of Forgiveness Applied Within Family Dyads." *Journal of Family Therapy*, in press.

Worthington, E. L., Jr. "The Pyramid Model of Forgiveness: Some Interdisciplinary Speculations about Unforgiveness and the Promotion of Forgiveness." In *The Foundation of the Scientific Study of Forgiveness*, ed. E. L. Worthington, Jr. and Michael E. McCullough. Radnor, PA: The John Templeton Foundation Press, 1998.

Worthington, E. L., Jr., and F. A. DiBlasio. "Promoting Mutual Forgiveness within the Fractured Relationship." *Psychotherapy* 27 (1990): 219-23.

Appendix K
RFC Anger Management (Case of Bill W.)

The incident with Bill W. described in the case study on anger was both unique and universal. While few people may have had this particular experience, everyone has had negative experiences with anger, either from others or within themselves. Now, compare what you have just read with the following account involving anger.

This incident occurred during the early part of the first century A.D. A man stood in the doorway of the temple in Jerusalem and likewise began to shout rebukes to the group gathered there. However, the circumstances in this case were quite different. You see, rather than using God's house as a place of worship, the merchants and money-changers had corrupted its spiritual purpose and were instead using the site for material gain. So offended was Jesus at their callous disregard for the holy place that the Scriptures report he literally drove the people out of the temple with a whip made of leather cords (John 2:13-16). Did Jesus actually hit anyone? We are not told. One thing that we do know, however, is that he was angry —very angry. The fury of his words and physical actions was such that it cleared the entire temple area.

Here are two dramatic accounts of anger, somewhat similar in expression yet markedly different in their appropriateness. In the first case the anger would be deemed unjustified and destructive, the other justified and constructive. One man stood indicted, the other vindicated. What made the difference?

Isn't Anger Bad?

To begin an examination of this question, I would suggest that in both cases the *initial* anger experienced by these men was neither good nor bad. In other words, generally speaking, emotions as such are not best viewed from a moral perspective. Instead, it is how we choose to cultivate, assess, express, and if necessary redirect these God-given responses that matters.

After years of intensive study, researchers have concluded that the basic function of all emotions is survival. Feelings are an innate part of the human condition, with anger so basic that we witness it in the cries of a newborn infant. Along with fear, anger is the most elemental in humanity's basic survival kit of feelings. Often referred to corporately as our preparedness states, these two emotions are familiar experiences to us long before we learn to experience a variety of other feelings states, such as love. In fact, some people do not learn how to love until quite late in life, if at all. Feelings are also experienced at various levels of intensity. For example, negative feelings may increase in stages from annoyance to anger, from anger to rage, or from apprehension to fear and from fear to terror. Conversely, positive feelings may range from fondness to attraction, from attraction to love or from stimulation to excitement, and from excitement to exhilaration.

Seen in this way, feelings can be regarded as gifts, serving to punctuate and enrich our lives while providing us with essential feedback necessary for adaptive living. They are like barometers alerting us to changes in our internal climate, guiding our interactions with others, and encouraging our own self-care. If we were to experience the absence of feelings, either positive or negative, we would be left without vital information necessary to navigate our relationships and attend to our spiritual and emotional needs.

For example, anger serves a critical function in our lives by promoting actions aimed at protection during times of danger or threat. This protective function operates automatically when something or someone we value, including ourselves, is at risk or in jeopardy. Let's consider an example. Suppose you are a parent watching your child play her first soccer game and you hear the coach screaming criticisms at her from the sidelines. Chances are good that you will find yourself getting angry, especially if this behavior continues over time and/or the criticisms seem unwarranted. Now, let me ask you a question. Why did you get angry? Because she is your daughter and you don't want her to get hurt. Right? (Even if you are not a parent, you may find this illustration evokes the same response since most people value the innocence of childhood and the sensitive nature of their formative experiences.) You are concerned that she may lose her fragile self-confidence, lose interest in the game, or suffer damage to her sense of self-worth. Since you value all of these and are threatened by their potential loss, you get angry. So, is this wrong? Most people would say "no," at least not yet. Why? Because your anger at this point is basically a recognition that you care and rather than being a bad thing actually provides the energy or motivation you may need to take corrective action. As a result, you may find yourself taking time to check out how these criticisms are affecting your daughter and, if necessary, offer extra reassurance. If the coach continues this behavior, you may choose to talk directly to him or even as a last resort move your child to another team. What is important to recognize and affirm is that your anger is a vital motivating mechanism that propels protective action. Without it, we and those we love would be left at times without an adequate defense.

Another point worthy of consideration is that anger is primarily a *secondary emotion* since it is triggered by one or more *primary emotions* such as fear, hurt, shame, or frustration. Anger serves to defend us against these feelings. Therefore, when we experience a threat from strong negative emotions like these, anger often ensues to help protect us from these feelings of tension or vulnerability. The entire process operates so quickly that we are often unaware of the presence of these initial feeling states, leading us to conclude that some event in our environment, for example the coach, made us angry. What is technically more accurate and beneficial for anger resolution is to recognize that the coach triggered the primary emotion of frustration, which in turn prompted the protective response of anger. Such an understanding of the nature of anger will lead us to look at primary rather than secondary emotions, subsequently focusing our corrective energies on the causes rather than the effects of trying events.

As an experiment, ask yourself the next time you get angry what feeling of vulnerability preceded your anger? While experiences vary, any variety of negative feeling states such as fear, hurt, shame, or frustration may be precipitating the anger response. Once again, these emotions are considered primary emotions since they serve as triggers to anger, alerting our bodies to the need for a defensive response. You might say that these negative feelings are like smoke and that anger is like a fire alarm. This alarm system not only alerts us to the presence of potentially dangerous smoke but also mobilizes resources to respond to the threat. Left without this response system, the well-being of our emotional, spiritual, and physical selves would be at serious risk. We will see how the awareness of viewing anger as a resource as well as recognizing its secondary nature are both central to promoting a redemptive response.

Isn't Anger a Choice?

Another consideration needs to be made in light of this discussion with regard to anger. I believe that the *onset* of anger is *not* volitional. To support this conclusion, I offer the following information.

Studies in human behavior have demonstrated that when a precise region of the brain called the amygdala is electrically stimulated, normally mild-mannered subjects become aggressive. When the stimulus is discontinued, they return to their normal, albeit apologetic, state. Other studies investigating the use of various chemical substances on aggressive behavior have similarly demonstrated that certain drugs, particularly alterations in certain hormone levels, will promote a higher level of angry responses.

Distinguished physiologist K. E. Moyer states that "certain hostility circuits appear to be sensitized by particular hormone balances and when these circuits are sensitized, a variety of environmental conditions will evoke hostile feelings and behavior. These environmental situations may involve frustration, stress in many forms, pain, or, if these circuits are highly sensitized, simply the presence of an attackable entity" (K. E. Moyer, *The Psychobiology of Aggression*, 1976).

This brief synopsis of the physiology of anger strongly suggests that given the right form of stimulation, human beings are hardwired, if you will, to experience anger. But there is more. Scientists have estimated that the human brain has ten thousand miles of nerve fibers per cubic inch which serve to connect billions of nerve cells or neurons. Within this astonishingly complex web of circuitry, we are told that the neurons are communicating signals back and forth at the rate of approximately one thousand impulses per second. As a result of this physical make-up, when any of our five senses are triggered in a way that indicates danger or threat, within the course of a microsecond our body begins to respond in ways that will help to promote our survival. Since a delay in responding may jeopardize survival in many situations, our bodies must respond quickly—so quickly, in fact, that our rational abilities must be bypassed initially in the service of survival.

What we are talking about here is often referred to as the fight or flight response. When our bodies experience alarm, they instantly pour adrenaline into our bloodstream to speed up our heartbeat and increase our blood pressure. Red blood cells, fueled by an increase in available sugars, bring more oxygen to the brain and muscles. Breathing accelerates in response to increasing demands by the body for oxygen and to reduce levels of carbon monoxide in the blood. Digestion slows as blood is redirected to the brain and muscles. Pupils dilate for better vision. Blood clotting increases in response to the possibility that an injury may be sustained. All of this occurs without invitation or conscious prompting. Were the body to engage the higher order functions of human reasoning, it might risk serious injury as the following event will illustrate.

When I was six years old, my parents took our family to Florida one winter on vacation. We stayed in a rented house located in a quiet suburban neighborhood that belonged to some friends of my parents. As my father and I were going out to the car one morning we ran into a neighbor who was walking his large German Shepard dog. As the pair walked up to where we were standing in the street, my father complimented the owner on his dog and quickly interjected, "Is he friendly?" No sooner had the owner said yes than the dog growled, lunged sideways and took my arm in his mouth. Just as quickly, my father somehow managed to retrieve my arm, place himself between me and the dog, and assume a combative posture and demeanor in anticipation of more aggression. Fortunately, the owner was able to steer the dog away and, after checking for injuries and offering apologies, quickly left with dog in tow. It all happened so quickly that there was no time to think, only respond to the natural and automatic proclivities of a parent protecting his child and my own instinctive desire to survive. Had my father failed to act quickly, serious injury may have followed.

Did my father have to think about his need to respond aggressively? I don't believe he did, at least not initially. While his actions may have been consistent with a carefully reasoned approach to such an unexpected chain of events, there was no time for his responses to be processed by the rational faculties of the highly developed human mind. Such deliberation and processing take time. As we have seen, when any of our five sense are alerted to a perceived threat to something that we value, our bodies automatically and immediately respond with an increase in tension leading to anger. Indeed, science continues to affirm what the psalmist proclaimed: we are fearfully and wonderfully made.

The *onset* of anger then is *not* a choice. The case of Bill W. helps to highlight this fact. As it turned out, Bill had made many resolutions and promises over the years to discontinue or control his anger, often in a state of deep contrition. While his repentant attitude was commendable, it was never sufficient to curtail his anger. We cannot tell ourselves to *not* be angry and have it work, anymore that we can tell ourselves to **be** angry.

As evidence of this fact, try right now to tell yourself to be angry. Really focus on your desire to be angry. Does it work? It's difficult isn't it? In order to be even moderately successful at this you must choose to reflect on some troubling issue from your past or in the present that has stirred your anger. But this means that your anger is already there and all you have done is give it recognition by selectively focusing your attention on that issue. This demonstrates again that the *onset* of anger is not volitional since it requires a threat, either real or imagined, to something of value to us in order for it to be triggered. At this point we are ready to offer the following definition of anger:

> ***Anger*** *is a feeling of displeasure, which represents a normal response to the perception of being threatened or attacked, accompanied by both physiologic and behavioral responses.*

Notice that this definition avoids the use of adjectives like extreme, intense, strong, or severe to modify the feeling of displeasure. Contrary to commonly offered definitions of anger, which often give the word a derogatory connotation, this description avoids extreme terminology, allowing for a more balanced and therefore positive evaluation of this feeling state. The tragic consequences of viewing anger only as an unmitigated evil can be witnessed in Bill's exaggerated sense of guilt. While he is correct in assuming responsibility for how he responds to his anger or any unreasonable perceptions which may needlessly trigger this feeling, his unrealistic goal to never be angry again will only serve to fuel frustration leading to more anger and/or self-debasement in the future. In addition, by not limiting the identification of anger to only an extreme feeling, we are now free to recognize that anger occurs at various levels of intensity. Anger may range from weak to strong, from mild to intense. So while I may be only moderately angry, I am nevertheless still angry.

The Bible and Anger

If asked for your opinion of anger prior to this discussion, whether it was good or bad, what would your initial response have been? If you are like most folks, you would have been inclined to see anger as bad. You may still feel that way, not only because anger is a negative and uncomfortable feeling personally but also because destructive examples of its use are everywhere. According to a report published in 1994 by the U.S. Department of Justice, homicide rates remain near historic highs despite modest declines in recent years. Domestic violence by most accounts has reached epidemic proportions, with emergency response services being pressed beyond their capacity. Terror and violence stalk our streets and invade our living rooms each evening on the network news.

And then there is the anger that never qualifies for network programming but is no less insidious in our lives. Customers standing in the limit 10 express check-out lane carrying 20 items, drivers cutting us off in traffic, and the passing insult of a co-worker, leave us with accumulations of negative feelings that pull us down and exhaust our energy. With so many examples of destructive and/or debilitating anger, how can we develop a balanced view of this negative emotion? Why should we even value a balanced view? Aren't destructive uses of anger so prominent that little will be lost if we fail to see its positive use? Won't considering the positive aspects of anger just give license to those people already misusing it, indirectly encouraging the further perpetration of their injustices on others?

To gain a better perspective on these and other questions, let's turn to the supreme standard for the evaluation of the moral and ethical proprieties of all our emotions and behaviors, the Bible. What does the Bible have to say about anger? Does it support the conclusion presented by some that anger is a sin?

We are introduced to the damaging results of anger early in Genesis chapter 4 where we read that Cain slew his brother Abel. Because they were the first- and second-born children of Adam and Eve, respectively, we are quickly introduced to the negative repercussions of the Fall. Notice the progression of events outlined in Genesis 4:3-7.

> [3]*In the course of time Cain brought some of the fruits of the soil as an offering to the LORD. [4]But Abel brought fat portions from some of the firstborn of his flock. The LORD looked with favor on Abel and his offering, [5]but on Cain and his offering he did not look with favor. So Cain was very angry, and his face was downcast. [6]Then the LORD said to Cain, "Why are you angry? Why is your face downcast? [7]If you do what is right, will you not be accepted? But if you do not do what is right, sin is crouching at your door; it desires to have you, but you must master it."*

Why was Cain's offering not accepted? We are not told. Perhaps God's response, If you do well, will you not be accepted? implies that Cain had not followed certain instructions for the offering ritual. If this were the case, then maybe his anger was in response to his guilt or shame. Or maybe he felt displaced and rejected by his younger sibling's approval and was manifesting an intense form of sibling rivalry. In either case, Cain was threatened by what occurred and got angry.

What is important to realize, for our purposes, is that even though Cain was very angry, he was not accused of sinning. God didn't say, Because you are angry you have sinned. Instead, He said sin is crouching at the door. Clearly, anger was not the problem here. It was what Cain ultimately chose to do with his anger that led to sin. We might even say that as anger increases so does our susceptibility to sin, since any strong emotion may compromise our self-control. But one does not necessarily lead to the other. This distinction is critical.

However, the fact that these two, anger and sin, are brought together so early in our biblical narrative has led some to an unfortunate conclusion. Some have suggested the following understanding of this passage:

Cain was angry + Cain murdered Abel + Murder is a sin =
Anger is a sin

There are many problems with logic of this type. First, as we have seen, this is not what the Scriptures say. Second, correlation does not mean causation. Just because anger and murder tend to go together does not mean that one causes the other or that anger is necessarily bad. Students of statistics are well aware of the limitation of correlational studies, being cautious that outcomes demonstrating strong positive or negative relationships are always subject to what are called confabulating variables.

A further examination of the Old Testament reveals that not only does it not condemn the emotion of anger, it also recognizes anger as an emotion commonly exhibited by our Lord. The anger of the Lord is referred to numerous times in the Old Testament. Clearly, even to imply that anger is sinful is an unacceptable conclusion based on this alone. However, what we do find time and again is the implicit or explicit admonition in the Scriptures to safeguard our anger from unacceptable or unwarranted expression. The New Testament also offers a variety of insights which can serve to guide our understanding and view of anger. Of particular use is Ephesians 4:26-27:

> [26]*"In your anger do not sin": Do not let the sun go down while you are still angry,* [27]*and do not give the devil a foothold.*

It is also important to consider that while many cases can be cited demonstrating how people overreact and use their anger destructively, there are also many people who under react and fail to use their anger assertively. These are individuals who benefit from the use of assertiveness training.

Steps to Success in Dealing with Anger

> *Create in me a new heart, O God, and renew a steadfast spirit within me. (Psalm 51:10)*
>
> *Do not be conformed to this world but be transformed by the renewing of your mind. (Romans 12:2)*

(STEP 1)   (STEP 2)

R - *Recognize* anger in yourself and others; recognize your need of God's strength/help.

E - *Empathize* with others and show love in your responses. (STEP 3)

N - *Notice* your reactions to anger and circumstances that give rise to anger. (STEP 4)

E - *Evaluate* the situation differently and give yourself time to consider your response.

W - *Work* in the present.

A - *Accept* responsibility for finding appropriate ways to express anger; *avoid* choices and circumstances that limit impulse control.

L - *Love* is demonstrated in self-control. (2 Peter 1:5; Galatians 5:22)

Appendix L
RFC Premarital Counseling Guidelines

Being ordained to marry someone is not only a privilege, but a great responsibility. A minister has the responsibility to withhold the decision to marry a couple until he is assured in his own mind that the marriage has a good chance of making it. If our practice becomes one of marrying anyone who comes to us to be married, then we really become no different from a justice of the peace or a marry-for-profit wedding chapel. (H. Norman Wright, *The Premarital Counseling Handbook*, 85)

Goals of Premarital Counseling

- Establish rapport with couple
- Review relationship history and challenge faulty information about marriage
- Help couples to better understand themselves and their mates
- Encourage appropriate growth and change
- Assist in separation from parents by reviewing the emotional, functional, and financial aspects of leaving and cleaving
- Teach communication and conflict resolution skills
- Plan for further marriage enrichment
- Work to establish or encourage a spiritual foundation
- Assess the need for an individual referral
- Help the couple decide whether or not to marry

Points to Remember

- Most couples spend more time researching the purchase of a new automobile or home than on preparing for their marriage. Pastors should set significant requirements on who they will marry to help emphasize the importance of preparation. These include a minimum number of well-organized premarital sessions; scheduling the premarital sessions a generous length of time prior to the wedding; a restriction on wedding showers prior to the completion of the premarital sessions; and so forth.
- Examining family-of-origin issues is one of the most important tasks of good premarital counseling.

- Effective premarital counseling should result in a significant percentage of marriage candidates postponing or ending their marriage plans. Estimates vary, but experience suggests that 25-35% of couples who participate in structured premarital counseling sessions will decide to delay or discontinue their wedding plans.
- Unlike working with distressed married couples, the goal of effective premarital counseling is for couples to leave the sessions feeling unsettled about their decision to marry. Only when they begin to question their initial decision will they come to understand whether their relationship is built on more than just infatuation.
- Pastors need to educate their churches on their premarital expectations and requirements for marrying couples.

Outline of Sessions

[ ] = Ideas and information to supplement or use in place of the PREPARE/ENRICH Inventories. Couples should complete the assigned pages prior to the beginning of the session.

Session 1: Preliminary Issues. Establish rapport; present outline of sessions; review couple's relationship and personal history using Norman Wright's "Challenging Questions" from his *Premarital Counseling Handbook*, 138-39; review expectations for premarital counseling; administer appropriate PREPARE/ENRICH Inventory.

Session 2: God's Plan for Marriage. Have partners describe their personal relationship with Jesus Christ and their spiritual life in general; encourage joint prayer and Bible study; discuss critical Scriptures related to marriage (i.e., *Divine Origin*: Genesis 2:18-25; *Honorable in All*: Hebrews 13:4; 1 Corinthians 7:36b, 28a; *Marriage is for Life*: Matthew 19:3-6; Mark 10:8; Romans 7:2; 1 Corinthians 7:10, 11, 39; *Warning Against Being Unequally Yoked*: 1 Corinthians 7:39; 2 Corinthians 6:14; *Roles*: Ephesians 5:23-33). How does the couple understand the principle of leaving and cleaving? Review the emotional, functional, financial, and spiritual implications of this idea [refer to pages 82-86 in Wright's *Before You Say 'I Do'* premarital manual].

Session 3: Communication and Conflict Resolution. Have the couple complete Communication Exercise I found on pages 7 and 9 of the *Building a Strong Marriage Workbook (BSMW)*. Use the results of the PREPARE/

ENRICH Inventory to discuss strength and growth areas. A number of experts agree that the future of the couple is largely dependent on how they handle conflict. Then have the couple complete Communication Exercise II and Review 10-Steps for resolving couple conflict in the BSMW [refer to pages 56-67 in Wright's *Before You Say 'I Do'* premarital manual].

Session 4: Family-of-Origin and Personality Issues. Refer to the results of the PREPARE/ENRICH Inventory to compare personality and family-of-origin (family map) styles. Discuss strengths and potential growth areas. Remind the couple that while each of them will change over the years, the decision to marry should not be based on the hope that their partner or their families will be significantly different or better in the future. Are they content with their partner as they are now? Have the couple take home the "Budget Worksheet" from the BSWM to complete for the next session [refer to pages 52-55 in Wright's *Before You Say 'I Do'* premarital manual].

Session 5: Roles/Responsibilities and Financial Management. Refer to the results of the PREPARE/ENRICH Inventory to begin the discussion. Usually there are a number of surprises in both areas. This may present another opportunity to utilize earlier communication exercises to resolve differences. Review the "Budget Worksheet" completed since the last meeting. Help the couple define their short- and long-term financial goals [refer to pages 42-51 in Wright's *Before You Say 'I Do'* premarital manual].

Session 6: Intimacy Issues and Leisure Activities. Introducing the discussion of sex can be a delicate matter. Helpers may begin asking the couple where they have gathered information about sex over the years. What person or persons have talked with them or what books have they read? Refer to the results of the PREPARE/ENRICH Inventory to assess strengths and growth areas [refer to pages 78-81 in Wright's *Before You Say 'I Do'* premarital manual]. Finally, ask the couple to use a 1-10 scale to rate how confident they are in their initial decision to marry. Those who respond with a number less than 8 should be encouraged to resolve their ambivalence before finalizing their decision. [Couples who re-affirm their marriage commitment should be encouraged to complete the appendix in Wright's *Before You Say 'I Do'* premarital manual.]

Follow-up Session (approximately six months following the wedding): Review positive aspects of the couple's relationship. Then identify needed growth areas by quickly reviewing the topics covered in the premarital sessions. The counselor may give the couple the "marital evaluation form" found in Wright's *Premarital Counseling Handbook* to facilitate this discussion. Set goals for identified growth areas. If serious problems emerge, refer to a counselor.

Required Reading

Couple: David H. Olson, *Building a Strong Marriage Workbook*, 1996. (Return with scored PREPARE/ENRICH Inventories.)

                H. Norman Wright, *Before You Remarry: A Guide to Successful Remarriage*, 1999.

                H. Norman Wright, *Starting Out Together—A Devotional for Dating and Engaged Couples*, 1996.

                H. Norman Wright and Wes Roberts, *Before You Say "I Do": A Marriage Preparation Manual for Couples*, 1997.

Counselor: H. Norman Wright, *The Premarital Counseling Handbook*, 1992.

                Ronald W. Richardson, *Family Ties That Bind: A Self-Help Guide to Change Through Family of Origin Therapy*, 1995.

                (All the previously listed couple books)

Suggested Reading

Couple: Larry Burkett, *Money Before Marriage: A Financial Workbook for Engaged Couples*, 1996.

                Linda Dillow and Lorraine Pintus, *Intimate Issues*, 1999. [For women]

                Les and Leslie Parrott, *Saving Your Marriage Before It Starts: Seven Questions to Ask (Before and After You Marry*, 1995.

                Douglas E. Rosenau, *A Celebration of Sex: A Guide to Enjoying God's Gift of Married Sexual Pleasure*, 1994.

                H. Norman Wright, *So You're Getting Married*, 1985.

Counselor: H. Norman Wright, *Marriage Counseling: A Practical Guide for Pastors and Counselors*, 1995.

Counseling Sessions

- A suggested premarital counseling schedule would include a total of six sessions ranging from 1 to 1½ hours in length. A final session should be scheduled for six months following the marriage to monitor marital adjustment and encourage continued progress.
- As part of the counseling experience, the couple should read *Before You Say 'I Do': A Marriage Preparation Manual for Couples* by Norman Wright, 1997.

Testing

- When possible, couples will benefit from being required to take the **Prepare/Enrich Marriage Inventory**. Ministers or counselors who want to do premarital counseling should take the brief course designed to prepare someone to administer these instruments properly. This inventory will greatly assist couples who want to find a more objective way to measure their current level of compatibility.

Appendix M
RFC Chemical Dependency Checklist

IDENTIFYING INFORMATION:

Name:_____ Age:_____ Residence:_____

Date of Admit:_____ Date of Assessment:_____ Referring Doctor:_____

Occupation: _____ Marital status:_____

Number of children and their ages: _____ Religion:_____

PRESENTING PROBLEMS:

Events precipitating consultation:_____

Brief history of the problem:_____

Previous psychiatric history:_____

Previous participation in any support groups such as AA / NA / OA / Alanon, etc._____

PSYCHOSOCIAL SUMMARY:

Family history of drug abuse and their attitude toward it:_____

What kind of relationship do you have with your father and mother?_____

With your spouse?_____

With your children?_____

Interpersonal relationships: (i.e. close friends? long-term friends? using friends?)_____

Medical history:_____

History of blackouts:_____

DRUG OR ALCOHOL USE HISTORY:

First experience with drugs or alcohol:_____

First intoxication from mood-altering substance:_____

List of Drugs Ever Used: * = Drug or drugs of choice

Name of Drug	Age at First Experience?	Date of last use?	Amount of last use?	(1) Route of Administration; (2) Most Consumed/Used in a 24-Hour Period of Time?

Describe any legal proceedings you have been involved with . . . DWI, arrests, bankruptcy, etc.

Do you have any legal matters pending at this time?

What is your opinion of your alcohol or drug use?

Do you believe you have a problem with it?

Have you ever experienced paranoia, delusions, or hallucinations?

IMPRESSIONS and RECOMMENDATIONS : (Include affect, dress, mood, etc.)

Appendix N

RFC Referral Guidelines

Helpers should consider making referrals under the following circumstances:

1. The problem lies outside the expertise of the helper or he simply don't understand what's going on;
2. The client fails to show signs of improvement after several sessions (3-5 sessions is a common framework used by many non-professional counselors);
3. The client demonstrates bizarre or extremely aggressive behavior, is severely anxious or depressed, needs legal advice, appears to be severely disturbed, has severe financial needs, or stirs strong sexual feelings or feelings of dislike in the counselor;
4. The helper has too much contact with the client in other arenas leading up to or during the counseling process to maintain the needed level of objectivity (often broadly referred to in the counseling literature as "dual relationships");
5. Scheduling demands on the helper preclude giving adequate attention to the needs of the client;
6. Strong feelings of anger, dependency, attraction, disgust, impatience, and so forth continue to be experienced by the counselee, the helper, or both (often referred to as transference and counter-transference, respectively);
7. When the client has chosen unilaterally to terminate counseling but is still judged by the helper to critically need assistance (Under such circumstances, the helper should preferably write a letter suggesting, if possible, three alternative referral sources. The letter should be sent "certified mail" to insure its receipt and protect the helper against any charges that she failed to demonstrate adequate care for the client.);
8. An unresolvable conflict has arisen or there is a significant discrepancy between the values of the therapist and the client;

9. Personal factors in the life of the helper significantly compromise his ability to provide adequate assistance (i.e. poor health, recent divorce, excessive stress, burnout, ongoing family conflicts, etc.);

10. The client is distinctly suicidal or homicidal;

11. The client has a severe alcohol or substance abuse problem that would likely require more clinical expertise and/or medical intervention to manage properly; and/or

12. The client is psychotic or clearly compromised in his or her ability to judge reality (i.e., suffering from hallucinations, delusions, etc.).

Under any of the above circumstances, the counselor should make every attempt to refer the counselee to other helpers who are both competent and Christian. In the event that the community in which the helper resides does not have such persons, then every attempt should be made to refer the individual, couple, or family to someone of equal or greater competence who will respect the religious orientation of the client. Many problems are not closely related to a client's value issues or belief systems and can be handled effectively by non-Christians. Helpers should spend a good deal of time getting to know their referral sources in the community, identifying those that are at least sympathetic with the religious values represented among their clients. Such investments on the part of helpers will greatly enhance the effectiveness and quality of their referral ministry.

Notes

1. All scriptural references come from the New International Version (NIV) unless otherwise indicated.

2. Oates, 1986, 31.

3. Crabb, 1984, 27.

4. Thornton, 1964, 16.

5. While we cannot fully evaluate the meaning of this statement without knowing how it was delivered, the serpent was described in verse 1 as "the most crafty beast." This observation suggests that the inflection, tone of voice, posture, and appearance of the deceiver all joined his carefully selected words in attacking the credibility of God.

6. Trust (faith) is seen here as the *choice* of placing firm confidence in the integrity of another person, object, or idea, stemming in part from previous experiences which have engendered such confidence. Appropriate trust is not born in a vacuum but is based in part on experiences or revelations from the past. In a sense, it is choosing to allow the faith potential God has given each of us to flow freely in response to trust engendering revelations.

7. Fossum and Mason, *Facing Shame,* 5.

8. Kaufman, *Shame: The Power of Caring,* 8.

9. The awareness of being limited, by itself, does not make shame a toxic experience. In fact, being aware of our limits as human beings represents a useful and healthy form of shame (see also 2 Thessalonians 3:14; Albers, 8; Erikson, 251-54). However, when that limitedness is presented as being bad or a reflection of our personal inadequacy, shame becomes toxic.

10. God's image in persons is represented by all of his attributes, which find full expression in Christ (Colossians 1:15), i.e., goodness, lovingkindness, trustworthiness, faithfulness, justness, and so forth. By distorting humanity's purity through deceptive messages and resulting toxic emotions, Satan has managed to spoil the essential relational qualities necessary for persons to live in harmony and balance with one another.

11. Proverbs 16:18.

12. Paul's admonition to the Galatians (6:1-5) challenges them to take responsibility for evaluating their *own* conduct before God. Such an examination *may* result in persons feeling an appropriate sense of "pride in themselves" (v. 5 NIV) or "rejoicing in himself" (KJV) regarding a particular behavior if it has been compared against and met the standards outlined in God's Word. However, it will also result in a sense of humility since we can never *fully* meet the standards for holiness set by God. Conversely, when a person begins to evaluate his or her behaviors using another person's conduct as the standard, this misplaced and misguided comparison will often result in a faulty conclusion, namely that he or she is better than others (pride). The story of the Pharisee and the tax collector (Luke 18:9-14) highlights the inherent spiritual risks of making comparisons with others the standard for determining our goodness or merit before God. Spiritual pride, thinking by our merit we are acceptable to God or thinking we are better than someone else, is really just shame buried beneath a veneer of self-deception.

13. Robert Albers reminds us that human finitude is not a curse but a gift that frees us from the anxiety of having to be like God (92).

14. While the focus of attention has purposely been restricted to the mistrustful and shameful aspects of this interchange, several distorted messages and corresponding negative emotional experiences are evidenced here.

15. Augustine's Confessions.

16. Chapter 3, verse 11 reveals a critical observation regarding the origin of shame. God's question to Adam, "Who told you that you were naked?" assumes someone, in this case Satan, had through his communications made unacceptable their previously acceptable condition of nakedness. Both the Scripture and experience demonstrate that the sense of unacceptability or inferiority witnessed in shame stems from interpersonal communications that are either intended to or inadvertently diminish the listener.

17. Matthew 12:24.

18. Matthew 7:3.

19. Genesis 3:17.

20. Brazilian psychiatrist Norberto Keppe suggests that the most common human mental illness is what is called a theomania: a delusion in which a persons believe that they can be, or in severe cases, literally *are* God. While full-blown delusions of this type are frequently observed in inpatient psychiatric settings (i.e., believing oneself to be Christ, etc.), more subtle manifestations of this common but erroneous human tendency are witnessed in the belief that we are somehow the masters or our fate, really are in control of our lives, can or should be perfect at something, are betters than others, etc.

21. A compelling description of this human tendency is offered by Ernest Becker in *Escape from Evil* (New York: Free Press, 1975), 91. He concludes that the cause of evil in human affairs is the desperate but largely unconscious attempt to control life born out of the shame of personal insignificance.

22. If God were to highlight sins in heaven, the leading one would no doubt be lovelessness.

23. "Divine balance" is defined here as a spiritual state of relational harmony characterized by the ability to love others as well as ourselves guided by our preeminent love relationship with God through Jesus Christ. By virtue of the redemption offered in Christ and the enabling power found through the indwelling power of the Holy Spirit, the attributes of God's image in humanity may once again find unlimited expression. In counseling, the practical extension of encouraging love is working to identify those thoughts and actions that serve to promote the spiritual best interest of the object of one's love.

24. The most complete definition of love found in the Bible comes from 1 Corinthians 13. In counseling, these verses find practical expression as we seek to help the clients identify those thoughts and actions that will serve to promote the spiritual best interest of the object of their love. In other words, our thoughts and actions are tangible expressions of how we "value" or "love" God, self, and others.

25. Thornton, *Theology and Pastoral Counseling*, 27.

26. Alter, *Resurrection Psychology*, 70.

27. Evidence regarding humankind's need for reconciliation with God, self, and others is found throughout the Scriptures (see also Ephesians 2:14-22 regarding Christ's work in promoting reconciliation between God, Jews, and Gentiles).

28. The significant problem of self-hatred among people, including Christians, has been highlighted by a number of well-known Christian thinkers, including Brennan Manning—"One of the most shocking contradictions in the American church is the intense dislike many disciples of Jesus have for themselves. . . . In my experience, self-hatred is the dominant malaise crippling Christians and stifling their growth in the Holy Spirit" (*Abba's Child*, 19-20); and Henri Nouwen—"Over the years, I have come to realize that the greatest trap in our life is not success, popularity, or power, but self-rejection" (*Life of the Beloved*, 21).

29. In his exegesis of Romans 7 and 8, Martin Luther highlighted the paradoxical nature of the Christian life in the Latin phrase he popularized, "simul justus et peccator," which means that Christians are at the same time sinners and saints. Christians forever walk in the shadow of the cross and therefore carry an ongoing consciousness of their sin (guilt). However, it is that same cross (i.e., Christ's atonement) which makes us righteous and affirms our great sense of worth to God (2 Corinthians 5:21).

30. Luke 5:16, 9:10; Matthew 14:13.

31. Matthew 16:34.

32. An excellent resource for helping individuals establish their sense of worth before God is *The Search for Significance* by Robert S. McGee.

33. Developmental researchers refer to this process as bifurcating our realities, dividing our worlds into dichotomous/dualistic structures or categories. Examples would include: me/mother, we/others, jock/nerd, love/hate, happy/sad, good/bad, and so forth.

34. Chuck Kelley, Faculty Workshop, Fall 2001.

35. 1 Corinthians 9:22.

36. Devotional Day—May 26.

37. *parakaleo*—to beseech, exhort, encourage or comfort; *noutheteo*—to put in mind, to warn, and to confront; *parmutheomai*—to have a positive attitude, to cheer up, to encourage; *antechomai*—to be available, to cling to, to hold fast, to take an interest in, to hold up spiritually or emotionally; and *makrothumeo*—to be patient or to have persistence.

38. Others listed in order of relative importance were (1) extratherapeutic or client contribution factors (40%); (2) relationship factors between the client and the counselor (30%); and (4) model and technique factors (15%).

39. Other relevant verses would include: "For as he thinketh within himself, so is he . . ." (Proverbs 23:7 ASV) and "Do not conform any longer to the pattern of this world, but be transformed by the renewing of your mind. Then you will be able to test and approve what God's will is—his good, pleasing and perfect will" (Romans 12:2).

40. Cognitive-behaviorists (Beck, 1979; Burns, 1999; Greenberger, 1995, Thurman, 1989; et al.) are rightly credited for emphasizing and developing this scriptural principle.

41. 1Corinthians 12:15b.

42. 1 Corinthians 13:1.

43. The 3-stage/3-step design of the RFC counseling process reflects an appreciation of the counseling model offered by Gerard Egan in his influential book *The Skilled Helper*, 6th ed., 1997.

44. "Giving back" to clients can involve four kinds of reflective responses: paraphrasing, reflecting feelings, reflecting meanings, and summative reflections. A good discussion of these reflective responses can be found in *People Skills* by Robert Bolton, 49-61.

45. While each intervention arguably could be understood as reflecting other RFC principles, only the primary RFC principle being emphasized is given for each strategic intervention.

Bibliography

Counseling Resources

Albers, R. H. *Shame: A Faith Perspective*. New York: The Haworth Press, 1995.

Alberti, R. E., and M. L. Emmons. *Your Perfect Right: A Guide to Assertive Living*. San Luis Obispo, Calif.: Impact Publishers, 1995.

Arterburn, S., and D. Stoop. *The Life Recovery Bible*. Wheaton: Tyndale House, 1995.

Augsburger, D. W. *Caring Enough to Forgive—Caring Enough Not to Forgive*. Ventura, Calif.: Gospel Light Publishing, 1981.

_____. *Helping People Forgive*. Louisville: Westminster John Knox Press, 1996.

Backus, W. *Good News about Worry*. Minneapolis: Bethany House, 1991.

Beck, A. *Cognitive Therapy of Depression*. New York: Guilford Press 1979.

_____. *Cognitive Therapy of Substance Abuse*. New York: Guilford Press, 1993.

Beck, A. *Prisoners of Hate: The Cognitive Basis of Anger, Hostility, and Violence*. Scranton, Pa.: Harper Collins, 1999.

Beck, A., and G. Emery. *Anxiety Disorders and Phobias: A Cognitive Perspective*. New York: Basic Books, 1985.

Bolton, R. *People Skills*. New York: Simon & Schuster, 1979.

Bongar, B., A. L. Berman, R. W. Maris, M. M. Silverman, E. A. Harris, and W. L. Packman, eds. *Risk Management with Suicidal Patients*. New York: The Guilford Press, 1988.

Bowlby, John. *A Secure Base: Parent-Child Attachment and Healthy Human Development*. New York: Basic Books, 1990.

Bruce, A. Balmain. *The Training of the Twelve.* Oak Harbor, Wash.: Logos Research Systems, Inc., 1995.

Burns, D. *Feeling Good: The New Mood Therapy.* New York: Avon, 1999.

Carkhuff, R. *The Art of Helping in the 21st Century.* 8th ed. New York: HRD Press, 2000.

Carter, L. *Heartfelt Change.* Chicago: Moody Press, 1993.

Chapman, G. *The Five Love Languages: How to Express Heartfelt Commitment to Your Mate.* Chicago: Northfield Publishing, 1992.

_____. *Hope for the Separated: Wounded Marriages Can Be Healed.* Chicago: Moody Press, 1992.

_____. *The Other Side of Love: Handling Anger in a Godly Way.* Chicago: Moody Press, 1999.

Chevalier, A. J. *On the Client's Path: A Manual for the Practice of Solution-Focused Therapy.* Oakland, Calif.: New Harbinger Publications, Inc., 1995.

Childs, B. H. *Short-Term Pastoral Counseling: A Guide.* Nashville: Abingdon Press, 1990.

Clinebell, H. *Understanding and Counseling: Persons with Alcohol, Drug, and Behavioral Addictions: Counseling for Recovery and Prevention Using Psychology.* Nashville: Abingdon Press, 1998.

Cloud, H., and J. Townsend. *Raising Great Kids: Parenting with Grace and Truth.* Grand Rapids: Zondervan Publishing House, 1999.

Coleman, P. *The Forgiving Marriage.* Chicago: Contemporary Books, 1989.

Collins, G. R. *Christian Counseling.* Dallas: Word Publishing, 1988.

_____. *Christian Counseling: A Comprehensive Guide.* Revised ed. Dallas: Word Publishing, 1988.

_____. *The Biblical Basis of Christian Counseling for People Helpers.* Colorado Springs: Navpress, 2001.

Conway, J., and S. Conway. *When a Mate Wants Out: Secrets for Saving a Marriage.* Grand Rapids: Zondervan Publishing, 1992.

Cosgrove, M. P. *Counseling for Anger.* Resources for Christian Counseling, vol. 1. Nashville: Word Books, 1988.

Coyle, Philip A. "A Critical Analysis of Family Therapists' Clinical Behaviors." Ph.D. diss., New Orleans Baptist Theological Seminary, 1987.

Crabb, Larry. *Basic Principles of Biblical Counseling.* Grand Rapids: Zondervan Publishing House, 1975.

_____. *How to Deal with Anger.* Colorado Springs: Navpress, 1991.

Crabb, Larry. *The Marriage Builder: A Blueprint for Couples and Counselors.* Grand Rapids: Zondervan Publishing, 1992.

de Shazer, S. *Clues: Investigating Solutions in Brief Therapy.* New York: W. W. Norton & Company, 1988.

DiBlasio, Frederick A. Workshop presented at the Annual Convention of the American Association for Marriage and Family Therapy, 1997.

Dobson, J. C. *Love for a Lifetime: Building a Marriage That Will Go the Distance.* Portland, Oreg.: Multnomah Press, 1987.

_____. *The New Dare to Discipline.* Wheaton: Tyndale House Publishing, 1996.

_____. *Emotions: Can You Trust Them.* Ventura, Calif.: Gospel Light Publications, 1997.

_____. *Home with a Heart.* Wheaton: Tyndale House Publishing, 1997.

Doherty, W. J. *Soul Searching: Why Psychotherapy Must Promote Moral Responsibility.* New York: Basic Books, 1995.

Drakeford, J. W. *Integrity Therapy.* Nashville: Broadman Press, 1967.

Drakeford, J. W., and C. V. King. *Wise Counsel: Skills for Lay Counseling.* Nashville: The Sunday School Board of the Southern Baptist Convention, 1988.

Egan, G. *The Skilled Helper: A Problem-Management Approach to Helping.* 6th ed. Pacific Grove, Calif.: Brooks/Cole Publishing Company, 1997.

Enright, R. D., and J. North. *Exploring Forgiveness.* Madison: University of Wisconsin Press, 1988.

Erikson, Erik H. *Childhood and Society.* New York: W.W. Norton & Company, 1985.

Flanigan, B. *Forgiving the Unforgivable: Overcoming the Bitter Legacy of Intimate Wounds.* Foster City, Calif.: IDG Books Worldwide, 1994.

Fleischman, M. J., A. M. Horne, and J. L. Arthur. *Troubled Families: A Treatment Program.* Champaign, Ill.: Research Press, 1983.

Flournoy, R. L., F. Minirth, F., and P. Meier. *100 Ways to Obtain Peace: Overcome Anxiety.* Old Tappan, N.J.: Fleming H. Revell Co., 1993.

Fossum, Merle A., and Marilyn J. Mason. *Facing Shame: Families in Recovery.* New York: W. W. Norton & Company, 1986.

Gilbert, B. *The Pastoral Care of Depression: A Guidebook.* Binghamton, N.Y.: Haworth Pastoral Press, 1998.

Godin, A. *The Pastor as Counselor.* New York: Holt, Rinehart and Winston, 1965.

Gold, M. *Good News about Depression: Cures and Treatments in the New Age of Psychiatry.* New York: Random House, 1995.

Gottman, J. *Why Marriages Succeed or Fail.* New York: Simon & Schuster, 1994.

Greenberger, D., and C. A. Padesky. *Mind Over Mood: A Cognitive Therapy Treatment Manual for Clients.* New York: Guilford Press, 1995.

Hands, D. R., and W. L. Fehr. *Spiritual Wholeness for Clergy.* Foreword by S. Howatch. New York: The Alban Institute, 1993.

Hargrave, T. D. *Families & Forgiveness: Healing Wounds in the Intergenerational Family.* New York: Brunner/Mazel Publishers, 1994.

Harley, W. R., Jr. *His Needs, Her Needs.* Old Tappan, N.J.: Fleming H. Revell, Co., 1995.

Hart, A. *Counseling the Depressed.* Waco: Word Books, 1987.

Hart, T. N. *The Art of Christian Listening.* New York: Paulist Press, 1980.

Headrick, J. A. "Developing a Pastoral Counseling Model That Utilizes Selected Brief Therapy Techniques and Communication Skills Training in Working with the Marital Problems of Couples. Ph.D. diss., New Orleans Baptist Theological Seminary, 1987.

Heaton, J. A. *Building Basic Therapeutic Skills: A Practical Guide for Current Mental Health Practice.* San Francisco: Jossey-Bass Publishers, 1998.

Hemfelt, R., and R. Fowler. *Serenity: A Companion for Twelve Step Recovery Complete with New Testament Psalms and Proverbs.* Nashville: Thomas Nelson, 1991.

Hiltner, S. *The Counselor in Counseling.* New York: Abingdon-Cokesbury Press, 1952.

Hulme, W. E. *Pastoral Care and Counseling.* Minneapolis: Augsburg Publishing House, 1981.

Kelsey, M. *Prophetic Ministry.* New York: Crossroad, 1982.

Kemp, C. F. *The Caring Pastor.* Nashville: Abingdon Press, 1985.

Kirwan, W. T. *Biblical Concepts for Christian Counseling.* Grand Rapids: Baker Book House, 1984.

Kniskern, J. W. *When the Vow Breaks: A Survival and Recovery Guide for Christians Facing Divorce.* Nashville: Broadman & Holman Press, 1993.

Lahaye, T. F., and B. Phillips. *Anger Is a Choice.* Grand Rapids: Zondervan Publishing House, 1982.

Leitch, J. S. *Suicide Prevention: A Narrative Guide for Professionals.* Oklahoma Department of Human Services, Integrated Family Services, Field Operations Division, 1990.

Leman, K., D. Jackson, and N. Jackson, N. *Becoming the Parent God Wants You to Be*. Colorado Springs: Navpress, 1998.

Lynch, W. R. *Images of Hope: Imagination as Healer of the Hopeless*. Baltimore: Helicon Press, 1965.

Madden, M. C. *The Power to Bless*. Revised ed. New Orleans: Insight Press, 1999.

Manning, B. *Abba's Child: The Cry of the Heart for Intimate Belonging*. Colorado Springs: NavPress, 1994.

_____. *Lion and Lamb: The Relentless Tenderness of Jesus*. Colorado Springs: NavPress, 1986.

_____. *The Ragamuffin Gospel: Embracing the Unconditional Love of God*. Colorado Springs: NavPress, 1993.

_____. *Reflections for Ragamuffins: Daily Devotions from the Writings of Brennan Manning*. Edited by Ann McMath Weinheimer, Ed. Colorado Springs: NavPress, 1998.

Markman, H., S. Stanley, S., and S. Blumberg. *Fighting for Your Marriage*. San Francisco: Jossey-Bass, 1994.

Marshall, J. R. *Social Phobia: From Shyness to Stage Fright*. New York: Basic Books, 1995.

Martin, D. G. *Counseling and Therapy Skills*. 2d ed. Prospect Heights, Ill.: Waveland Press, 1983.

Matthews, W. J., and J. H. Edgette. *Current Thinking and Research in Brief Therapy: Solutions, Strategies, Narratives*. Vol. 2. Philadelphia: Taylor & Francis, 1998.

May, G. *Addiction and Grace*. San Francisco: Harper San Francisco, 1991.

McCullough, M. E., S. J. Sandage, and E. L. Worthington, Jr. *To Forgive Is Human: How to Put Your Past in the Past*. Downers Grove, Ill.: InterVarsity Press, 1997.

McDowell, J., and B. Hostetler. *Josh McDowell's Handbook on Counseling Youth: A Comprehensive Guide for Equipping Youth Workers, Pastors, Teachers, and Parents*. Nashville: Word Books, 1996.

McIntosh, I. F. *Pastoral Care and Pastoral Theology*. Philadelphia: Westminster Press, 1972.

McMinin, M. R. *Psychology, Theology, and Spirituality in Christian Counseling*. Wheaton: Tyndale House Publishers, Inc., 1996.

Menninger, K. A. *Whatever Became of Sin?* New York: Hawthorne Books, 1973.

Miller, K. *A Hunger for Healing: The Twelve Steps as a Classic Model for Christian Spiritual Growth*. San Francisco: Harper San Francisco, 1992.

Miller, K. *A Hunger for Healing Workbook.* San Francisco: Harper San Francisco, 1992.

Minirth, F. B., and P. D. Meier. *Counseling and the Nature of Man.* Grand Rapids: Baker Book House, 1982.

Moon, G. *Homesick for Eden: A Soul's Journey to Joy.* Ann Arbor, Mich.: Servant Publications, 1997.

Morris, D., with G. Lewis. *Forgiving the Dead Man Walking.* Grand Rapids: Zondervan Publishing House, 1998.

Moyer, K. E. *The Psychobiology of Aggression.* New York: Harper and Row, 1976.

Narramore, B. *Help! I'm a Parent: How to Handle Temper Tantrums, Sibling Fights, Questions about Sex, and Other Parenting Challenges.* Grand Rapids: Zondervan Publishing House, 1995.

Narramore, C. M. *The Psychology of Counseling.* Grand Rapids: Zondervan Publishing House, 1960.

Nouwen, H. J. M. *The Wounded Healer: Ministry in Contemporary Society.* New York: Image Books, Doubleday, 1972.

Oates, W. E. *An Introduction to Pastoral Counseling.* Nashville: Broadman Press, 1959.

_____. *The Presence of God in Pastoral Counseling.* Waco: Word Books Publisher, 1986.

Oates, W. E., and A. Lester. *Pastoral Care in Crucial Human Situations.* Valley Forge: Judson Press, 1969.

Oden, T. C. *Kerygma and Counseling.* Philadelphia: Westminster Press, 1966.

Oglesby, W. B., Jr. *Referral in Pastoral Counseling.* Nashville: Abingdon, 1978.

Orlinsky, D. E., and K. I. Howard. "Process and Outcome in Psychotherapy." In S. L. Garfield and A. E. Bergin, eds., *Handbook of Psychotherapy and Behavior Change,* 3d ed., 311-81. New York: Wiley, 1896.

Patton, J. *Pastoral Counseling: A Ministry of the Church.* Nashville: Abingdon Press, 1983.

Powell, P. W. *The Life Beyond.* Tyler, Tex.: Paul Powell, 1998.

Pruyser, P. W. *The Minister as Diagnostician.* Philadelphia: Westminster Press, 1976.

Ray, W., and R. Rivizza. *Methods Toward a Science of Behavioral Experience.* 2d ed. Belmont, Calif.: Wadsworth, 1985.

Reisser, P. C. *The Focus on the Family Complete Book of Baby and Child Care.* Wheaton: Tyndale House Publishing, 1999.

Richardson, R. W. *Family Ties That Bind*. North Vancouver, British Columbia: International Self-Counsel Press Ltd., 1984.

Roberts, R. C., and M. R. Talbot. *Limning the Psyche: Explorations in Christian Psychology*. Grand Rapids: William B. Eerdmans Publishing Company, 1997

Rosenau, D. *A Celebration of Sex*. Nashville: Thomas Nelson, 1996.

Savage, J. *Listening & Caring Skills in Ministry: A Guide for Pastors, Counselors, and Small Group Leaders*. Nashville: Abingdon Press, 1996.

Sears, M., and W. Sears. *The Complete Book of Christian Parenting & Child Care: A Medical & Moral Guide to Raising Happy, Healthy Children*. Nashville: Broadman & Holman Publishers, 1997.

Schroeder, T. W. *Pastors Counseling Manual for Ministry to Those Who Must Sustain a Loved One in Crisis*. St. Louis: Concordia Publishing House, 1981.

Sheehan, D. *The Anxiety Disease*. New York: Bantam Books, 1983.

Sizemore, F. H. *Suicide: The Signs and Solutions*. Wheaton: Victor Books, 1988.

Smalley, G., and D. Silvestro. *Love Is a Decision: Thirteen Proven Principles to Energize Your Marriage and Family*. New York: Pocket Books, 1993.

Smedes, L. B. *Art of Forgiving: When You Need to Forgive and Don't Know How*. San Francisco: Harper San Francisco, 1996.

_____. *Forgive and Forget: Healing the Hurts We Don't Deserve*. New York: Harper & Row, 1984.

Smith, D. *Integrative Therapy*. Grand Rapids: Baker Book House, 1990.

Sphar, A. "An Investigation of the Relationship between Internalized Shame and Dualistic Thinking in Students at the New Orleans Baptist Theological Seminary." Ph.D. diss., New Orleans Baptist Theological Seminary, 1988.

Stewart, C. W. *The Minister as Family Counselor*. Nashville: Abingdon Press, 1979.

Stone, H. W. *Brief Pastoral Counseling: Short-Term Approaches and Strategies*. Minneapolis: Fortress Press, 1994.

Switzer, D. K. *Pastoral Care Emergencies: Ministering to People in Crisis*. Mahwah, N.J.: Paulist Press, 1989.

Tan, S.-Y. *Understanding Depression*. Grand Rapids: Baker Book House, 1995.

Taylor, C. W. *The Skilled Pastor: Counseling as the Practice of Theology*. Minneapolis: Fortress Press, 1991.

Taylor, G., and R. Wilson (contributor). *Exploring Your Anger: Friend or Foe?* Strategic Christian Living Series. Grand Rapids: Baker Book House, 1997.

Thornton, E. E. *Theology and Pastoral Counseling.* Englewood Cliffs, N.J.: Prentice-Hall, Inc., 1964.

Thurman, C. *The Lies We Believe.* Nashville: Thomas Nelson Publishers, 1989.

Walter, J. L., and J. E. Peller. *Becoming Solution-Focused in Brief Therapy.* New York: Brunner/Mazel Publishers, 1992.

Warren, P., J. Capehart, and S. Dengler. *You & Your A.D.D. Child: How to Understand and Help Kids with Attention Deficit Disorder.* Nashville: Thomas Nelson, 1995.

Weeks, G. R., and S. Treat. *Couples in Treatment: Techniques and Approaches for Effective Practice.* New York: Brunner/Mazel, Publishers, 1992.

Weil, B. E. *Adultery, the Forgivable Sin: Healing the Inherited Patterns of Betrayal in Your Family.* New York: Birch Lane Press, 1993.

Weissman, M. M., J. C. Markowitz, and G. L. Klerman. *Comprehensive Guide to Interpersonal Psychotherapy.* New York, New York: Basic Books, 2000.

Westberg, G. E. *Good Grief: A Constructive Approach to the Problem of Loss.* Philadelphia: Fortress Press, 1971.

Wheat, E. *First Years of Forever.* Grand Rapids: Zondervan Publishing, 1988.

_____. *Intended for Pleasure.* Old Tappan, N.J.: Fleming H. Revell Co., 1997.

_____. *Love Life for Every Married Couple.* Grand Rapids: Zondervan Publishing, 1983.

White, J. R. *Grieving: Our Path Back to Peace.* Minneapolis: Bethany House Publishers, 1997.

White, J., and G. Smalley, G. *What Kids Wish Parents Knew About Parenting: What You Need to Know Before It's Too Late.* Monroe, La.: Howard Publishing, 1998.

Whitlock, G. E. *Preventive Psychology and the Church.* Philadelphia: Westminster Press, 1973.

Wicks, R. J., and R. D. Parsons. Clinical Handbook of Pastoral Counseling. Vol. 2. Mahwah, N.J.: Paulist Press, 1993.

Wilson, S., and L. Crabb. *Into Abba's Arms.* Carol Stream, Ill.: Tyndale House Publishers, 1998.

Wimberly, E. P. *Using Scripture in Pastoral Counseling.* Nashville: Abingdon Press, 1994.

Worthington, E. L., Jr. *Dimensions of Forgiveness*. Radnor, Pa.: Templeton Foundation Press, 1998.

_____. *Hope-Focused Marriage Counseling: A Guide to Brief Therapy*. Downers Grove, Ill.: Intervarsity Press, 1999.

_____. *Marriage Counseling: A Christian Approach to Counseling Couples*. Downers Grove, Ill.: InterVarsity Press, 1993.

_____. "The Pyramid Model of Forgiveness: Some Interdisciplinary Speculations about Unforgiveness and the Promotion of Forgiveness." In E. L. Worthington, Jr. and M. E. McCullough, eds., *The Foundation of the Scientific Study of Forgiveness*. Radnor, Pa.: The John Templeton Foundation Press, 1998.

Worthington, E. L., and K. Worthington. *Helping Parents Make Disciples: Strategic Pastoral Counseling Resources*. Grand Rapids: Baker Book House, 1996.

Wright, H. N. *After You Say 'I Do.'* Eugene, Oreg.: Harvest House, 1999.

_____. *Before You Remarry*. Eugene, Oreg.: Harvest House, 1999.

_____. *Before You Say I Do: A Marriage Preparation Manual for Couples*. Eugene, Oreg.: Harvest House, 1997.

_____. *Marital Counseling*. San Francisco: Harper & Row Publishers, 1981.

_____. *Self-Talk, Imagery, and Prayer in Counseling*. Vol. 3. Waco: Word Books, 1986.

Wright, N., G. J. Oliver, G. J., and S. Dahl. *Fears, Doubts, Blues, and Pouts: Stories About Handling Fear, Worry, Sadness, and Anger*. Colorado Springs: Chariot Victor Publication, 1999.

Yalom, I. D. *Love's Executioner & Other Tales of Psychotherapy*. New York: Harper Perennial, 1989.

Zondervan Publishing Company. *Recovery Devotional Bible: New International Version*, 1993.

Preaching Resources

Allen, R. J., ed. *Patterns of Preaching: A Sermon Sampler*. St. Louis: Chalice Press, 1998.

Allen, R. J., B. S. Blairsdell, and S. B. Johnson. *Theology for Preaching*. Nashville: Abingdon Press, 1997.

Alter, R. *The Art of Biblical Narrative*. New York: Basic Books, Inc. Publishers, 1981.

Anderson, L. *Dying for Change*. Minneapolis: Bethany House, 1990.

Aycock, Don M., ed. *Herald to a New Age: Preaching for the Twenty-First Century*. Elgin, Ill.: Brethren Press, 1985.

Bailey, R. *Jesus the Preacher*. Nashville: Broadman Press, 1990.

Bailey, R., and J. L. Blevins. *Dramatic Monologues: Making the Bible Live*. Nashville: Broadman Press, 1990.

Bailey, R. W. *The Minister and Grief*. New York: Hawthorn Books, Inc., 1976.

Barna, G. "The Pulpit-meister: Preaching to the New Majority." *Preaching* 12, no. 4 (1997): 11-13.

Bauer, C. *Handbook for Storytellers*. Chicago: American Library Association, 1977.

Baumann, D. J. *An Introduction to Contemporary Preaching*. Grand Rapids: Baker Book House, 1972.

Bausch, W. *Storytelling: Imagination and Faith*. Mystic, Conn.: Twenty-third Publications, 1985.

Baxter, B. B. *The Heart of the Yale Lectures*. New York: The Macmillian Company, 1947.

Bennett, B. *Thirty Minutes to Raise the Dead: How You Can Preach Your Best Sermon Yet—This Sunday*. Nashville: Thomas Nelson Publishers, 1991.

Blackwood, A. W. *Preaching from the Bible*. New York: Abingdon-Cokesbury Press, 1941.

_____. *Biographical Preaching for Today*. Nashville: Abingdon Press, 1954.

Blackwood, J. R. *The Soul of Frederick W. Robertson*. New York and London: Harper & Brothers Publishers, 1947.

Bridger, F., and D. Atkinson. *Counseling in Context*. London: Harper-Collins Publishers, 1994.

Broadus, J. A. *On the Preparation and Delivery of Sermons*. 4th ed. Revised by V. L. Stanfield. San Francisco: Harper and Row, Publishers, 1979.

Brokoff, J. R. *As One with Authority*. Wilmore, Ky.: Bristol Books, 1989.

Brooks, P. *Lectures on Preaching*. New York: E. P. Dutton, 1877.

_____. *Lectures on Preaching*. Grand Rapids: Zondervan Publishing House, n.d.

Brown, C. R. *The Art of Preaching*. New York: Macmillan, 1922.

_____. *The Social Message of the Modern Pulpit*. New York: Scribners, 1906.

Brown, D. M. *Dramatic Narrative in Preaching*. Valley Forge, Pa.: Judson Press, 1981.

Brown, H. C. *A Quest for Reformation in Preaching.* Waco: Word Books, Publishers, 1968.

Brown, H. C., Jr., H. G. Clinard, and J. J. Northcutt. *Steps to the Sermon: A Plan for Sermon Preparation.* Nashville: Broadman Press, 1963.

Brown, H. C., Jr., H. G. Clinard, J. J. Northcutt, and A. Fasol. *Revised Steps to the Sermon: An Eight-Step Plan for Preaching with Confidence.* Nashville: Broadman & Holman Publishers, 1996.

Brueggemann, W. *Finally Comes the Poet: Daring Speech for Proclamation.* Minneapolis: Fortress, 1989.

Bryson, H. T. *Expository Preaching: The Art of Preaching through a Book of the Bible.* Nashville: Broadman & Holman Publishers, 1995.

Buechner, F. *Telling the Truth: The Gospel as Tragedy, Comedy, Fairy Tale.* San Francisco, Harper and Row, 1977.

Bugg, C. *Preaching from the Inside Out.* Nashville: Broadman Press, 1992.

Buttrick, D. *Homiletic: Moves and Structures.* Philadelphia: Fortress Press, 1987.

Caldwell, F. H. *Preaching Angels.* New York: Abingdon Press, 1954.

Campbell, B. *Toolbox for (Busy) Pastors.* Nashville: Convention Press, 1998.

Carson, D. A. *Telling the Truth: Evangelizing Postmoderns.* Grand Rapids: Zondervan, 2000.

Chappell, Bryan. *Christ-Centered Preaching: Redeeming the Expository Sermon.* Grand Rapids: Baker, 1994.

Chappell, C. G. *Anointed to Preach.* Nashville: Abingdon-Cokesbury Press, 1951.

Chartier, M. R. *Preaching as Communcation: An Interpersonal Perspective.* Nashville: Abingdon Press, 1981.

Claypool, J. *The Preaching Event.* Revised ed. New Orleans: Insight Press, 2000.

Cleland, J. T. *Preaching to be Understood.* Nashville: Abingdon, 1965.

Coffin, H. S. *Preaching in a Day of Social Rebuilding.* New Haven: Yale University Press, 1918.

Cothen, J. *Equipped for Good Work.* Gretna, La.: Pelican Publishing Company, 1981.

Cox, J. W. *Preaching.* San Francisco: Harper & Row, 1985.

Craddock, F. *Overhearing the Gospel.* Nashville, Abingdon Press, 1978.

_____. *Preaching.* Nashville: Abingdon Press, 1985.

Craft, C. H. *Communication Theory for Christian Witness.* Nashville: Abingdon, 1983.

Criswell, W. A. *Criswell's Guidebook for Pastors*. Nashville: Broadman Press, 1980.

Crum, M., Jr. *Manual on Preaching*. Wilton, Conn.: Morehouse-Barlow, 1988.

Dale, R. W. *Nine Lectures on Preaching*. New York: A. S. Barnes & Co., 1878.

Davis, H. G. *Design for Preaching*. Philadelphia: Muhlenberg, 1958.

Dawn, M. J. *Reaching Out without Dumbing Down*. Grand Rapids: William B. Eerdmans, 1995.

DeBrand, R. E. *Guide to Biographical Preaching*. Nashville: Broadman Press, 1988.

Dockery, D. *The Challenge of Postmodernism*. Wheaton: Victor Books, 1995.

Dodd, C. H. *The Apostolic Preaching and Its Development*. New York: Harper and Row, 1964.

Duduit, M., ed. *Handbook of Contemporary Preaching*. Nashville: Broadman Press, 1992.

Erickson, M. J., and J. R. Heflin. *Old Wine in New Wineskins: Doctrinal Preaching in a Changing World*. Grand Rapids: Baker Books, 1997.

Eslinger, R. L. *Narrative Imagination: Preaching the Words That Shape Us*. Minneapolis: Fortress Press, 1995.

Fant, C. E., and W. Pinson, Jr., eds. *A Treasury of Great Preaching*. Vol. 6. Dallas: Word Publishing, 1995.

Farmer, H. H. *The Servant of the Word*. Philadelphia: Fortress, 1964. (Original work published 1941.)

Farris, S. *Preaching That Matters*. Louisville: Westminster John Knox Press, 1998.

Fasol, A. *Essentials for Biblical Preaching: An Introduction to Basic Sermon Preparation*. Grand Rapids: Baker Book House, 1989.

_____. *With a Bible in Their Hands*. Nashville: Broadman & Holman Publishers, 1994.

Fee, G. D., and D. Stuart. *How to Read the Bible for All It's Worth: A Guide to Understanding the Bible*. Grand Rapids: Zondervan, 1982.

Fisher, D. *The 21st Century Pastor*. Grand Rapids: Zondervan Publishing House, 1996.

Ford, D. W. C. *The Ministry of the Word*. Grand Rapids: William B. Eerdmans, 1979.

Ford, L. *The Christian Persuader*. Minneapolis: World Wide Publications, 1966.

Forde, G. O. *Theology Is for Preaching*. Minneapolis: Fortress Press, 1990.

Forsyth, P. T. *Positive Preaching and the Modern Mind*. New York: Hodder and Stoughton, 1907.

Fosdick, H. E. *The Modern Use of the Bible*. New York: Macmillan, 1924.

_____."What Is the Matter with Preaching." In L. Crocker, ed. *Art of Preaching: An Anthology*, 39-50. Springfield: Charles C. Thomas, 1971.

Freeman, H. *Variety in Biblical Preaching: Innovative Techniques and Fresh Forms*. Waco: Word Books, 1986.

Fry, J. *Homiletics*. Philadelphia: Board of Publications of the General Council, 1919.

Galli, M., and C. B. Larson. *Preaching That Connects: Using the Techniques of Journalists to Add Impact to Your Sermons*. Grand Rapids: Zondervan, 1994.

Garrison, W. *The Preacher and His Audience*. Westwood, N.J.: Revell, 1954.

Garvie, A. E. *The Christian Preacher*. New York: Charles Scribner's Sons, 1921.

Gericke, P. *Sermon Building: A Guided Learning Book*. El Paso: Carib Baptist Publications, 1973.

Gladden, W. *Tools and the Man*. Boston: Houghton Mifflin, 1893.

Goodman, T. *The Intentional Minister*. Nashville: Broadman and Holman, 1994.

Gossip, A. J. *In Christ's Stead*. London: Hodder & Stoughton, 1921.

Gowan, D. E. *Reclaiming the Old Testament for the Christian Pulpit*. Atlanta: John Knox Press, 1980.

Greidanus, S. *The Modern Preacher and the Ancient Text: Interpreting and Preaching Biblical Literature*. Grand Rapids: William B. Eerdmans Publishing Company, 1988.

Hall, E. E., and J. R. Heflin. *Proclaim the Word!* Nashville: Broadman Press, 1985.

Hamilton, D. L. *Homiletical Handbook*. Nashville: Broadman Press, 1992.

Hasselgrave, David. *Communicating Christ Cross-Culturally: An Introduction to Missionary Communication*. 2d ed. Grand Rapids: Zondervan Publishing House, 1991.

Hemphill, K. *The Antioch Effect*. Nashville: Broadman and Holman, 1994.

Henderson, D. W. *Culture Shift: Communicating God's Truth to Our Changing World*. Grand Rapids: Baker Books, 1998.

Holbert, J. C. *Preaching Old Testament: Proclamation and Narrative in the Hebrew Bible*. Nashville: Abingdon Press, 1991.

Horne, C. F. *Dynamic Preaching: How to Make Your Preaching Life-Changing and Powerful.* Nashville: Broadman Press, 1983.

Horne, C. S. *The Romance of Preaching.* New York: Revell, 1914.

Horseman, C. *Good News for a Postmodern World.* Cambridge: Grove Books, 1996.

Hybels, B., S. Briscoe, and H. Robinson. *Mastering Contemporary Preaching.* Portland, Oreg.: Multnomah Press, 1989.

Jackson, E. N. *A Psychology for Preaching.* Great Neck, N.Y.: Channel Press Inc., 1974. (Original work published 1961.)

Jefferson, C. E. *The Building of the Church.* New York: Macmillan, 1910.

Jones, E. D. *The Royalty of the Pulpit.* New York: Harper & Brothers Publishers, 1951.

Jones, I. T. *Principles and Practice of Preaching.* New York: Abingdon Press, 1956.

Jowett, J. H. *The Preacher: His Life and Work.* New York: G. H. Doran, 1912.

Kaiser, W. C., Jr. *The Old Testament in Contemporary Preaching.* Grand Rapids: Baker Books, 1973.

_____. *Toward an Exegetical Theology: Biblical Exegesis for Preaching and Teaching.* Grand Rapids: Baker Book House, 1981.

Keck, L. E. *The Bible in the Pulpit: The Renewal of Biblical Preaching.* Nashville: Abingdon Press, 1978.

Kemp, C. F. *The Preaching Pastor.* St. Louis: Bethany Press, 1966.

Kennedy, G. *God's Good News.* New York: Harpers, 1955.

Killinger, J. *Fundamentals of Preaching.* Philadelphia: Fortress Press, 1985.

Klem, H. *Oral Communication of the Scriptures.* Pasadena: William Carey Library, 1982.

Koller, C. W. *Expository Preaching without Notes.* Grand Rapids: Baker Book House, 1962.

Kraft, C. *Christianity in Culture: A Study in Dynamic Theologizing in Cross-Cultural Perspectives.* Maryknoll, N.Y.: Orbis Books, 1991.

Kromminga, C. G. "Remember Lot's Wife: Preaching Old Testament Narrative Texts." *Calvin Theological Journal* 18 (1983): 32-46.

Larsen, D. L. *The Anatomy of Preaching: Identifying the Issues in Preaching Today.* Grand Rapids: Kregel Publications, 1999.

_____. *Telling the Old, Old Story.* Wheaton: Crossway Books, 1995.

Lewis, R. L., with G. Lewis. *Inductive Preaching: Helping People Listen.* Westchester, Ill.: Crossway Books, 1983.

Liefield, W. E. *From Text to Sermon.* Grand Rapids, Zondervan, 1984.

Loscalzo, C. A. *Apologetic Preaching*. Downers Grove, Ill.: InterVarsity Press, 2000.

Lowry, E. L. *Doing Time in the Pulpit: The Relationship between Narrative and Preaching*. Nashville: Abingdon Press, 1985.

Luccock, H. E. *Communicating the Gospel*. New York: Harper & Brothers, Publishers, 1954.

Lueking, F. D. *Preaching: The Art of Connecting God and People*. Waco: Word Books, 1985.

Lutzer, E. *Pastor to Pastor: Tackling the Problems of Ministry*. Grand Rapids: Kregel Publications, 1998.

MacArthur, J., Jr. *Rediscovering Pastoral Ministry*. Dallas: Word Publishing, 1995.

MacArthur, J., Jr., and The Master's Seminary Faculty. *Rediscovering Expository Preaching*. Dallas: Word Publishing, 1992.

Macchia, S. A. *Becoming a Healthy Church: 10 Characteristics*. Grand Rapids: Baker Books, 1999.

Macgregor, H. C. *The Making of a Preacher*. Philadelphia: Westminster, 1946.

Malphurs, A. *Developing a Vision for Ministry in the 21st Century*. 2d ed. Grand Rapids: Baker Books, 1999.

Massey, J. E. *Designing the Sermon: Order and Movement in Preaching*. Nashville: Abingdon, 1980.

Maxwell, J. *Developing the Leader within You*. Nashville: Thomas Nelson, 1993.

Mawhinney, B. *Preaching with Freshness*. Eugene, Oreg.: Harvest House, 1991.

McConnel, F. J. *The Prophetic Ministry*. New York: Abingdon, 1930.

McDill, W. *The 12 Essentials for Great Preaching*. Nashville: Broadman & Holman Publishers, 1994.

McDonough, R. M. *Leading Your Church in Long-Range Planning*. 2d ed. Nashville: Convention Press, 1975.

Meyer, F. B. *Expository Preaching: Plans and Methods*. Grand Rapids: Baker Book House, 1980. (Original work published 1912.)

Miller, C. *The Empowered Communicator: 7 Keys to Unlocking an Audience*. Nashville: Broadman & Holman Publishers, 1994.

_____. *The Empowered Leader: Ten Keys to Servant Leadership*. Nashville: Broadman and Holman Publishers, 1995.

Miller, D. G. *Fire in Thy Mouth*. Nashville: Abingdon Press, 1954.

_____. *The Way to Biblical Preaching*. Nashville: Abingdon Press, 1957.

Mitchell, H. H. *Celebration and Experience in Preaching*. Nashville: Abingdon Press, 1990.

_____. *The Recovery of Preaching*. San Francisco: Harper & Row, 1977.

Mitchell, J. P. *Visually Speaking*. Louisville: Westminster John Knox Press, 1999.

Morgan, G. C. *Preaching*. Old Tappan, N.J.: Fleming H. Revell, Co., 1937.

Morgan, P. *Story Weaving: Using Stories to Transform Your Congregation*. St. Louis: CBP Press, 1986.

Niles, D. T. *The Preacher's Task and the Stone of Stumbling*. New York: Harpers, 1955.

Noyes, M. P. *Preaching the Word of God*. New York: Scribner, 1943.

Olford, S. F., and D. L. Olford. *Anointed Expository Preaching*. Nashville: Broadman and Holman, 1998.

Ong, W. *Orality and Literacy: The Technologizing of the Word*. New York: Routledge, 1982.

Oxnam, G. B. *Preaching in a Revolutionary Age*. New York: Abingdon-Cokesbury, 1944.

Peck, T. "Salvaging the Old Testament Biographical Sermon." *Preaching* 15, no. 6 (2000): 28-30.

Pepper, G. W. *A Voice from the Crowd*. New Haven: Yale University Press, 1915.

Perry, L. M. *Biblical Preaching for Today*. Chicago: Moody Press, 1990.

_____. *Biblical Preaching for Today's World*. Chicago: Moody Press, 1973.

_____. *Biblical Sermon Guide*. Grand Rapids: Baker Book House, 1979.

Piper, J. *The Supremacy of God in Preaching*. Grand Rapids: Baker Book House, 1990.

Pitt-Watson, I. *Preaching: A Kind of Folly*. Philadelphia: Westminster, 1978.

_____. *A Primer for Preachers*. Grand Rapids: Baker Book House, 1986.

Rainer, T. S. *Eating the Elephant*. Nashville: Broadman and Holman Publishers, 1994.

Read, D. H. C. *The Communication of the Gospel*. London: SCM, 1952.

_____. *Sent from God: The Enduring Mystery of Preaching*. Nashville: Abingdon, 1974.

Reid, C. H. *The Empty Pulpit: A Study in Preaching as Communication*. New York: Harper & Row, 1967.

Robinson, H. W. *Biblical Preaching: The Development and Delivery of Expository Messages.* Grand Rapids: Baker Book House, 1980.

_____. *Making a Difference in Preaching.* Grand Rapids: Baker Books, 1999.

Robinson, H., S. Briscoe, and B. Hybels. *Mastering Contemporary Preaching.* Portland, Oreg.: Multnomah, 1989.

Rosenberg, B. *The Art of the American Folk Preacher.* New York: Oxford University Press, 1970.

Rust, E. C. *The Word and Words: Towards a Theology of Preaching.* Macon: Mercer University Press, 1982.

Salmon, B. *Storytelling in Preaching: A Guide to Theory and Practice.* Nashville: Broadman Press, 1988.

Sample, T. *Hard-Living People and Mainstream Christians.* Nashville: Abingdon Press, 1993.

Samples, B. *The Metaphoric Mind.* Reading, Mass.: Addison-Wesley Publishing Co., 1976.

Scherer, P. *For We Have This Treasure.* New York: Harper, 1944.

Schreiter, R. *Constructing Local Theologies.* Maryknoll, N.Y.: Orbis Books, 1985.

Shoemaker, H. S. *Retelling the Biblical Story: The Theology and Practice of Narrative Preaching.* Nashville: Broadman Press, 1985.

Skinner, C. *The Teaching Ministry of the Pulpit: Its History, Theology, Psychology, and Practice for Today.* Grand Rapids: Baker Book House, 1973.

Sleeth, R. E. *God's Word and Our Words: Basic Homiletics.* Atlanta: John Knox Press, 1986.

Spradley, J. *Culture and Cognition: Rules, Maps and Plans.* San Francisco: Chandler, 1972.

Stevenson, D. E. *In the Biblical Preacher's Workshop.* Nashville: Abingdon Press, 1967.

Stewart, J. S. *A Faith to Proclaim.* New York: Scribners, 1953.

_____. *Heralds of God.* Grand Rapids: Baker, 1972. (Original work published 1946.)

Stott, J. R. W. *Between Two Worlds: The Art of Preaching in the Twentieth Century.* Grand Rapids: William B. Eerdmans Publishing Company, 1982.

Sweazey, G. E. *Preaching the Good News.* Englewood Cliffs, N.J.: Prentice-Hall, 1976.

Taylor, G. *How Shall They Preach.* Elgin, Ill.: Progressive Baptist Publishing House, 1977.

Taylor, W. M. *The Ministry of the Word.* New York: Anson D. F. Randolf and Co., 1876.

Thompson, W. D. *Preaching Biblically: Exegesis and Interpretation.* Nashville: Abingdon Press, 1981.

Tizard, L. J. *Preaching: The Art of Communication.* New York: Oxford University Press, 1959.

Troger, T. H. *Ten Strategies for Preaching in a Multimedia Culture.* Nashville: Abingdon Press, 1996.

Turner, T. A. *Preaching to Programmed People.* Grand Rapids: Kregal Resources, 1995.

Van Der Geest, H. *Presence in the Pulpit: The Impact of Personality in Preaching.* Translated by D. W. Stott. Atlanta: John Knox, 1981.

Vine, W. E. *Vine's Complete Expository Dictionary of Old and New Testament Words.* Edited by Merrill F. Unger and William White, Jr. Nashville: Thomas Nelson, 1996.

Vines, J., and J. Shaddix. *Power in the Pulpit: How to Prepare and Deliver Expository Sermons.* Chicago: Moody, 1999.

Warren, R. *The Purpose Driven Church.* Grand Rapids: Zondervan, 1995.

Watson, J. I. M. *The Cure of Souls.* New York: Dodd Mead, 1896.

Whitesell, F. D. *The Art of Biblical Preaching.* Grand Rapids: Zondervan Publishing House, 1950.

_____. *Preaching on Bible Characters.* Grand Rapids: Baker Book House, 1955.

Wiersbe, W. W. *Preaching and Teaching with Imagination.* Wheaton, Ill.: Victor Books, 1994.

Willhite, K., and S. M. Gibson, eds. *The Big Idea of Biblical Preaching: Connecting the Bible to People.* Grand Rapids: Baker Books, 1998.

Willimon, W. H. *Biblical Sermons: How Twelve Preachers Apply the Principles of Biblical Preaching.* Grand Rapids: Baker Book House, 1989.

_____. *Christianity in Culture: A Study in Dynamic Biblical Theologizing in Cross-Cultural Perspectives.* Maryknoll, N.Y.: Orbis, 1979.

_____. *Contextualization: Meanings, Methods, and Models.* Grand Rapids: Baker Book House, 1989.

_____. *God's Human Speech: A Practical Theology of Proclamation.* Grand Rapids: William B. Eerdmans Publishing Company, 1997.

_____, ed. *Handbook of Contemporary Preaching.* Nashville: Broadman Press, 1992.

_____. *The Homiletical Plot: The Sermon as Narrative Art Form.* Atlanta: John Knox Press, 1980.

Willimon, W. H *How to Preach to People's Needs*. Grand Rapids: Baker Book House, 1956.

_____. *The Intensive Word: Preaching to the Unbaptized*. Grand Rapids: William B. Eerdmans, 1994.

_____. *Learning to Preach like Jesus*. Wheaton: Crossway Books, 1989.

_____. *A Manual for Biblical Preaching*. Grand Rapids: Baker Book House, 1981.

_____. *Marketplace Preaching: How to Return the Sermon to Where It Belongs*. Grand Rapids: Baker Books, 1995.

_____. *Ministry in an Oral Culture: Living with Will Rogers, Uncle Remus, and Minnie Pearl*. Louisville: Westminster/John Knox Press, 1994.

_____. *Ministry Nuts and Bolts: What They Don't Teach Pastors in Seminary*. Grand Rapids: Kregel Publications, 1997.

_____. *A New Hearing: Living Options in Homiletic Method*. Nashville: Abingdon, 1987.

_____. *Overhearing the Gospel*. Nashville: Abingdon Press 1978.

_____. *Paul the Preacher*. Nashville: Broadman Press, 1991.

_____. (2000). *Postmodern Pilgrims*. Nashville: Broadman and Holman.

_____. *The Preacher's Portrait: Some New Testament Word Studies*. Grand Rapids: William B. Eerdmans Publishing Company, 1961.

_____. *Preaching with Purpose: The Urgent Task of Homiletics*. Grand Rapids: Zondervan Publishing House, 1982.

_____. *The Pulpit Is Waiting*. Gretna, La.: Pelican Publishing Company, 1998.

_____. *Spirit, Word, and Story: A Philosophy of Preaching*. Dallas: Word Books, 1989.

_____. *U.S. Lifestyles and Mainline Churches: A Key to Reaching People in the 90's*. Louisville: Westminster/John Knox Press, 1990.

_____. *The Way to Biblical Preaching*. New York: Abingdon Press, 1957.

_____. *With a Bible in Their Hands: Baptist Preaching in the South, 1679-1979*. Nashville: Broadman & Holman Publishers, 1994.

_____. *The Witness of Preaching*. Louisville: Westminster/John Knox Press, 1989.

Index

About the Authors

Asa R. Sphar III, Ph.D. currently serves as Professor of Psychology and Counseling at New Orleans Baptist Theological Seminary (NOBTS) and as their Director of Clinical Training for their counseling programs. In addition, he is Director of Counseling Services of New Orleans, a private outpatient counseling center serving six separate locations in the New Orleans area. He holds the following degrees: Master of Divinity (M.Div.) in Psychology and Counseling, Master of Arts in Marriage and Family Therapy (MAMFC), and a Doctor of Philosophy (Ph.D.) in Psychology and Counseling. At the completion of his graduate studies he received the Outstanding Student Award and the Broadman Seminarian Award for his graduating class. His other credentials, memberships, and recognitions include the following: Licensed Professional Counselor; National Certified Counselor; Approved Supervisor/Clinical Member of the American Association for Marriage and Family Therapy (AAMFT); Charter Member of the American Association of Christian Counselors (AACC); Clinical Member of the Fellowship of Christian Counselors and Therapists (FCCT); Certified Pastoral Counselor Educator (CPCE); and a Member of the Christian Association for Psychological Studies (CAPS). Dr. Sphar and his wife Donna will celebrate their 25th wedding anniversary this year. They have two daughters, ages 17 and 21.

Argile Smith, Ph.D., is also on the faculty at New Orleans Baptist Theological Seminary. Presently he serves as Professor of Preaching, occupying the J. D. Grey Chair of Preaching and the Chair of the Division of Pastoral Ministries. Prior to joining the faculty, he was the pastor of Trinity Heights Baptist Church in Shreveport, LA. Having been involved in pastoral ministry since 1977, he currently serves as bi-vocational pastor of Faith Baptist Church in New Orleans. He has published a variety of articles on topics related to pastoral ministry and preaching as well as a number of Bible study guides. He holds the Master of Divinity (M.Div.) and Doctor of Philosophy (Ph.D.) degrees. He is a member of the Evangelical Homiletics Society. He and his wife, Connie, have been married for twenty-seven years, and they have three sons, ages 16, 20, and 22.

CPSIA information can be obtained at www.ICGtesting.com
Printed in the USA
LVOW06s1423260214

375265LV00001BA/26/P